THEO-POETICS

D1599362

THEO-POETICS

Hans Urs von Balthasar
and the Risk
of Art and Being

ANNE M. CARPENTER

Foreword by
Peter J. Casarella

University of Notre Dame Press
Notre Dame, Indiana

Library of Congress Cataloging-in-Publication Data

Carpenter, Anne M., 1984– author.
Theo-poetics : Hans Urs von Balthasar and the risk of art and being /
Anne M. Carpenter ; foreword by Peter J. Casarella.
    pages   cm
Includes bibliographical references and index.
ISBN 978-0-268-02378-2 (paperback) — ISBN 0-268-02378-6 (paper)
1. Balthasar, Hans Urs von, 1905–1988. 2. Theology.
3. Theology—Methodology. 4. Religion and poetry.   I. Title.
    BX4705.B163C37   2015
        230'.2092—dc23
        2015031757

∞ *The paper in this book meets the guidelines for permanence and durability*
of the Committee on Production Guidelines for Book Longevity of
the Council on Library Resources.

For Beatrice, whom Dante learned to love

CONTENTS

FOREWORD

What we typically understand by interdisciplinary work can itself be too limited. If we are thinking about taking a figure or idea from one field and comparing it to another figure or idea on the other side of the departmental fence, then we are still thinking within the limits of disciplines alone. Or perhaps we have made the effort of convening experts from two or more fields. I know from experience in my own academic foxhole that this is no small feat. Scholars need to be convinced that the new interchange will outweigh the risk of moving outside of the comfort zone of one's chosen discipline.

Hans Urs von Balthasar never accepted an academic position. Besides the writing of a dissertation on an unusual topic even for a cross-disciplinary field (one which he himself considered to be liable to the charge of *"Methodensyncretismus"*),[1] he never had to wage these battles or face these quandaries from within an academic setting. But this does not mean that his work can be viewed as liberated from all disciplinary constraints. In fact, there are many passages in his vast oeuvre in which despite his occasional demurrals he clearly intends to be read as a professional theologian. His writings on poets, novelists, and metaphysicians, by the same token, were seldom written just for a churchly audience. He was the quintessential man of letters who desired to be read by anyone who was reading those whom he was reading, above all by the authors themselves.[2] In this sense, von Balthasar raises rather than lowers the bar for expertise in a specialized field.

None of this gets to the issue of what von Balthasar considered essential, that is, his distinctive approach to *"katholische Integration."*[3] Von Balthasar thought of this form of integration as the enhancement rather than the washing out of distinctions. It had little to do with applying a

Catholic brand to the finished product either in the name of the institutional Church or a cultural Catholicism. His approach started from a different point of view. A poet became more of a poet when read theologically. A theologian became more of a metaphysician when seen in light of the transcendentals of beauty, truth, and goodness. The search for the transcendentals could not take place after the investigation of the literary character of a text. The discernment of an ecclesial mission could not be placed alongside the task of a writer as an endeavor to be pursued on weekends.

This approach meant, above all else, that no one element of the truth for Christian thinking and acting could be isolated from the mix. Von Balthasar considered "exegetical rationalism" and the explicit politicization of theology to be good examples of that phenomenon.[4] Both being human and the being of the world had to be considered anew in terms of the likeness of God in worldly being as a whole (*die Gottabbildlichkeit des weltlichen Seins im Ganzen*). The application of the *analogia entis* to catholicity could not be achieved, according to von Balthasar, simply by reviving the Neoplatonic dynamics of a primordial *eidos* and its worldly image. From his exchange with Karl Barth, von Balthasar clarified to himself and others that Jesus Christ is not an abstract point of mediation between the infinite and the finite. The Incarnate Word's enfleshment offers Jesus Christ as the one who stands in the middle of the personal, social, and natural cosmos and radiates a distinctive mission for each of his followers.[5]

In this context Anne Carpenter targets the "theo-poetics" of the Swiss theologian. This is not his terminology, and she is aware of the liberties taken by others in applying this word to von Balthasar's aesthetics. As a term, I believe it was coined about forty years ago by a scholar of religion at Harvard, Amos Wilder, whose brother's plays were of more than a little interest to the Swiss theologian.[6] Roberto Goizueta gave the term an important Latino valence in his landmark book *Caminemos con Jesús*.[7] Goizueta was looking for an idiom to highlight the beauty and goodness of Mexican street processions on Good Friday in San Antonio, Texas. Carpenter, by contrast, uses the term to examine the poetic shape of theology in von Balthasar. She boldly constructs her own hieroglyphs to offer a port of entry to each chapter with full confidence that paying attention to the actual construction of an intrinsically elusive word will not diminish in any way the metaphysical depth of the task at hand.

Carpenter's interpretations of von Balthasar's readings of diverse authors are invitations to consider anew what he has bequeathed. She does not peg him to a particular school or ignore his deep roots in *Germanistik* (German cultural studies), in *The Spiritual Exercises* of St. Ignatius of Loyola, or in German Catholic theological scholarship of the first half of the twentieth century. She guides the reader to consider the most fundamental of questions about von Balthasar's oeuvre: "If it's not systematic theology, then what kind of theology is it? If it's not a practical mandate for interdisciplinary cooperation, then what kind of integrative thinking is needed?" With these significant questions in mind, she examines his approach to, for example, the proto-Thomistic Christocentric metaphysics of Maximus the Confessor, Rilke and Heidegger on the encounter with self before death, Dante on the beauty of Christ, Hopkins on the grace of self-offering, and even the inimitable Erich Przywara on the polarities that undergird the analogy of being. She also considers the consequences of focusing on poetic practices for a theory of language and for politics. Von Balthasar needed to raze the bastions that demarcate fields of learning and social conventions. The former student of German cultural life thrust himself into the heart of the world once he faced the call to contemplate Christ's own mission. Carpenter with fresh eyes asks whether and how this introverted student of the German lyric lived up to that daunting, world-embracing standard.

Carpenter has done von Balthasar's growing readership a great favor precisely by not determining too neatly the outcome of the inquiry. Her analysis yields a roadmap rather than an endpoint. She explores the development of his thought in its context and lays out with all necessary precision an argument about how to find the place where for von Balthasar Christology, metaphysics, and poetry find their center. In the end, she concludes:

> There is a way in which artists should still be allowed to be artists, and theologians to be theologians. Their desires meet at the crossways of authentic transcendence, before the God who redeems all that is and all that we desire.[8]

Von Balthasar labors to sketch out the crossways of authentic transcendence knowing that this intersection, like the streets of San Antonio during the celebration of Good Friday, will be a place where strangers will get to know one another for the first time. Each pilgrim will retain her most sacred dignity but also be changed immediately and forever with a glance toward a common destiny within Christ's glorified body. Accompanying us patiently toward this intersection is one of the great and exciting achievements of this exceptional work of scholarship.

Peter J. Casarella

NOTES

1. Hans Urs von Balthasar, *Geschichte des eschatologischen Problems in der modernen deutschen Literatur* (Freiburg i. Br.: Johannes, 1998), 13 n. 1: "The more detailed justification of this syncretism of methods will follow in the larger publications." Translation my own. This was written in his dissertation of 1930. The amplification appeared in the multivolume *Apokalypse der deutschen Seele* from 1937–39.

2. Manfred Lochbrunner, *Hans Urs von Balthasar und seine Literatenfreunde: Neun Korrespondenzen* (Würzburg: Echter Verlag, 2002).

3. See Holger Zaborowski, "Katholische Integration: Zum Verhältnis von Philosophie und Theologie bei Hans Urs von Balthasar," in *Hans Urs von Balthasar—Vermächtnis und Anstoß für die Theologie*, ed. Magnus Striet and Jan-Heiner Tück (Freiburg i. Br.: Herder, 2005), 28–48. The adjective is only capitalized at the beginning of titles. In writing the term *katholische Integration*, one is neither distancing nor melding the two distinct terms in English: "catholic" and "Catholic." Because of this interesting ambiguity, I left the phrase in German in the text.

4. Cf. Holger Zaborowski, "Katholische Integration," 37.

5. Zaborowski writes: "Denn jede christliche Form der Vermittlung und der analogischen In-Entsprechung-Setzung steht unter dem Anspruch des einen Mittlers, von dem her Christen ihre je eingene Sendung verstehen: Jesus Christus" (37–38). "Each Christian form of mediation and of the inner, analogical setting into place of a correspondence stands within the claim of a mediator, from whom every Christian understands his or her own mission. Jesus Christ is this mediator."

6. Amos Niven Wilder, *Theopoetic: Theology and the Religious Imagination* (Philadelphia: Fortress, 1976). Von Balthasar refers to Amos Wilder in *Theo-Dramatik II, 2, Die Personen in Christus* (Einsiedeln: Johannes Verlag, 1978), 83. The engagement with Thornton Wilder in the *Theo-Drama* was more substantive, positive, and frequent. See, for example, *Theo-Dramatik I: Prolegomena* (Einsiedeln: Johannes Verlag, 1973), 76–80 and *Theo-Dramatik II, 1, Der Mensch in Gott* (Einsiedeln: Johannes Verlag, 1976), 40ff. Interestingly, David L. Schindler reported to me that von Balthasar ordered Thorton Wilder's collected works through him and that they were on his desk awaiting the writing of a new full-scale monograph when von Balthasar passed away. The significance of the relationship between the two brothers has now been carefully analyzed in Christopher J. Wheatley, *Thornton Wilder & Amos Wilder: Writing Religion in Twentieth-Century America* (Notre Dame, IN: University of Notre Dame Press, 2013).

7. Roberto S. Goizueta, *Caminemos con Jesús: Towards a Hispanic/Latino Theology of Accompaniment* (Maryknoll, NY: Orbis, 1995).

8. Quote from Carpenter's Conclusion.

ABBREVIATIONS

Apokalypse I–III *Die Apokalypse der deutschen Seele*, vols. 1–3

GL I–VII *Glory of the Lord*, vols. 1–7

Herrlichkeit *Herrlichkeit: Eine theologische Aesthetik*, vols. 1–5

ST *Summa Theologica* (Thomas Aquinas)

TD I–V *Theo-Drama*, vols. 1–5

Theologik I–III *Theologik*, vols. 1–3

TL I–III *Theo-Logic*, vols. 1–3

Full reference information can be found in the bibliography. It must be noted that Ignatius Press is, as of the completion of this study, in the midst of republishing Hans Urs von Balthasar's trilogy of works. The first volume of *Glory of the Lord* is the only volume in a new print. The citations in this book are from the previous print edition, whose page numbers match the majority of current scholarship.

Introduction

Ond'ella a me: "Per entro I mie' disiri,
che ti menavano ad amar lo bene
di là dal qual non è a che s'aspiri,

quai fossa attraversati o quai catene
trovasti, per che del passare innanzi
dovessiti così sogliar la spene?"
—Beatrice to Dante, *Purgatorio*,
Canto XXXI, 22–27

Hans Urs von Balthasar (1905–1988) was a Swiss-Catholic theologian of great importance in the twentieth century. His formal education included a doctorate in literature, which resulted in a massive three-volume work on the state of German literature and philosophy entitled *Die Apokalypse der deutschen Seele* (The Apocalypse of the German Soul)—and licentiates in both theology and philosophy. Throughout his life, von Balthasar continued to display a thoroughgoing interest in art and theology. With a background particularly attuned to this link, von Balthasar set out to "recover" the transcendental of beauty in theology, which he argued had been a consistent facet of Christian theology from the beginning but which had been lost or obscured in modern theology. This project is his "theological aesthetics."

Any confrontation with von Balthasar's work must therefore respond to his unique knowledge of both theological propositions *and* art. This is a difficult balance to keep, and scholarship has struggled to attend to both von Balthasar's theological claims and his poetic manner of claiming them. My task in this work is twofold: a careful exploration of von Balthasar's use of poetry and poetic language and a detailed analysis of his philosophical presuppositions. My thesis is that Hans Urs von Balthasar uses poets and poetic language to make theological arguments, because this poetic way of speaking expresses metaphysical truth without reducing one to the other. Taken as a whole, this twofold task and its blended thesis serve both as an introduction to von Balthasar's entire oeuvre and as a scholarly response to a lacuna in work on von Balthasar's theology, a lacuna that opens wide into circles beyond his theology itself.

There is in modern theology the temptation to retreat increasingly into symbol and away from metaphysics, a temptation that exists alongside the desire to renew metaphysics at the cost of imagery-rich language. Metaphysics and language, being and image, are placed in opposition to one another. This book searches the thought of von Balthasar in order to show how such an opposition is false and how, indeed, metaphysics and language stand and fall together. We can show how this is so by investigating the nature of beauty.

Von Balthasar is considered to be one of the prime instigators of twentieth- and twenty-first century theology's renewed interest in aesthetics.[1] Von Balthasar's theology is both poetic and philosophical, and while this simultaneity is often admitted, it is never explained. Because von Balthasar's work has metaphysical import, it is necessary to evaluate his metaphysical outlook. We must ask, for example, how his metaphysic relates to the Thomist metaphysic in particular, since he himself places Aquinas's metaphysic at the "height" of ancient metaphysics in *Glory of the Lord IV*. At the same time, evaluating von Balthasar's metaphysic on the theoretical level and then relating it to his aesthetic insights is really only to confront the issue in the mode of philosophy. It is also necessary to understand the specifically *poetic* value of von Balthasar's work—both his use of artists and his artistic use of language. Von Balthasar has to somehow be appropriated in a manner simultaneously philosophical and poetic, and this is precisely the challenge. When von Balthasar "does" theology, he employs philosophy and poetry in tandem. His is a unique theological grammar, one that must be expressed on its own terms before being evaluated. In order to examine von Balthasar's theological contribution and evaluate its worth, *what he means* and *how he means it* are central concerns. The "what" is theological truth, and the "how" is a perplexing combination of theological and poetic language.

Von Balthasar presents us with a *theo-poetic* rather than sheer systematic theology, by which I mean that the almost mathematical discursive arguments of certain theological styles give way in von Balthasar to symbolic as well as discursive argumentation. In a given theological problem, von Balthasar is capable of using either imagery-rich reasoning, or more straightforward philosophical reasoning, or—as is most often the case—both at once. For him, "poetic" or more symbolic language expresses truth and persuades with a power like prose. Poetic language is in this way able to function within theological reasoning. The term "theopoetic" is thus drawn from von Balthasar's affirmation of poetic expression: when God speaks to us in the Incarnation, *all* qualities of human language—even being itself—are employed as a created "grammar" by which God expresses himself to us. So those aspects of language that are highly developed uses of analogy and symbol have a role to play in God's self-expression and in human attempts to discuss God. With God at the center of expression, poetry becomes capable of an authentic role in theological language. This theocentrism is why von Balthasar possesses what I am calling a *theo*-poetic. The emphasis here follows the logic of von Balthasar's trilogy as he himself titles its contents: a "theo-poetic" joins *Theo-Drama* and *Theo-Logic* as an explanation of their inner form (*Glory of the Lord*). Thus the term "theo-poetic," or theological poetic, as it is used in this book is to be sharply distinguished from the agnostic overtures of the "theo-poetic" movement, whose lineage is not to be found in the thought of von Balthasar.[2]

Rather than a retreat to symbol due to the questionable expressive power of language, a "theo-poetic" seeks out images because of a fundamental confidence in language's ability to express metaphysical reality. Von Balthasar's confidence in linguistic expression is rooted in his prior understanding of metaphysics as well as in his grasp of the relationship that persists between metaphysics and language. This relationship itself bears a profound Christological foundation, one that von Balthasar comes to emphasize when he writes *Glory of the Lord*. So his theo-poetic requires the interplay of three massive fields of knowledge: metaphysics, language, and Christology. It is this "interplay" of fields that we will spend the book untangling, opening the way to greater understanding of von Balthasar's unique theological poetic.

In chapter 1, we begin with the youthful von Balthasar and his early interactions with philosophy and art. His earliest work, *The Development of the Musical Idea*, presents us with an idealistic young man convinced of music's power to express divine reality. This idealism confronts the devastation of modern German art and philosophy, and indeed the Second World War, and develops into a sharp distinction between art and religion. In the caesura between art and religion, von Balthasar comes to emphasize the otherness of God and authentic transcendence over-against the confusion over transcendence and divinity that he detects in modern thought. Modernity in this way experiences a fundamentally *metaphysical* problem, one that leaves modern thought incapable of appropriating authentic transcendence. The poet Rainer Maria Rilke and the philosopher Martin Heidegger appear as major interlocutors here. Both philosophy and art threaten to disintegrate into a tragic obsession with death, unable to account for finitude and its demise save through resignation.

Chapter 2 explores the development of von Balthasar's major poetic-metaphysical concerns as he moves into *Glory of the Lord* and the trilogy. With many of the same worries, von Balthasar turns to theology in order to resuscitate art and philosophy through a theological account of beauty. This theological account has Christ as its center, allowing for von Balthasar to affirm the goodness of worldly contingency while avoiding the despair he suspects in modern theology. Dante Alighieri's *Divina Commedia* appears in this chapter in order to show how Christology redeems worldly beauty.

Chapter 3 makes a concerted effort to uncover the major characteristics of von Balthasar's metaphysical thinking. The chapter bends itself toward the major philosophical concerns that uphold von Balthasar's Christocentrism and which are enlivened by it. Thomas Aquinas, Karl Barth, and Martin Heidegger are the fundamental interlocutors in this chapter, and von Balthasar's interactions with the thought of all three allows him to firmly link Christology, metaphysics, and the expressiveness of language.

Chapter 4 reworks the themes of the three previous chapters into a properly "poetic" form, opening up a discussion over the relationship between language, metaphysics, and the art of poetry. D. Stephen Long's *Speaking of God* opens for us a way into von Balthasar's poetic view of language, allowing us to understand what is at stake in discussions of language and metaphysics together. Then we discuss the primary characteristics of a theological poetic, that which makes this theory of language especially poetic in form, and yet in such a way that it is ordered by theological presuppositions. Thomas Aquinas's *De veritate* leads the way here, allowing us to understand what it is that von Balthasar is suggesting about language and metaphysics.

Chapter 5 brings the book to a close by marshaling its themes into a focused evaluation of von Balthasar's "redeemed" theo-poetic as it comes to expression in the poetry of G. M. Hopkins. Here we explore Hopkins in contrast to Rilke and then move into a concentrated assessment of Hopkins's adherence to the metaphysical thought of John Duns Scotus. Von Balthasar resituates and reevaluates Hopkins's poetry in a new context, placing him in the school of Aquinas rather than Scotus and showing us in a final way how metaphysics is necessary for a vigorous understanding of language. Without the new context von Balthasar gives him, Hopkins's hope for a sacramental-poetic language disintegrates. With von Balthasar's renewed grasp of metaphysics, it is conceivable for him to use poetic language in his theology in a manner that Hopkins's intimates is possible.

A word should be said about the poems that open each chapter. Every poem is meant to express some of the essential themes of the chapter it begins, though those themes may not be immediately apparent. The poems prepare the reader for the text in a hieroglyphic fashion: that is, as an image and a word only made sense of in context and, indeed, best understood once the chapter itself has closed. No poem, save that of chapter 4, receives exegesis or contextual explanation. This is in order that the poems may still function *as poetry*, which is to say that they illuminate their themes at the intersection between words and meaning. By the end of the book, the reader will be better equipped to understand the role these poems play and how they recapitulate their theological and philosophical counterparts in the prose.

ONE

Beauty and Risk

Die Apokalypse der deutschen Seele and Von Balthasar's Early Work

The Law of Contingent Being

The world is consumed in invisible flame, devoured
by an inward law: the indivisible eternal hour
of eternal death. Life is ruins.
Swallowed by the earth,
whose growing vines clutch and draw
the living toward its open jaws.

Can you see?
The living fire that endures, the never-ending
blaze—forge-work of a decaying heart?
All the world is flame.
Persisting, consisting, in always-death;
bearing mortal sons to fuel its perseverance.

We, we sons, with our terrible desire.
The breathless need, the airless heat, learned

in a subterranean hearth. The dark fire that burns
beneath the ribcage of the blood-soaked earth.
Blood in our veins, circulating the physical want—
blood animating the flesh, keeping it hot.

We who eat to sustain the heat, who break flesh
and bone on white teeth. Who must eat
—can we be blamed?—
who must consume with ashen faces.
Death offered from open hands to open mouths;
death in libation to the uncompromising law.

Dread law, appalling logic.
The marrow of the earth is death—
a pale flame. And we daily take
the deadly turn. Participate
in the mysterious familiar rite.
We who daily die: covered in blood.

We, clothed in the flesh of the sustaining fire,
comprised of life's unfailing promise to end,
and glittering in the soft angles of desire.
Draw me close and see—touch and taste, beneath
the skin, the cauterizing wound, felt in heat.
The consuming measure that shivers and seethes.

We do not rise (you and I).
We with patient gestures slowly descend,
and caress the waking death that lives within,
the knotted fire, the ancient covenant,
sinking deeper with palatable nearness.
All the world is fire.

One of the most difficult facts to acknowledge about earthly beauty is
that it dies. Youth slips away; buildings and sculptures decay. We cannot
hold on to beauty as if it could be owned, controlled, preserved. This is
the problem confronted in this chapter and in von Balthasar's earliest

writings on beauty. That is, what is beauty, and what does it mean to speak of beauty when beauty is everywhere and appears as if clothed in death? After all, beauty *fades*. How, then, do we perceive reality through it? This question echoes the themes of the German poet Rainer Maria Rilke in his *Duino Elegies*. The opening of Rilke's First Elegy leads to the following statement: *das Schöne ist nichts als des Schrecklichen Anfang* [beauty is nothing but the beginning of terror].[1] This sentiment is the controlling idea through all ten of the elegies, so that beauty is forever allied with an accompanying terror or tremendousness (*Schreckliche* can mean both). It is much like standing too close to the sun: here is a beauty whose very immanence overwhelms, whose grandeur is intrinsically bound to tragedy and to death. An elegy is a song of death. Is this what beauty must be?

For the poet Rilke and for the modern philosophers that von Balthasar spent his youth studying, finite being is thoroughly caught up in death. Inasmuch as all finite being tends toward death, earthly beauty also appears under the sign of death. Beauty—earthly beauty—does not last. Paintings fade, music is forgotten, the original ecstasy never again returns with the same intensity.

Still, we must wonder if the tragedy of beauty is inevitable. Or rather, we must wonder if earthly beauty's evanescence must always be called *tragic*: can the living finitude of earthly beauty betray an openness to what transcends it and not merely an openness to death? The "question" is as metaphysical as it is existential. It asks after our experience of the beautiful, certainly, but that experience itself begs for an understanding of the way the world is constructed. What a thing is informs how it is known. The metaphysical "risk" here rests in a struggle over several possible definitions of finitude and transcendence: what does it mean to be a finite creature, and what does it mean to be open to transcendence? The beauty expressed in art and literature signals a metaphysical question.

This question is buried everywhere in von Balthasar's earliest long work, *Die Apokalypse der deutschen Seele*.[2] We begin with this work and his other early writings, searching out the roots of von Balthasar's strange yet careful intersection between literature and philosophy, between image and logic. These early writings provide a portrait of his beginnings. Von Balthasar himself was a man who understood the importance of a beginning, and this is his own.[3]

So, like the opening reflection of *Glory of the Lord I*, it is fair to ask: what is the "first word" of von Balthasar's first work? The lengthy three volumes prove themselves unwieldy to read and unwieldy to summarize, serving the reader a bewildering critical assessment of different German philosophical and literary epochs. Von Balthasar moves through a large crowd of literary and philosophical figures, each a titan in respective ways: Heidegger, Hegel, Schelling, Nietzsche, Dostoyevsky, Rilke, Goethe, Barth, and so on. It is easy to wonder whether *Apokalypse* is simply a mess of open ends with no organizing principle at all. No first word.

Buried beneath the complex evaluations of immanence and transcendence, of philosophical success and failure, of Prometheus and Dionysius—all of which will be, in brief, reviewed—there still *is* a "first word." That word is "terror" (Rilke's *Schreckliche*), and for von Balthasar it becomes the rising critique of modern German thought from Idealism to *Lebensphilosophie* to existentialism. All is marked by *Schreckliche*, unable to account for beauty save with fear. Von Balthasar lays bare the fear that rests beneath modern German conceptions of the world, and in his critique makes more urgent the question over whether or not, or in what way, this modern anxiety perceives reality.

Several points both narrow the scope of this inquiry and help to shape terror as its first word, since it is by all means possible to choose another for von Balthasar's *Apokalypse*.[4] (1) The concern in my chapter is to relate von Balthasar's earliest views of beauty and art into a cohesive perspective, one marked more and more by sharp caution and yet hope. I will review his first articles on art, written before and after his dissertation, which will clarify the "risk" he grows to perceive. (2) Since the focus here is on the role of beauty, much of von Balthasar's critiques of German Idealism and other philosophers must be left aside for the sake of brevity. The outcome is a much more obvious insight into von Balthasar's caution, as if the dust had been cleared away. (3) One artist in particular takes center stage in my inquiry into *Apokalypse*, and that is Rainer Maria Rilke. There are several reasons, the first being that he is one of the few artists to appear throughout his dissertation instead of in one section. Rilke is also the final poetic voice permitted lengthy discussion before von Balthasar moves into his theological review with Karl Barth, and as such Rilke represents a kind of "height" to which von Balthasar has been building. What emerges after this extensive inquiry is a rather unusual affirmation for my book, which claims to lead to a theo-poetics: that beauty is filled with terror. More specifically, we will see that, for von Balthasar, *beauty without the Christian God can only be beauty-made-terror*.

I present the central themes of *Apokalypse* and examine these themes as they emerge in von Balthasar's earliest texts before his dissertation as well as after its writing. Then we examine the dissertation itself, and work in detail with its arguments. *Apokalypse* will frame von Balthasar's early texts for us, and it will leave us prepared to look into von Balthasar's renewed aesthetic efforts *Herrlichkeit*, which we will study in chapter 2.

APOCALYPTIC THEMES

Von Balthasar's expanded dissertation, *Die Apokalypse der deutschen Seele*, has several themes that will help to frame a basic sense of his early concerns with art and philosophy. Both art and philosophy are permitted to "speak" to one another in *Apokalypse*, which results in a developing concern over the role of contingency in concepts of transcendence. Both art and philosophy are oriented to transcendence, but the basic stance of each can be—and, in the case of modern German thought, *is*—distorted.

The most prominent theme in *Apokalypse* is detectible in the three titles of the volumes: I. *Der deustche Idealismus* (German Idealism), II. *Im Zeichen Nietzches* (In the Sign of Nietzsche), III. *Vergöttlichung des Todes* (Apotheosis of Death). Von Balthasar's overall arc moves from a survey of German Idealism in thinkers like Hegel, through the shattering of idealism in Nietzsche and other representatives, to the hopeless confrontation with death in figures such as Heidegger and Scheler.[5] Von Balthasar's argument is an "arc" to be found in the implicit narrative occurring between the figures that rise and speak in the pages of *Apokalypse*. The arc plays out, in a certain respect, as a downward spiral into increasing futility as German thought attempts to confront the world without the Christian God.

Death looms more and more as the inextricable end, and even the *condition for* life. Death becomes, as in Rilke, the "other side" of life. This last, negative note dominates the third volume. All the same, to characterize the arc as entirely hopeless would be misleading: von Balthasar sees in the confused attempt for transcendence an inverted—or perhaps negatively verifying—affirmation of the *real* human orientation toward transcendence. Such a desire or orientation—an "openness"—is both genuine and, to the extent that it is affirmed in the figures reviewed, laudable.

What idealism and existentialism both forget is a fundamental relationship between God and the world, eventually leading to the atheist position of one such as Nietzsche or to the ambiguously atheist in one such as Rilke. The identity of God and the world—either in the direction of idealism or of existentialism—leads to the evisceration of real transcendence. Now transcendence must be found, somehow, *in* the world—and in two respects: as a potency for transcendence (which von Balthasar desires to affirm), and as an inward capacity for the fulfillment of that transcendence (which von Balthasar denies).[6] Both affirmation and denial operate simultaneously in von Balthasar's evaluations of his various interlocutors, and he will emerge with hope for the modern situation and sharp caution. The *hope* is for a recovery of the desire for transcendence, already so pronounced. The *caution* is against every effort to totalize that desire, every effort to absolutize the essentially created. He turns to the Christian God to correct what is lost or distorted and to bring what is authentic into fullness.

The arc working through *Apokalypse* moves in two alternate directions, which von Balthasar names the "Prometheus Principle" (*Prometheus-Prinzip*) and the "Dionysius Principle" (*Dionysosprinzip*), rather oddly borrowing from Nietzsche.[7] What marks the Promethean movement in German literature and philosophy is the attempt to "raise" the earthly to the heavenly, a movement that von Balthasar accuses German Idealism in general of attempting. It desires a view of the "whole," which von Balthasar is not against so long as the incomparable God remains determinative of the "whole." Humanity becomes the middle point (*Mittlerpunkt*) between God and the world, stretched across a double dialectic (*doppelten* δια): between the absolute God and a negated world and between an absolute world and a negated God (*Gott-Alles zu Welt-Nichts und von Welt-Alles zu Gott-Nichts*).[8] Von Balthasar characterizes this as the "grabbing and mastering of opposites," one that leads eventually to a profound resignation to the "pain" (*Schmerz*) found in attempting to navigate the various poles of existence. In order to prevent despair, the very imperfection of the world is absolutized: resignation becomes the perfection of the imperfect.[9]

The Dionysian inverts the Promethean: now heaven is "brought down" to earth, an attempt that von Balthasar uses to characterize existentialism or *Lebensphilosophie*. It begins with Nietzsche, though "beginning" here is not chronological, but philosophical: Nietzsche sets himself against all the certainties of Idealism, and buries himself in the contradictions of contingency. All the figures of the Dionysus principle do much the same, so that the "resignation" of German Idealism is in many ways much more radicalized. Now pain itself is exalted—Dionysus is crucified, quite apart from Christian ideals—and contingency made central.[10] The focus is no longer on life and the mind, or the life of the mind, but on life itself, on existential pain.[11] This is one of the reasons why poets begin to play a major role in the Dionysus sections of the dissertation, since they most of all ask their questions and render their answers in an existential mode. Kierkegaard is another major figure here, set against Nietzsche and alongside him, as an example of a furious attempt to redeem Christianity in the face of the grand Dionysian desire to submerge all things into a painful contingency.[12]

Both points of view, the Promethean and Dionysian, drive toward what von Balthasar calls an "eschatology" (*Eschatologie*) or "end problem" (*Endproblem*) for the German "soul" (*Seele*). It is not at first clear what he means by any of these terms, since he is applying them in the most unusual of ways. Von Balthasar moves through his argument by considering the various endpoints and "end problems" of every figure he meets. He is at once "reading" German history as if it were a narrative laced with meaning—tending toward an end—and at the same time resisting its every turn toward self-determining self-transcendence.[13]

Von Balthasar begins *Apokalypse* by acknowledging that art, philosophy, and theology all "penetrate" a complex eschaton that pertains to every level of existence.[14] This is an essentially theological presupposition, insisting that all of creation tends toward an end and that all forms of human knowledge attempt to grasp that end. Art and philosophy do not penetrate the eschaton in a manner identical to theology, however, and von Balthasar moves to contrast the medieval understanding of the eschaton from the modern. The Middle Ages are characterized, like the modern German thought von Balthasar is about to explore, by a *total view* of the eschaton: it includes all things in its reach. In the medieval mind, the eschaton is individual, it is ecclesial, and it elevates nature.[15] Every aspect of creation is touched, and this is what makes it total.

If in the Middle Ages the eschaton is primarily the work of God, the modern age places human beings at the middle point.[16] Aidan Nichols describes the contrast in terms of the Dionysus principle: "The Christian soul focuses eschatologically on a reality beyond it, namely Christ. . . . The Dionysian soul focuses on its own inner existence."[17] This, for von Balthasar, is the root of a dangerous shift, one that totalizes the human perspective and, while still driving toward an "eschaton" of sorts, has nowhere to go. As we will see with the third and final volume of *Apokalypse*, the result of this kind of eschaton is to end in nonbeing (*Nichtsein*). By reason of his argument, von Balthasar places himself at odds with what he understands to be the modern era's desire for a self-sustaining eschaton.[18]

The "end," the "apocalypse" von Balthasar is out to describe and critique is really a "final attitude."[19] What von Balthasar attempts to iterate in *Apokalypse* are the concrete perspectives of each of the philosophers and literary figures he examines. While each has a distinctive standpoint, von Balthasar permits them to stand together as a testament to a building tragedy. The dark turn is laid to rest, as if from the outside, by Karl Barth, whose stubbornly theological stance—in a work of irony, perhaps—vindicates what was lost in the Middle Ages.[20] It is the *theological*, specifically the *Christological*, that rescues art and its possibilities for von Balthasar and that redeems the possibilities of human nature. A human nature that—as we will see—is in German thought trapped more and more in inevitable tragedy.

Key in von Balthasar's account of the welling modern tragedy, and its possible redemption, is the poet Rilke. Von Balthasar's analysis of Rilke stretches across the poet's entire corpus, including fragments that were never completed. His poetry serves as a commentary from the opening pages of *Apokalypse*. Von Balthasar begins his work with the use of a quotation from Rilke's "First Elegy":

But did you come to terms with it? Were you not always
still distracted by expectation, as everything called
a beloved to you?[21]

This passage in the elegy unfolds along the outlines of a nameless longing, one for which Rilke seeks a direction. In von Balthasar's eyes, Rilke
is describing the "openness" with which all knowledge penetrates the eschaton. It seems at first that a beloved might be an answer to the longing
that opens up the human being, but in his elegies Rilke rejects such a
solution as one instead to be overcome. A beloved in the end withers beneath the pull of much stronger longing (the theme of "Third Elegy"),
whose tidal forces are cause for fear. Beauty is thus still associated with
terror (*Schreckliche*), and love—at least, this kind of love—is not enough
to rise to its heights.

It is significant that von Balthasar begins his project by quoting from
this, the first of the elegies, the one that begins with beauty's terror.
Though he never speaks of Rilke or his other interlocutors in terms of
terror specifically, the concept—or rather, its threat—looms throughout
Apokalypse. Both the Prometheus and Dionysius impulses in German
thought unhinge the created world from its proper relationship with its
Creator, and the result for either is a rising confrontation with the pain
and anxiety (*Angst*) of existence. This *anxiety* more clearly emerges in
existentialism (the Dionysian), which is itself a reaction to German Idealism. From the outset, von Balthasar perceives an inner threat in both
impulses: the threat to make the intra-historical the absolute standpoint
(*Absolutheitsstandpunkt*), or the threat of a Gnosticism that raises earth
to heaven by making humanity an absolute.[22] The result is vacillation
between calm and agitation, between love and fear.[23]

Rilke appears in the opening pages of *Apokalypse* to represent the
struggle of both sides—really, the struggle of the human heart for authentic redemption—as von Balthasar introduces his argument. The poet
is a major figure in the Dionysius principle, and von Balthasar refrains
from alluding to him again until the second volume—the volume describing what is Dionysian. Rilke emerges as a guide in the opening
pages of this volume, as the poet describes his "circling" existence. Von
Balthasar uses this image as a way to describe the peculiar struggle

experienced by the Dionysius principle: contingent existence itself, rendered absolute, does not cease its search for fulfillment as perhaps might be hoped, but rather continues that search in an endless loop of contradiction. Von Balthasar describes that contradiction in the following terms:

> The radical finitude of the world is not then like a last frontier, where it encounters life in the end and where it must resign itself, but finitude is from the beginning, in increasing measure, the inward and irremovable contradiction between "ground" and "form."[24]

The poem that von Balthasar uses to depict the contradiction is from Rilke:

> I circle for thousands of years long,
> in the circle around God, around the most ancient tower,
> and still I did not know: I am a falcon, a storm
> over a greater song.[25]

So Rilke has managed to grasp the perilous cycle, the endless turn of pure contingency, and here exalts it as the highest form of life. This is what von Balthasar calls the "enchantment between angst and seduction."[26] Von Balthasar spends the rest of the second volume examining the ways in which his interlocutors succumb to this circling dialectic, his governing image. Other poets—taking the stage with more prominence after Rilke's opening note—move across von Balthasar's stage (especially Goethe), rising up to crystalize the Dionysius principle. Everywhere the finitude of life is not simply an ending horizon, but is also the *ground* for existence, so much so that von Balthasar moves to the next volume of *Apokalypse*: the divinization (apotheosis) of death. Here is finitude at its most radical exaltation.

Everywhere, von Balthasar "circles" like Rilke over what it means to be a contingent being, a creature of God. To lose an authentic perspective over creatureliness—the loss of what it means to be a creature, always in relationship to a Creator—is to consign oneself to an endless and futile search for fulfillment. It is fundamentally a loss of authentic metaphysics, which results in existential agony and fear. Though assured Christologically that our circling in the end cannot be futile, von Balthasar himself struggles with how art, and the aspects of contingency and transcendence with which it is concerned, might find a place in our desire for redemption. Von Balthasar's restless circling is situated in his early works on art, wherein he is convinced of art's power and yet increasingly concerned that it is not mistaken for the final answer to our disquiet.

THE EARLY VON BALTHASAR AND ART

Overture: Music and Metaphysics

Von Balthasar's first published work was on music. *Die Entwicklung der musikalischen Idee. Versuch einer Synthese der Musik* (The Development of the Musical Idea. An Attempt of a Synthesis of Music), published in 1925 when von Balthasar was but twenty, provides the earliest glimpse into the mind of this young scholar.[27] Of all the arts, von Balthasar was most invested in music from an early age. Blessed with perfect pitch and fair skill as a pianist, music remained throughout his life his most primordial art—and by "art" I mean to invoke the old Latin sense of *ars*: a work that is effort, skill, and knowledge. Music is the primordial *ars* of von Balthasar's intelligence.

The precocious twenty-year-old scholar presents an optimistic view of music's capacities in *Die Entwicklung der musikalischen Idee*. Von Balthasar characterizes the arts in general as possessing a capacity to mediate the divine. The opening of the book fixates most of all on music as the greatest of the arts because it is the most "immediate" (*unmittelbarste*), capable of presenting us with the mystery of existence in the most intimate fashion.[28] It can do so because it speaks to us without words (literally, with the un-word-like: *unworthaft*), gathering together sounds in an almost word-like fashion—word-like because it can communicate and because we can "hear" the meaning in the sound—and yet without actual words. Indeed, lyrics layered into music only highlight the mysterious un-word-like speech quality of music. In this way, music can express more-than-words (überwörtlich).[29]

This sentiment evokes a cheerful confidence in music's abilities, one Aidan Nichols notes as a "rather naïve version of Christian Romanticism."[30] Von Balthasar optimistically relates the development of music through rhythm, into melody, and into harmony, each progressive addition lending music greater perfection to its inner form. The young man is perhaps at his most effervescent when he discusses the perfection of meaning in art, which he describes as the objectification of the metaphysical and the divine. This perfection comes to ever-greater completion by the agency of the divine light that speaks from above:

> What is this maximum, this perfection of meaning? It is the *greatest* objectification of the metaphysical, the divine, because through nothing other than the divine primordial light (*Urlicht*) itself is each meaning, each idea, spoken from above. It stands at the middle-point of a circle, from the individual arts radiating outward, and so the divine itself is through radiance carried (*fortgerissen*) here and there in time and space, [and] in ever perfected developing form (*entwickelnden Form*) brought to ever brighter illumination (*hellerem Aufleuchten*).[31]

Von Balthasar is here at his most guileless, willing as he is to draw such strong lines of continuity between the divine light of God and the developing forms of music and the arts. He very nearly threatens to unite the two entirely. The metaphysical—by which he means reality itself—is dramatically brightened in music, lit up from the inside like filament flaring in a light bulb. Then it is not only this-worldly reality that we perceive in art, but also the radiance of God himself. The young von Balthasar here verges on the Dionysian.

The development of music is not without its flaws, however, and von Balthasar cautions himself and his reader to some degree. He insists very early that the eternal is never quite grasped in the arts, so that they are marked not only by closeness to the divine but also by an eternal longing and tragedy (*ewige Sehnsucht und Tragik*).[32] Von Balthasar eventually contends that art is "in itself tragic" because it is touched on all sides by unbearable longing and its own contingency.[33] His immense optimism— never again revisited with quite the same ardent flare—receives a kind of shapeless restriction, a vague admission of contingency never quite fleshed out by the young man here. His later works treat these questions with increasing urgency.

What is contiguous between this early book and von Balthasar's later treatises is, first, the lasting question of art's positive contributions and intrinsic limitations. Here, too, is a window into a mind extremely willing to consider the development of an internal idea or the form of an entire phenomenon—in this case, the form of music itself—and shaping his understanding of that development based on his perception of its intrinsic qualities, which is a habit that von Balthasar would never abandon. This is a tendency in his thought that troubles more than a few, the most articulate version of which can be found in Karen Kilby's *Balthasar: A (Very) Critical Introduction*.[34]

We can see the origins of von Balthasar's thinking of the whole here in his very first writing. *Die Entwicklung die musikalischen Idee* is populated everywhere by a discussion of *Form* and *Idee*, both used as near-synonyms with an implied meaning: there is a certain internal unity by which the arts, and music in particular, cohere.[35] This is how art's development can be discerned and evaluated. So he can refer to the essence (*Wesen*) of the musical idea (*Idee*).[36] Kilby is concerned that "in his very affirmation of the fragmentariness, the perspectival nature, of all theology, von Balthasar frequently positions himself *above* it."[37] It is clear that Kilby is correct—and at the same time incorrect. The von Balthasar of this very early publication and the von Balthasar of later years adores grasping the fullness or wholeness of a field, a being, a world. At the same time, the musical emphasis—which he never quite seems able or willing to abandon—interprets this wholeness apart from Kilby's concern that von Balthasar has taken the position of God. In music, the note is never comprehensible in itself and the whole musical work is never understood without its notes: we can see this in von Balthasar's optimism at the "lighting" of being and in its "tragedy." That is to say, the whole is always known in the fragments, and not otherwise. While much too naïve in its expression at this early stage, we will see von Balthasar's thought expand to welcome Kilby's critique and sidestep it.

To continue the comparison between von Balthasar's earliest work and his later works, we can note that his interest in art's ability to illuminate metaphysical reality follows him through the rest of his life.[38] Von Balthasar works under the conviction that art is intimately entwined with reality and that it expresses that reality—not as simple mimicry, but in such a way that it clarifies and magnifies that reality. Such a conviction places art in constant contact with metaphysics and philosophy, and in no simple fashion. Much of his dissertation is spent in the middle of the complex contact points between philosophy and art. He is utterly convinced that the two speak to one another. This eventually leads him to insist that the beauty of the arts, indeed beauty itself, provokes an encounter with truth, a prominent theme in *Glory of the Lord*.[39] Third, the *physicality* of the arts is never to be forgotten, since they are characterized by the shaping of material things in order to express what is immaterial. This "physicality" needs to be stressed from the outset.

Developments: Art and Religion

Von Balthasar did not remain as naïve toward art's relationship with religion as he was when he was twenty. Two years later, in 1927, von Balthasar published two articles that relate art and religion: "Kunst und Religion" ("Art and Religion"), and "Katholische Religion und Kunst" ("Catholic Religion and Art").[40] Each shows distinctive growth in his apprehension of the question of art's relationship to religion. The contours of both are similar enough for a brief review.

In "Kunst und Religion," von Balthasar shows increased reservation toward art. The essay navigates similar concerns to *Die Entwicklung die musikalischen Idee*, that is, an affirmation of art's desire for transcendence. Now it is framed differently. "Kunst und Religion" begins with a sharp distinction between art and religion—even the title forms an introductory caesura—and maintains that distinction, a remarkable turnaround compared to von Balthasar's earlier and rather extravagant entwining of the two. He notes from the outset a tension between art and religion and furthers that tension by insisting that an absolutized aestheticism, one that sets out to capture the essence of religion, cannot persist.[41] At the same time, a Puritan rejection of art cannot serve as the correct counter-response. There must be some relationship between art and religion, beyond the negative relationship of a caesura and yet without straying into a relationship of identity. Von Balthasar seats the meeting-place between art and religion in the human person, particularly in his or her "vulnerability" (*Gefährdetheit*).[42] But what does he mean by *vulnerability*?

Von Balthasar expands on the concept of "vulnerability" in "Katholische Religion und Kunst." Vulnerability does *not* mean that the unity between art and religion can be found in the unity of the subject. According to von Balthasar, understanding it as such threatens to obscure the difference of each, since in the subject art and religion still operate in a distinguishable way.[43] Within the human person, the aesthetic and religious do not exist on a continuum. Art—and here he sounds like Søren Kierkegaard—is not a bridge to the religious.[44] Instead, there is an "abyssal difference" (*abgründige Verschiedenheit*) between the two.[45] If art desires to absolutize itself, to take the place of religion, then it can only end tragically. Art's transcendence is dissolved into an endless spiral if art is rendered absolute, because it is not in fact absolute at all. Like the mythical Icarus, it collapses to the earth in an attempt to embrace what is not its own. This is art's temptation toward tragedy. Here von Balthasar hints at a major theme that he will discuss in *Apokalypse*: the theme of art and philosophy's titanic reach to claim the absolute, and the failure of that reach.

Instead of a continuum or an identity, the vulnerability that characterizes both art and religion is one of analogous surrender: the artistic surrender to the aesthetic, and the religious surrender to God.[46] The vulnerable attitude of each is typified by surrender, and though not identical, the two are capable of being analogously linked. There is something *like* religious surrender in aesthetic surrender. The inverse is also true, even as the mutual likeness of the aesthetic and religious surrenders divides them because the aesthetic cannot be identified with the religious. This distinction through analogy is why von Balthasar argues that Catholicism is at once emphatically *not* an aesthetic religion and yet *is* a place *for* the artist.[47] Religion cannot be identified with the aesthetic at any point, but this does not serve to alienate art so much as give it a place to operate. What is important to understand is that the relativization of art that occurs in von Balthasar's refusal to identify it with the religious emerges from an attempt to preserve and vivify it. By knowing what its surrender is not, we also know what it is, and when it is rightly understood, aesthetic surrender can then serve to illuminate religious surrender. In his focus on surrender, von Balthasar foreshadows claims to be found in both *Glory of the Lord* and *Theo-Drama*. "Surrender," and its concomitant term "kenosis," is a key phrase in the understanding of both parts of the trilogy.

Glory and *Drama* argue that authentic faith and freedom take place in the form of surrender to God in willing, graced obedience.[48]

Von Balthasar further foreshadows himself in a move for Christology. Because the analogous unity of aesthetic and religious surrender is ultimately to be found in God, von Balthasar expands that claim to argue that Christ himself unites art and religion, since he is the fullness and over-fullness (*die Fülle und der Überfluß*) of what is worldly.[49] In making such an argument, von Balthasar echoes a typical Catholic attitude toward the Incarnation, which is that the Incarnation affirms and elevates the natural without destruction. In the Incarnation, especially on the cross, we encounter a surrender that encompasses both aesthetic and religious surrender, because Christ's surrender is entirely to God. Moreover, his surrender on the cross plumbs the depths of aesthetic tragedy and out-bounds it, ultimately relativizing tragedy because the good is always metaphysically prior.[50] God himself is Goodness itself, and created being is good. This gives the Good priority over any tragedy. The way von Balthasar works toward the triumph of tragedy through tragedy in this text sounds eerily like his claims in *Mysterium Paschale* and *Theo-Drama*, though these are decades away.

The emphasis on Christology helps to nuance von Balthasar's developing position toward art. Though he now adopts a less naïve appropriation of the relationship between art and transcendence—carefully and consistently distinguishing this relationship from that of religion—he also sees more clearly the way Christ helps to retain a positive relationship between art and religion instead of a merely negative one. As von Balthasar's thought continues to progress, Christ will play a more and more central role in the navigation between art, philosophy, and competing views of transcendence.

Radical Caution and Radical Hope: Risking Art in Modernity

Von Balthasar's gravest risks, at least as far as *art* is concerned, occur in a pair of articles published in 1940: "Die Kunst in der Zeit," and its response, "Antikritik."[51] These were written just after the last volume of *Apokalypse* was published in 1939, and they stand apart from von Balthasar's work on art in the twenties in both time and tone. Both of the 1940 essays raise the issue of modernity and its value to Christianity in the context of Christian art and modern art in particular. Unlike the earlier articles, these two are almost entirely negative (vitriolic, even) about the state of modern art, and here von Balthasar seems to be near despair. Yet he also insists on radical hope, and the tension between these two dispositions paints a picture of a man who values art profoundly, but also senses danger in it.

The first of these articles, "Die Kunst in der Zeit," discusses the dilemma of modern art as a struggle between real creativity and nihilism. This struggle is felt in the current era, according to von Balthasar, as a need to emerge from a stagnant artistic tradition ("worn clothes," *abgetragene Kleider*) to achieve authenticity (*Echten*).[52] Art in the modern era is in a crisis, a crisis with its past. It struggles with a past that has become, in von Balthasar's view, bereft of fruitfulness. The question is not so much how art might shed its past, but rather how it might come into fruitful contact with its own tradition.

It would appear that the art popular at the time of his writing fit this "crisis" with the past: first Dadaism, which was founded in Switzerland and characterized by radical anarchism; this developed into Surrealism, with its discomfiting juxtapositions and conscious embrace of Hegelian and Marxist thought; both were followed by Abstract Expressionism, which sought to express content without form.[53] All three are heavily characterized by a deliberate separation from past art forms, and their political undertones make their break from tradition more thorough than those previous breaks of the past. Von Balthasar does not desire such an estrangement, and sees these artistic breaks as nihilistic, not as authentic developments.[54] Together they are a rupture, one rooted in the Enlightenment. As far as von Balthasar is concerned, Enlightenment individualism becomes in the modern era the phenomenon of a "tradition-less human being" (*traditionslosen Menschen*), a "pure individual" (*reine Individuums*).[55] The radical atomization of the modern era is not a cultural reinvigoration; it is the loss of culture itself. It is the rejection of the "tradition-character" (*Traditionscharakter*) of human existence.[56]

Von Balthasar is acerbic about the current state of art—a sharp cry from the blithe young man waxing poetic about the development of music in 1925—and his alarm is palpable. He notes the way artistic development becomes more and more an effort to express "personality," which is not in this case a compliment. It is the "deification of the artist," the glorification of *genius*.[57] Modern art strives to have no history, since its only history is that of the individual artist who is glorified. Art's effort to be more radically self-revelatory draws from the old forms of art like an oil pump: it contributes nothing of itself while it drains the past in service of its drive for the hyper-personal. But von Balthasar's language is much starker than this. He calls the modern deification of the artist a "vampiric attrition" (*vampyrische Verschleiß*), the "art of depletion" (*Art von Raubbau*), an art that consumes past forms in a "desperate disguise of its own sterility" (*verzweifelter Deckmantel der eigenen Sterilität*).[58] Art is dead, or in any case persists in life while in fact being lifeless.

The current state of art could not be more hopeless, and perhaps in this way von Balthasar betrays the heavy malaise of the war raging at the edges of Switzerland's borders at the time he writes. Indeed, his commentary touches on the political as well as on the theological. In the case of the latter, he works hard to imply that theology has reached a similar crisis of depletion, a destructive lack of historical memory. He wonders if there is a way out of art's thorough death, and here his aesthetic-theological reflection takes up political themes. Repeatedly, he rejects mere "homeland protection" (*Heimatschutz*) as insufficient to the invigoration of art, working his rejection in a double meaning: he disallows both the physical defense of a country and a mere repetition of past ages in art as the "answer" to art's (or theology's) degeneration.[59] It would be the physical defense of a dry husk. His focus in this article is on aesthetic loss, though the theological and the political (with its representative extremes in the Third Reich and communist Russia) loom as half-said.

More than anything, von Balthasar desires to place the individual in the context of the fullness of tradition—and for him this relativizes not only the individual (who can no longer be deified), but also the community, since the past helps to place both in proper relationship to one another. Neither is absolute. Thus, as a counter to other options available to art for resuscitation, von Balthasar encourages a new "living link with the whole history" of culture:

> Homeland protection [*Heimatschutz*] is not enough. Adequacy can only be a new living link with the whole history [of art]. This would be the opposite of historicism. Anyone who wanted to build the Romanesque, Gothic, or Baroque again would only deny the spirit

of the style, which was a spirit of vitality, inventiveness and was forward-looking.[60]

The revitalization of art, therefore, involves the regrafting of modern awareness back onto the history it has rejected. It must be grafted onto the "whole history," not some part of it, and certainly not its mere repetition; these latter two options would only repeat the "vampiric" reuse of prior forms.

The response to von Balthasar's article was a firestorm to which he responded a few months later in "Antikritik." He was attacked for being too negative, and indeed for being too far-reaching in his bitter criticism. In defending himself, von Balthasar first clarifies his intention, which was to reveal the dire situation in which art finds itself:

> This fatal situation—perhaps at its highpoint today, with critical implications for the history of the world, engulfing as it does not just individuals but also lands and nations—this situation, which no individual himself can "do something about," has been in the wings for a long time because of the growing divergences [*Auseinanderentwicklung*] that have developed between the individual and the community [*Masse*].[61]

Von Balthasar's first act is to insist that the crisis of art, and indeed of theology, has been a long time in coming. Shades of *Razing the Bastions'* stark tones and long historical reach are detectible here in the mode of an aesthetic critique. Von Balthasar's criticism extends fully into theology this time, since theology has also abandoned Patristic and Scholastic tradition for the sake of objective factual research (*sachlich objektiven Forschung*)—not only in German scholarship, but also in scholarship done in English and the Romantic languages.[62] So, though there is a grave crisis in art, von Balthasar means to show how there is a similar crisis in the realm of theology.

Responding to criticism of his dark views, von Balthasar claims that he is not being defeatist or fatalist. Instead of "frivolous optimism" (*leichtfertigen Optimismus*), he wrote "Die Kunst in der Zeit" in an effort "to learn to see" (*sehen zu lernen*); that is, to assess the situation honestly. This, he says, is the first way to overcome the problem.[63] His hope for the reinvigoration of art and of theology repeats an emphasis on wholeness already seen in "Die Kunst in der Zeit." The wholeness this time takes up a fully theological attitude, so that the secular powerlessness (*Ohnmächtigwerden*) of spirit currently in sway will be met by and indeed turn out to be a sign of the "powerlessness [*Ohnmächtigwerden*] of that Almighty Spirit himself, who in this powerlessness and futility redeemed the world and spiritualized power: 'When I am weak, then I am strong.'"[64]

In a significant footnote, von Balthasar returns again to the atomized individual and posits not its opposite as his solution—that would contradict his previous article—but rather puts forward the idea of a *whole individual*: "only the highest power of creative personalities . . . will regenerate our art, and even our religious art."[65] Again, von Balthasar's resolution to the "crisis" is to resist an extreme elevation of either the (history-less) individual or the (totalized) community. If "Die Kunst in der Zeit" and "Antikritik" are taken together as a complete argument, then it is true to say that the former's "whole history" is meant to enable the latter's "creative personality."

With his emphasis on the wholeness of history rather than its distortion and on the creative personality that results in someone who lives related to history, von Balthasar reiterates in broad strokes the underlying concerns in *Apokalypse*. He decries a suffocating self-aggrandizement in art that cuts it off from genuine creativity and that cuts it off from the wealth of its own past. Caught in the glorification of what is absolutely individual, it bleeds the vitality of the past as well as the present. Von Balthasar implies that the absolutization of art, a concern of his as early as "Katholische Religion und Kunst," prevents it from achieving the genuine newness that it desires. Theology, too, is trapped in an analogous myopia, which threatens to cut it off from contact with the tradition and with modern concerns. As an alternative to the current state of art and theology, von Balthasar appears to desire something like the evaluation of tradition Yves Congar would hold in *The Meaning of Tradition*, or rather, something like John Henry Newman's illative sense in *Grammar of Ascent*.[66] In the case of the former, the past cannot be merely repeated, but rather must receive creative newness through its interaction with the present. In the latter, Newman's illative sense permits affirmation to take place without totalized, "scientific" answers that exhaust the present question of its complexity and newness. Both are ways of overcoming theological myopia.

Von Balthasar's radical hope in the face of his devastating critiques of both theology and art is that the profound place of vulnerability each has found itself occupying will in grace turn out to be a strength and an opportunity. Though concerned, deeply concerned, over the radical historical nihilism of art and theology, von Balthasar is not afraid to uncover the threat in all its various discolorations because he does not fear that either will be ultimately destroyed. Every disfiguration he detects is also a potential avenue for grace: historical nihilism could be transformed into a new richness in our attitude toward the past, and stifling individualism could be transformed into the authenticity of creative personality.

DIE APOKALYPSE DER DEUTSCHEN SEELE

As we move to consider the ideas contained in von Balthasar's expanded dissertation, it is helpful to remember the essays that bracket its publication. The early optimism that permeated von Balthasar's writing is braced by strong caution and, after the dissertation, profound concern over that path modern art and theology then appeared intent on taking. Everywhere beneath von Balthasar's incisive critiques of German philosophy and literature is a concern that something has *gone wrong*, but also a concern to hold onto a radical hope for the modern era. To understand these concerns more clearly, we look now to the expanded dissertation itself: *Apokalypse der deutschen Seele*.

Background

Von Balthasar completed his dissertation in German literature in 1929 (it was published in 1930), and thereafter joined the Jesuits. His time with the Jesuits denotes a fundamental change in the direction of his life, one in which the deeply religious and immensely talented young man became a man dominated by theological concerns. As the 1930s unfolded, he trained with the Jesuits in both philosophy and theology, studying in Fourvière and Pullach and guided from afar by Erich Przywara in Munich. He received licentiates in each discipline, but never a doctorate in either one. The geographical variance of his training at this time also influenced him in new ways. His experience in France was particularly fruitful to him, magnifying his appreciation for not only theology, but also, in the words of Peter Henrici, for "the great men of her literature—Péguy, Bernanos, and above all Claudel, with whom he had an unforgettable personal encounter."[67] Here, too, he came to know Thomas Aquinas to a greater degree as well as the "sawdust Thomism" of the era.[68] Von Balthasar also began reading patristic writings with great intensity, out of which emerged three books on three figures in particular: Origen, Gregory of Nyssa, and Maximus the Confessor.[69] The young Jesuit novice, then priest, thus gained familiarity with whole new realms of philosophy, literature, and theology—all while never ceasing to forget his first great project. He expanded his original dissertation into three volumes, published from 1937 to 1939.

It is impossible to underestimate the importance of von Balthasar's intellectual growth in this decade. In the 1930s, von Balthasar is "stretched" on an elemental level: the very resources that he seeks as his first principles receive fundamental expansion. With a heavily philosophical dissertation on German literature already behind him, the young Jesuit scholar adds to an extensive appreciation of art, adds as well to his philosophical training, and most of all enters the realm of the fully theological, the last of which sees his first written contributions near the end of this decade. He grows at the very roots of his intellectual skills. His dialogue with the Church Fathers, for example, never ceases from this point forward; his interest in literature is never again strictly German; his affirmations of the analogy of being remain bound to both Thomas and Przywara. When he broadens his dissertation and publishes it as *Die Apokalypse der deutschen Seele*, the work now bears the unmistakable markings of his own intellectual growth. The original work's theological "tilt" becomes a fully theological a priori, one that critics at the time noticed with derision.[70] Von Balthasar's expanded dissertation, though still ostensibly pertaining to an eschatology of the German soul, is no longer really about the German soul *alone*, if it ever was meant to be purely German at all. His deep knowledge of German philosophy and literature is now placed entirely at the service of a much broader theological vision, one with greater risks, risks that von Balthasar finally highlights when he reaches to the theology of Karl Barth near the end of *Apokalypse*.[71]

It is to this broader vision that I turn in order to frame von Balthasar's *Apokalypse* as a whole. The lengthiest scholarly interaction with *Apokalypse* comes in the form of Aidan Nichols's *Scattering the Seed*, a work that reviews von Balthasar's earliest philosophical writings. Nichols and Alois M. Hass have done the most to review and summarize *Apokalypse*, alongside a collection of critiques in *Letzte Haltungen*.[72] A full summary of von Balthasar's expanded dissertation rests in Nichols's *Scattering the Seed*, and I will not recapitulate it here. Instead, I will highlight certain essential themes that lead into von Balthasar's evaluation of poetry and philosophy (broadly construed), especially his evaluation of Rilke's poetry.

Rilke, Heidegger, and the Absolute Unity of Death and Life

As we have already seen, Rilke haunts all three volumes of *Apokalypse* until finally coming to the fore as perhaps the ultimate figure of artistic tragedy. The poet Rilke is paired with Martin Heidegger, who is in his way the ultimate philosophical tragedy.[73] In *Apokalypse*, the two men are presented as kindred spirits: the philosopher who saw philosophy end in poetry, and the poet who became dominated by (philosophical) questions of life and death. Here philosophy and poetry finally meet on the same horizon, and it is interesting to note that von Balthasar diagnoses each with the same ailment. The reason for the failure is, in von Balthasar's eyes, *not* because philosophy and poetry have greeted one another in these two figures—as if the shared coherence of poetry and philosophy must by necessity result in failure. Rilke and Heidegger fail, rather, because their worldviews are significantly *flattened*, and their understandings of transcendence—either philosophical or poetic, or perhaps philosophical-poetic—suffer for it. They each make what is an essentially *metaphysical* error, which is to view the universe entirely according to contingency, thus "flattening" a more classic hierarchy of being. But this metaphysical error is also, in von Balthasar's read, poetic: it distorts Rilke's art as much as Hiedegger's philosophy.

My focus is on Rilke's role in *Apokalypse* and not Heidegger. My question is with respect to poetry, even as Heidegger parallels it in his philosophy. Even so, describing aspects of von Balthasar's critique of Heidegger's philosophy as it relates to *Apokalypse*'s interpretation of Rilke will be helpful to us.

Von Balthasar divides his analysis of Heidegger and Rilke into three major themes: (1) Being in the World, (2) Decay and Death, (3) Creation from Fear. All three contribute to an evaluation that focuses on the way in which both figures totalize qualities of contingent existence. For both Rilke and Heidegger, the finitude of life, which is primarily marked at its utmost limit in death, is exalted as the highest and most eternal condition for reality itself. So both Rilke and Heidegger become prime examples of the Dionysius principle, which gives permanence and transcendence to the finite.

In von Balthasar's eyes, Heidegger accomplishes the elevation of contingency into the absolute through his discussion of *Dasein*, which gives death not only ontological weight but also ontological permanence: it is that by which and in which life persists. Here von Balthasar, who is writing in the 1930s, recalls many of the major themes in Heidegger's *Being and Time* (1927). Of particular relevance is Heidegger's characterization of *Dasein*, of Being-in-the-world, as always impending toward its end: *Dasein* is Being-towards-the-end as much as it is also in-the-world. Death always "stands before us," and because of this it gives to *Dasein* its "ownmost possibility" for authenticity and wholeness. Heidegger explains himself in the following way:

> Death is a possibility-of-Being which *Dasein* itself has to take over in every case. With death, *Dasein* stands before itself in its ownmost potentiality-for-Being. This is a possibility in which the issue is nothing less than *Dasein's* Being-in-the-world. Its death is the possibility of no-longer-being-able-to-be-there. If *Dasein* stands before itself as this possibility, it has been *fully* assigned to its ownmost potentiality-for-Being. When it stands before itself in this way, all its relations to any other *Dasein* have been undone. This ownmost non-relational possibility is at the same time the uttermost one.[74]

So for the Heidegger of *Being and Time*, death existentially and ontologically determines *Dasein* not merely when it occurs, but also through every stage of authentic existence. Death is at once totalizing and individualizing. Piotr Hoffman summarizes Heidegger's point of view: "Death totalizes me, for due to death my identity will become complete. Death individualizes me, for it imposes upon me the one and only experience that is inescapably mine."[75] It is this point of view that has von Balthasar concerned.

Dasein is always anticipating death. This anticipation is not, Heidegger stresses, a continual worry over death. It is, rather, the fundamental existential-ontological orientation of *Dasein* in its wholeness.[76] For von Balthasar, Heidegger's discussion of death and its relationship to *Dasein* is far too determinative of each: nowhere is either relativized, except in terms of the other. Death is to be understood through *Dasein*, and *Dasein* through death. Heidegger imitates Rilke's circling falcon, which has no resting-place. What individuates *Dasein* also renders it inescapably indeterminate and solitary, at least until its death.[77]

Rilke renders much the same conclusion through his poetry, and in the poet's case von Balthasar sees a figure who deliberately sets himself as far apart from Christianity as possible and yet without knowing draws himself close to it again. In Rilke, the emphasis leans more and more on *surrender* (*Hingabe*), as opposed to Heidegger's *anticipation* (*Vorlaufen*): the subject, finding itself already in the world (akin to Heidegger's being-in-the-world), must—in order to really be authentic—continually surrender itself to the conditions of its existence, most of all the conditions of its death. For Rilke, surrender to death is an effort filled with dread, and alternately praise.[78] Rilke describes a final attitude (an "apocalypse") in which death plays a fundamental, even constitutive, role.

For von Balthasar, Rilke's poetry revolves around several "ground motives" (*Grundmotive*): God and death, love and anxiety (*Angst*), angels and time, transfiguration and risk. These motives do not change, instead increasing with intensity and urgency, and for von Balthasar, his section on Heidegger and Rilke does much the same.[79] Always, the focus remains on contingent being that can perceive nothing but its own demise, and in horror and exaltation lifts that death to a quasi-divine status. Because he perceives Rilke and Heidegger's basic point of view in this way, von Balthasar describes Rilke's position as a radical phenomenology: the poet asks questions about worldliness, temporality, and perishableness—as phenomenology would—and asks after their possible perpetuation.[80]

Von Balthasar shows detailed knowledge of Rilke's works through his citations, and among these there emerge two central texts that were also Rilke's last: *Sonnets to Orpheus* and *Duino Elegies*.[81] Both works revolve around the three themes outlined in von Balthasar's section on

Heidegger and Rilke, and both serve as the poet's final reflections on death before his own. Von Balthasar takes them up as the banners for Rilke's ultimate poetic achievements, and he orders the rest of the poet's works around these two.

Sonnets to Orpheus exploits the Greek myth of Orpheus in order to discuss the nature of existence. Orpheus, according to the myth, is a great poet and musician admired by humans and gods alike for his skill. His beloved Eurydice, the inspiration for his art, dies. Orpheus's sorrow is so powerfully expressed in his music that he is permitted to visit her in the underworld and take her back with him on one condition: he must not look back to make sure she follows him, or she will be lost to him forever. But of course Orpheus cannot resist, and he turns back to see her vanish before his eyes. Rilke was fascinated by the myth before he wrote *Sonnets*, and it receives some treatment in his poem "Orpheus. Eurydice. Hermes."[82]

The organizing image in *Sonnets* is music, another theme with which Rilke was fascinated early and which receives expansion here.[83] Von Balthasar is quick to highlight the theme.[84] Orpheus is presented as the ultimate poet-musician, so much so that the figure of Orpheus becomes a symbol of the divine ("the god"). The god of the *Sonnets* lives according to the "law" of music: music, in order to be *musical*, must always persist by always dying. This law describes the nature of a note, which, to be played, must rise into being and fall to silence again as another note emerges in the melody. Only together, in the whole dialogue between notes and silence—life and death—do we have song.

The myth of Orpheus, as expressed in Rilke's poetry, aligns the poet closely with Heidegger and at the same time differentiates him from Heidegger. Orpheus approximates the way *Dasein* is "thrown" and always-already in the middle of existence: the poet-god is scattered everywhere, and suffuses existence. Since Orpheus is at once living and dead, death is always determining the wholeness of existence, which again resembles Heidegger's characterization of *Dasein* in *Being and Time*. Nevertheless, the intermingling of death and life is for Rilke so thorough as to suggest in von Balthasar's eyes a distinctive understanding of time, which in turn nuances Rilke's conception of authenticity apart from Heidegger's. While in *Being and Time* Heidegger describes authenticity in terms of an openness to the death that determines *Dasein*'s wholeness and individuality, for Rilke authenticity is characterized rather as its *living in death*: this, for Rilke, is not only a question of the existential present (as with Heidegger), but also is cast as a type of eternity. Heidegger brackets out the question of eternal life; Rilke incorporates eternity fully into death. Rilke's subject, as von Balthasar explains, "lives as dead in the landscape of action."[85]

So for Rilke all of existence must be described as a rising song, much as the first sonnet begins: "There ascended a tree. O pure over-ascendancy! / O Orpheus singing! O tall tree in the ear!"[86] The nettled problem of growth and song are one, and Rilke establishes very early a total link between song and existence in this way. He becomes more forthright later: he claims that "song is existence,"[87] that existence is a breathing, invisible poem,[88] a place where transformation and departure are one.[89]

Von Balthasar highlights the way the first sonnet encapsulates Rilke's fundamental intentions. Drawing on its first lines about the tree, von Balthasar uses them to express one of his major concerns, which is how both Heidegger and Rilke *identify* existence, truth, and beauty. All three are not simply united, but also the same thing. Existence itself is absolutized, so that all of its transitory properties—and even its very *transitoriness*—are elevated to the status of totally governing characteristics. Note the comparison in von Balthasar's explanation:

> But as "truth" is existence for Heidegger, it is also the third transcendental, "beauty." Art is existence for Rilke: "song is reality." Because it [song] is its illuminating transcendence ("O pure transcendence! O Orpheus singing!") and thus the atmosphere of "divine" nothingness, "the room of praise" is being coming to itself.[90]

Rilke's *Sonnets to Orpheus*, perhaps better than any other work of his, describes the identity of contingent existence and beauty that von Balthasar diagnoses in both Heidegger and Rilke. Essentially, finitude becomes an unrestricted quality of all being; finitude becomes, for Heidegger and Rilke, a transcendental.[91]

The end result, for Heidegger, is the identity of being and nonbeing (*Sein* and *Nichtsein*). In *Being and Time*, Heidegger gives careful consideration to what he calls the "not" (or "nullity," *Nichtigkeit*) of *Dasein*. This nullity is experienced as *Dasein's* inability to be its own ground, which is felt as a "not."[92] Key for von Balthasar in the ontological identity of being and nonbeing is Heidegger's "What Is Metaphysics?" from 1929. Here, Heidegger quotes Hegel's *Science of Logic*, "Pure Being and pure Nothing are therefore the same," and argues that Hegel is correct, although for different reasons than Hegel himself thought. "Being itself is essentially finite," Heidegger reasons, "and reveals itself only in the transcendence of *Dasein* which is held out into the nothing."[93] What Heidegger means to achieve through his union of *Sein* and *Nichtsein* is a fully existential awareness of what is, for him, the central metaphysical question: "Why are there beings at all, rather than nothing?"[94] *Dasein* is always confronted with this question, and so is always "held out into the nothing" in a double sense: held out into the inevitability of its own death (as in *Being and Time*), and held out into the fact that its existence means always to be surrounded by the nullity of what it is not because it is finite (as in "What Is Metaphysics?").[95] So, for Heidegger, the identity of being and nonbeing—felt existentially, as it were, by *Dasein*—becomes the condition for the transcendence of *Dasein*. When *Dasein* "holds itself out into the nothing," it is placed in a position "beyond beings," and thus in a position of transcendence.[96] In this way, the unity of *Sein* and *Nichtsein* provide the possibility of transcendence, and in von Balthasar's mind Heidegger equates truth with finitude as such.[97]

Von Balthasar insists that the same can be said for Rilke in his *Sonnets*. In the *Sonnets*, Orpheus—the mythological poet and musician—becomes for Rilke a living-dying god. Von Balthasar highlights the metaphysical undertones in this poetic image, as when he looks to Rilke's discussion of the "Non-being's condition" (*Nicht-Seins Bedingung*) by which the reader is asked to imitate Orpheus.[98] The full context in Rilke is as follows:

> Be before all departure, as if it were behind
> you, like Winter, which even now pales.
> Beneath the snows is a Winter so endlessly consigned
> that, while frozen-over, your heart in truth prevails.

> Be always dead in Eurydice—, ascend in musical progression;
> in splendor climb backward into the absolute ground.
> Here, beneath the evanescence, be, in the wealth of declension,
> be a struck glass, which already annihilates itself in the sound.

Be, and know likewise Non-Being's condition,
the unending ground for your inner pulsation,
that you do this fully, this one time.

Which is also needed, like the hollow and silent
store of rich Nature, the unspeakable hum,
count yourself rejoicing in it and forget the sum.[99]

The poet asks his reader to be "always dead," to be "a struck glass," and here Rilke has achieved his most radical unity between life and death. In order to live, we must be "before all departure," which also means to always be departing. Elsewhere in the *Sonnets*, Rilke calls this manner of existing, Orpheus's manner of existing, the "silent friend of many distances" according to which we are always persisting in an intimate relationship with space and separation.[100] Von Balthasar claims it is the poet's way of trying to work through the problem of negation and distance—Hegel's distance.[101] Like Hegel, Rilke perceives a troubling distance that needs to be overcome; unlike Hegel, it is overcome through abiding death instead of a final synthesis.[102]

Von Balthasar's concern with Rilke is that his beautifully wrought poetry testifies to death as the ground and condition for life, and indeed for art. Later in his section on Rilke, von Balthasar makes the question more urgent:

What for Heidegger is the problem of being from nothing [*Nichts*], is for Rilke creation [*Schaffen*] from nothing, the creating [*schaffende*] nothing that is man. And as Heidegger brought the fear [*Angst*] of being by exceeding being as a whole, likewise does Rilke's fear of the "ground spring," the fabric and the bearing of creation. The *Book of Hours* already supplies crucial questions about the medium of the poet: is the absolute in which he breathes, which is substantial, God? Or is it substantial nothingness?[103]

Von Balthasar detects the inexorable logic of Rilke's poetry, which is that the empty "space" (realm, silence, *Nichtsein*) of death so thoroughly permeates life that it becomes the condition for human creativity.

Beyond a dualistic opposition between life and death, beyond a horizon that views them together as a "whole" out-of-nothing (Heidegger), Rilke's sensibilities draw death into the most intimate arenas of human effort.[104] Von Balthasar summarizes the turn through the poet's own eyes, in the very early *Book of Hours*, when Rilke begins to wonder whether the poet creates from nothing—from a kind of death. The poet himself becomes a space of life-from-death, and the collision between the two reaches a fever pitch at such a point. Rilke, in a later poem, describes it as a kind of self-surrender: "All the things to which I give myself / Grow rich and spend me."[105] But von Balthasar does not detect surrender at all, only power masquerading as surrender. Here the poet creates *ex nihilo*, like God.[106] This is a serious problem in von Balthasar's eyes, and two students of his early work are quick to note von Balthasar's reticence to accept Rilke's understanding of surrender. As Nichols says in *Scattering the Seed*: "Spontaneity and receptivity may not so much coalesce as prove mutually subversive, reciprocally destructive."[107] Or in Cyril O'Regan's words, von Balthasar has an "abiding sense from *Apocalypse of the German Soul* that German thought's most feminine gestures are contaminated with masculine urges, [and so] we are put on notice that the will to power can masquerade as *Gelassenheit*."[108]

The end result of Rilke's creative *ex nihilo* finds its fullest expression in the *Duino Elegies*. If the *Sonnets* discuss existence according to the theme of music and song, then in *Duino Elegies* that song (since an elegy is a poem-song) becomes a naked discussion of death. Both relate essentially the same metaphysical perspective, but under different modes. Von Balthasar is set on this link: "The Sonnets lead to inner plasticity by virtuosity, but the Elegies at the same time give the theory and metaphysic of this action."[109] So the *Sonnets* robe death in the glory of praise, while in the *Elegies*, Rilke has no patience anymore: beauty and terror are one. Death stands before Rilke as an angelic impossible, a titanic figure that the poet addresses and from whom he expects (indeed, demands)[110] no answer: "Every angel is terrifying."[111]

Themes already familiar from the *Sonnets* are repeated again in the *Elegies*: existence receives a paradoxical (non)solution yet again: "abiding is nowhere";[112] death is the presupposition for life.[113] Decay and menace, for the Rilke in von Balthasar's eyes, have the same character, an ontological character[114]—ultimately, everything must be inverted: "Negative is positive. Weakness is power."[115] Von Balthasar describes the inversion as an absolute agreement to a constant "Yes-No," a dialectic between life and death that can only be absolutized as a permanent relative.[116] This inversion is perhaps no better expressed in its tragic consequences than in the Second Elegy:

> Lovers, you, in your sufficiency in each other,
> I ask you. You grasp each other. Do you have evidence?
> I see that it happens in me, when my hands fold
> together or when my weary
> face rests itself in them. There is for me a little
> feeling. Still, for this who would yet risk to *be*?
> Yet you, you who rise with the other's
> ecstasy until, overwhelmed, he
> implores you: no *more*—; when underneath your hands
> you both become rich as aged wine;
> when you sometimes disappear because you
> so wholly soar beyond reach: I ask you. I know
> you touch each other so blessedly because at each caress
> your bodies do not shrink away, as you—tenderly—
> drown in one other; because beneath each other you sense
> tangible permanence. So you almost promise each other eternity
> in an embrace. And still, when you survive these first
> awful glances, the yearning through the window,
> the first shared moment, a walk through the garden:
> lovers, *are* you lovers after this? When you lift and join
> each to the other's mouth—: drink to drink:
> o how the drinker then strangely vanishes in the action.[117]

This section of Rilke's Second Elegy describes his pervading doubt that love can provide any real or sustainable comfort for the profound loneliness that characterizes existence. There is no refuge in another. In an earlier article on Rilke from 1933, von Balthasar describes the intensity of Rilke's loneliness, a loneliness that reduces love to an "eerie Doppelganger" (*unheimlichen Doppelgänger*).[118] Love has no force for Rilke, whose solitude is so peerless that the expectations for another are dissolved into an absolute distance: the absolute distance of Orpheus in the

Sonnets, or the eyeless gaze of the angels in the *Elegies*. The poet has become absolute, and absolutely alone.

The peerless solitude of Rilke's creativity is closely aligned with Heidegger's *Dasein* and bears an orientation to death that makes *Dasein* its ownmost and nonrelational. Both are characterized by radical individualization in the face of death, and here Rilke is more radical than Heidegger, with the latter's emphasis on care (*Sorge*) soothing *Dasein*'s existential aloneness. Such solitude is for von Balthasar the final standpoint of the Dionysian principle. It reflects the atomized, history-less individual he fears in his 1940 essays, and the aesthetic religion he distances himself from in his early writings on art. The worry here, for von Balthasar, is both artistic and metaphysical. Art has absorbed a sort of nihilism, so that it can—as in Rilke—no longer express anything but the beautiful terror of the angels. Such an attitude emerges out of an inability to conceive of a transcendence that is not entirely immanent to itself, which is a metaphysical as much as an artistic worldview. Beauty becomes the terrible mask for a new transcendental of being: death.

Terror is the most appropriate word to describe where Rilke and German thought appear to end. The term summarizes von Balthasar's judgment on the modern German "final attitude," an attitude that seeks its transcendence in itself and leads itself to ultimate failure. Von Balthasar's read of these various Dionysian thinkers, particularly Rilke, shows their awareness of their own tragedy. Rilke reaches desperately for love and finds solitude; the poet embraces surrender to pain in the last (tenth) elegy. For Rilke, this is his final expression of glory. For von Balthasar, Rilke has discovered the final expression of a tragedy. Beauty, with no anchor but the finite, becomes a horrific testament to inevitable failure.

Central to the union of horror and beauty—beauty *as terror*—is the identification of being and nonbeing, which for von Balthasar is also the totalization of contingent being. Since all that is, is finite, then finitude must grapple with its inherent limitation (for Heidegger, the "not" and ultimately death), which then forces finitude to embrace limitation as its grounds, means, and end. Death and life are cyphers of one another, since ultimately they are ontologically identical. Rilke grasps this ontological identity in his poetry, and through art reveals the metaphysical repercussions such a perspective has on beauty. Beauty is thus the handmaid of the terrible.

Von Balthasar is greatly concerned over the fate of beauty in modernity, and he himself "circles" between hope and despair. Or rather, he paints a scene that is equally dark and light, a sort of theological chiaroscuro. Beauty and metaphysics, art and philosophy, have come to a mutually resembled ruin: atomized, history-less, nihilist. They resemble one another because they are not so far apart. As von Balthasar comes to emphasize in his theological aesthetics, beauty itself is a transcendental—it is proper to metaphysics. His response to the twin failures of philosophy and art in the modern age, as characterized in *Apokalypse*, is the unusual unity of philosophy and art in *Glory of the Lord*. Here von Balthasar answers by *heightening* the relationship between each through theology.

As we will find in the next chapter, it is through his theological aesthetics that von Balthasar's evaluation of the modern age does not rest on this negative note, even as it remains aware of every risk. The most perceptible hint in this direction is von Balthasar's section on Karl Barth in *Apokalypse*, at first a counterintuitive claim and a contradictory move, given Barth's thorough reticence toward art. What von Balthasar sees in Karl Barth is a theologian who keenly defends exactly what Rilke loses: otherness. Specifically, the radical otherness of God.[119] Already von Balthasar had contrasted Rilke's failed sense of transcendence and intimacy with the Christian sense of each. As he says elsewhere, where Rilke cannot really love because there is no other except the one consumed in desire, Christian love "grows from the immanence of an absolute transcendence."[120] Barth grasps this absolute transcendence, though perhaps not its immanence.

Von Balthasar also adheres to a particular theological perspective for the sake of authentically understanding beauty. God is the first and last word, indeed the Word who protects and enables all human words. Von Balthasar, while praising the human desire that Barth at times places under deep suspicion, sees in Barth a truly *theological* aesthetic. It is this aesthetic, and no other, that can rescue the beautiful—and, through the beautiful, theology—from tragedy. It is this aesthetic to which we move in the following chapter.

TWO

The Redemption of Beauty

Von Balthasar and the Path to *Herrlichkeit*

Lazarus

I sucked air through dusty lungs, jaw
hanging open as in an endless scream.
Nerves wakened all fire and raw
as blood squeezed through collapsed veins.

I lurched, loose muscles sliding along
parched bone—tendons tightening in
sudden jolts. I had been alone.
Now I, now . . . oh, where had I been?

Dark solitude of wakeless sleep,
lying with the worms that over time
undid me: unwound each fleshly string
that over a lifetime I had meant to bind.

We are all undone, our faces rotted
to the skull. Time has no sympathy.

Nor do we: so quick to forget the dead
though we all die, and slowly.

I staggered to my feet, still harbored
by the earth that had swallowed me.
Still bound by a ragged shroud: forward,
onward, out of the watching dark—

into warm light on sore and squinting eyes,
eyes that saw the tear-stained cheeks of
the Son of Man, who looked at me and sighed:
"Oh Lazarus, I forget no one."

For all the darkness to be found in von Balthasar's *Apokalypse*, a world in which the human being lives in the shadow of total death without the Christian God, beauty has not died. Well into his theological career, von Balthasar begins a massive theological project: the trilogy (his "triptych"), of which the first word is *beauty*. If *Apokalypse* and *Glory of the Lord* are to be viewed together, then the first word of the latter is a response to the first word of the former: *beauty* responds to *terror*.

As we saw in the last chapter, what is "at risk" in the case of beauty is at once metaphysical and artistic, and indeed ultimately theological. The collapse of transcendence that von Balthasar recounts in his *Apokalypse* is at root metaphysical because the proper distinction between God and creation has been destroyed, and human thought, no longer able to imagine transcendence beyond the contingent existence it knows, submerges transcendence into contingency itself. Metaphysically, this means that—with figures like Heidegger—finitude becomes a transcendental of being, a transcendental alongside the one, the true, the good, and the beautiful. In art, the metaphysical error plays out in expressions of radical tragedy. With figures like Rilke, the evanescence of human existence is equated with its eternal destiny, so that the end of every human being is to be like Orpheus: persisting in death. In either case, what human nature is oriented to in a final and constitutive manner is death. In this way, the "openness" of the human spirit that defines its striving for transcendence is continually, painfully thwarted.

Art and metaphysics stand and fall together. To risk one is to risk the other. What von Balthasar has achieved in such a conviction is a most serious acknowledgement of beauty's status as a transcendental: if beauty really is a transcendental of all being, then an error with respect to being will mar beauty and thus those things indebted to beauty, especially art. Modern thought has distorted being, and thus also the beautiful.

Von Balthasar's response to the modern distortion of beauty is to shape his theological aesthetics. While still careful to distinguish between art and theology, and indeed philosophy and theology, the correct proportions of both art and philosophy are to be found in theology. To be specific, the true shape of human transcendence and fulfillment is to be found in Jesus Christ, the Word made flesh. Much as in the above poem, "Lazarus," Christ is the one who responds to death and shows us its defeat. In and through the Incarnate Word, created being is brought to the fullness it desires—and indeed brought to a fullness it can neither dream nor achieve by its own power. Here, here in Christ, is where von Balthasar locates the rich intersection between art and metaphysics, and in *Glory of the Lord* he allies the two in a unique and expressive theological language that supports his theological aesthetics.

In this chapter, we will see that *Glory of the Lord* is both a refutation and a redemption of the modern age. Modern art threatens to be, in von Balthasar's eyes, an art that glorifies the individual artist and so obscures its expression in its obsession with the absolutely unique, history-less individual. So, too, modern metaphysics empties being of its fullness to such a degree that the individual subject stands in a peerless, atomic tragedy. The individual stands *alone*. Von Balthasar is firmly set against this sort of ahistorical self-glorification. At the same time, such an obsession with the individual distorts what von Balthasar understands to be an essentially good and distinctive quality of the modern age: the emphasis on what is *personal*. This he desires to incorporate into his theological aesthetics, which is itself an excavation of what has been lost in the past—not for the sake of exalting the past *as past*, but rather for the sake of a vivified present.

FROM *APOKALYPSE* TO THEOLOGY: RISKING BEAUTY AND MODERNITY

How can von Balthasar, that great lover and defender of beauty, begin his career with the terror of a beauty distorted by modern thought? It would do us well to be irritated—cage-rattled, like Rilke's panther—at this point in time.[1]

> His gaze has grown so weary from the passing
> of the bars, that it bears nothing more.
> To him it is as if there are a thousand bars
> and behind a thousand bars no world.[2]

If we, and von Balthasar, are not merely to retreat into the past, then it becomes necessary to respond to the distortion of beauty with its proper proportions. In his response to modernity, von Balthasar carefully incorporates the highly personal (even phenomenological) into his theological aesthetic as much as he recalls the importance of the Thomist understanding of being. Beauty is his first word, and this is both a classical metaphysical invocation as well as a modern one.

One interpretive option is to see *Glory of the Lord* as a refutation of the failings uncovered in the artists discussed in *Apokalypse*. Given the false eschatologies of *Apokalypse*, *Glory of the Lord* responds with a true eschatology, one with a transcendent end to be found in the wholly transcendent God. In this way, the first epoch in the trilogy can be seen as a continuation of *Apokalypse's* cautionary evaluation of modern beauty and philosophy, a continuation that—unlike *Apokalypse*—responds with a rich account of the ways in which beauty can and should play a role in theology. *Glory of the Lord* in this context would be like the response of a doctor to a sick patient, a doctor who responds by telling the patient what real health looks like and how it can be achieved.

Another option is to see *Glory of the Lord* as a resuscitation of the modern age through the use of ancient theology and art (Augustine, Bonaventure, Dante) alongside the use of modern theologians and artists (artists and theologians of a different sort than most moderns from *Apokalypse*: Barth, Péguy, Hopkins, etc.). Here *Glory of the Lord* becomes the avenue by which the modern desire for the personal is redeemed through its contact with the objective glory of God, not for the sake of condemning what is personal, unique, and free, but rather for the sake of showing its authentic contours. In this case, *Glory of the Lord* is not a negative refutation or counterposition so much as it is an attempt to place the modern back into dialogue with the past it originally sought to refute on its own terms. We may recall the concerns for a "whole history" and "creative personality" from *Die Kunst in der Zeit* and *Antikritik*, and see von Balthasar's efforts as an attempt to provide the grounds for just that sort of wholeness and personality. This second option is by far von Balthasar's favored stance in *Glory of the Lord*, though elements of the first remain active throughout.

First, then, we must seek after the immediate outcome of *Apokalypse* and how *Glory of the Lord* is an inheritor of that outcome and a development beyond it. There are two articles that Aidan Nichols indicates as especially responsive to the problems emerging from *Apokalypse*: "The Fathers, the Scholastics and Ourselves" (1939) and "On the Tasks of Catholic Philosophy in Our Time" (1946).[3] These two writings serve to frame an important period of time in the development of von Balthasar's attitudes toward beauty, which leads us into the theological aesthetics. It should be emphasized that these articles were written in tandem with many of those writings reviewed in the last chapter, which means that von Balthasar was already working toward a more positive incorporation of modern concerns in theology even as he was heavily critiquing modernity.

"The Fathers, the Scholastics, and Ourselves"

The first of these articles, "The Fathers, the Scholastics, and Ourselves," is von Balthasar's appraisal of Patristic and Scholastic contributions to theology in the modern era, and of the modern era's contributions to theology. According to Nichols, von Balthasar writes with Jean Daniélou in mind: von Balthasar lauds the *Scholastics* as well as the Fathers, gently opposing Daniélou's more radical focus on the Patristic age.[4] So von Balthasar looks back on the three great ages of the Church (Patristic, Scholastic, modern), to examine the "innermost structural law" of each, measuring them "according to the structural law of what is essentially Christian as we encounter this norm in the Gospel."[5] This method of evaluation, which strives to draw out what is most distinctive in an era and relate it to a unifying norm, very much resembles the way von Balthasar would use the gestalt (form) of Christ to order his theological aesthetics decades later. As in his aesthetics, he first sets out to describe the "form" (here: "innermost structural law") of the Gospel.

Von Balthasar begins by insisting that human beings desire to be with God, but that this desire has been distorted into a desire to *be* God.[6] Original sin, here interpreted as the grasp to be God, is the falsification of an irreducible difference: God is incomparable and nothing can claim his place. In this essay, von Balthasar follows his mentor, Erich Przywara, whose work on the analogy of being reinforces its central role in any assessment of created existence. Von Balthasar's claims about desire and its distortion are metaphysically oriented, navigated as they are by the analogy of being. With the same argument, von Balthasar also stresses, as in *Apokalypse*, the importance of the human desire for transcendence (in *Apokalypse*, an "openness") and how it is necessary to distinguish between God and creature for the sake of the fulfillment of that desire. A failure to properly distinguish is also a failure to comprehend desire.

Against the sinful distortion of our desire and its proportionate metaphysical distortions stands the Incarnation. God and the world are not alike, and yet they do share likeness. Any similarity is governed by an "ever-greater" dissimilarity. This dissimilarity is "overcome" yet preserved in the Incarnation, where in Christ we can now really share in God's life as we desire, through "the absolute 'unmixedness' of the two natures, indeed precisely in their greatest separation."[7] The unique Christian norm has as its foundation the ineluctable difference between God and creation, and the union of the two in Christ without the destruction of their difference.[8] Von Balthasar thus reaches back to Chalcedon for his Christian norm and reads it as the abiding explanation of the Resurrection, uniting both the Resurrection and Chalcedon inasmuch as the first reveals that grace perfects nature and does not destroy it, and the second affirms and explains this conviction.[9] The difference between God and creation is not eliminated by the Incarnation; it is reinforced, and brought to fulfillment without admixture. Von Balthasar thus *stresses* the role of nature in the Christian norm, which, as Aidan Nichols notes, runs against the representation of the later von Balthasar "as the prophet whose contours are obliterated by the form of grace."[10] The norm that von Balthasar is looking for is the Incarnation, and it is a norm that illuminates the vitality of nature and not its poverty—or rather, it is a norm that illuminates the vitality of nature's poverty. With the Christian norm established, von Balthasar sets out to evaluate the great ages of the Church according to such a norm.

The Patristic era bears a unique place with respect to the other eras; Patristic theology is foundational in a way never again mirrored.[11] The Patristic age is marked, most of all, by an "immediacy" to the experience of the Gospel, an immediacy that continues to echo in its writings. This is why the age is a "wellspring of living water" for all ages. For all its greatness, however, von Balthasar detects a danger in the highly Platonic thought of the Fathers: that of a latent pantheism, a participation in divinity that in the end does not offer a strong enough distinction between God and creation.[12] The danger of distorting our unmixed sharing in divine life always looms on the horizon.

This is a danger that Scholasticism would help to correct through its careful application of Aristotelian concepts.[13] In an odd way, the Christian indebtedness to (Platonic) pagan ideas is rescued through indebtedness to other (Aristotelian) pagan ideas. But it is not Aristotelianism itself that von Balthasar is out to vindicate; it is created nature. Thomas Aquinas thus stands as the theologian of *nature*, a nature that is "*presupposed* before any gracious and unmerited participation in God can take place and in fact is the basis by which this participation can take place."[14] A presupposed nature helps to buttress the integrity of created being with respect to grace, and thus to distinguish creation from its creator even in the midst of salvation history. This also helps theology to defend the gratuity of grace, since the presupposition of human nature means that this nature does not require God's grace as necessary to itself.[15] Pantheism is eviscerated through a robust understanding of nature, which for von Balthasar helps to radicalize the intimacy of the "unmixed union" between God and creation in Christ.[16]

Yet it is the modern age that brings *both* the Patristic and Scholastic eras to purity, despite the modern age also being an age with profound flaws: "nowhere else does the legacy of original sin thrive more strongly, nowhere in fact does impotence, dissipation and dissolution, seem so present as here."[17] The modern age is characterized by progressive emphasis on the individual and the personal, and it is in *this* emphasis that the real relationship between creature and creator is made most naked.[18] Because the modern age is more aware of the various nettled struggles of an individual, humanity's sharp longing for God and the inadequacy of that longing's ability to fulfill itself are thrown in relief. So, despite a modern age often hostile to Christianity, von Balthasar claims that, "the point is not to fret how the authenticity of the Christian dispensation might be once more distorted and disfigured through original sin in quite unexpected ways. Rather, the real issue is the more exciting possibility: that this authenticity can be even more apparent in our time than perhaps ever before."[19]

"The Fathers, Scholastics, and Ourselves" presents us with a von Balthasar who, for all the critiques leveled against the literary-philosophical attitudes of the modern era in *Apokalypse*, sees purpose in this difficult age, and indeed, a positive contribution to Christianity. The role of the personal, of the individual, is the modern age's defining theological datum, and von Balthasar perceives in this emphasis a danger, but also an opportunity. Given the article's close proximity to *Apokalypse*'s lengthened publication, it is necessary to see in von Balthasar both an unwavering optimism alongside the darkness in *Apokalypse*. Von Balthasar's interest in what is personal has not yet received definition, except negatively: the person is not history-less, and not separated from others. What a person is, authentically speaking, receives definition in *Theo-Drama* and *Glory of the Lord*.

"The Tasks of Catholic Philosophy in Our Time"

"On the Tasks of Catholic Philosophy in Our Time" was written after the Second World War had ended. This is the same article that in Aidan Nichols's estimation gives the fullest fruits of *Apokalypse*.[20] Von Balthasar's tone has calmed compared to the sharp edges of "Die Kunst in der Zeit" and *Apokalypse*, but the risks are no less grave, since again von Balthasar puts to the question how natural knowledge (here: philosophy, whereas in *Apokalypse* it was also art) might still enliven the Church in the modern era. This is no small task in a time when the whole Church stands in "twilight . . . vis-à-vis the modern world."[21]

As in "The Fathers, the Scholastics, and Ourselves," von Balthasar makes the shaping light of Christ the formal starting point for his reflection, since it is in view of the cross and Resurrection that the "greatness of the Christian situation will be grasped," a greatness that takes seriously *both* being in the world and being subject to Christ.[22] Philosophy thus has a legitimate autonomy, an autonomy that Christianity by necessity affirms, an autonomy only properly conceived of as "open" to revelation.[23]

The openness that characterized *Apokalypse* as a chief concern here receives rehashing, this time under the explicit light of a viable Catholic philosophy. For its part, philosophy is driven by an eros for wisdom, and von Balthasar identifies this eros as the same desire that fuels theology's love for God; both fields are oriented to what is ultimate, and in that respect neither can be said to derive from separable desires.[24]

Is there not a confusion here, in the identity of philosophical and theological eros? After his great pains to distinguish between artistic surrender and religious surrender, their "abyssal difference," in "Katholische Religion und Kunst" and "Die Kunst in der Zeit," von Balthasar shows himself quite willing to unite the desire that drives both philosophy and theology. It is reasonable to think he could with equal fairness identify the eros of art and theology, and yet he does not. Here rests an inconsistency in his thought that has yet to play itself out in fullness, and we will see how it affects *Glory of the Lord* and also finds a more nuanced response there.

The resolution in *Glory of the Lord* is partly grasped in "Catholic Philosophy." Theology receives its light from the Triune God—that is, from revelation—and so always stands at an elevated horizon compared to philosophy, but the eros that occupies its study is a love irradiated by grace, not a new love entirely.[25] There is still, then, a distinction at hand between philosophy and theology while yet they are united in eros, though von Balthasar has not satisfactorily explained the distinction and union except with recourse to grace.

To return to topic, von Balthasar finds that in the modern age, Christianity is at a point of real vulnerability, a powerlessness that echoes that of "Antikritik."[26] Von Balthasar describes modern philosophy in terms similar to Rilke's circling (and futile) dialectic from *Apokalypse*: "the Christian-anti-Christian amalgam has been melted together in such an indissoluble fashion that dialectical thought can devote itself to all the games of endless speculation without ever needing to come to a decision."[27] As in his previous articles, von Balthasar's recommended response to the burden of a despoiled Christianity is to seek the tradition anew, opening it up to the modern era—a move *toward* vulnerability—in such a way that the tradition is illuminated in all its vitality as a response to modernity.[28] The old Scholastic real distinction between essence and existence, epitomized by Thomas Aquinas, comes to light again and vivifies the concerns of modern figures such as Hegel and Kierkegaard, showing their one-sidedness and at the same time permitting them to contribute.[29] As we will see, von Balthasar expands on the inversion of the Christian metaphysical task in his theological aesthetics.

Part of this inversion relates to a new emphasis on what is personal. Again like "The Fathers, Scholastics, and Ourselves," von Balthasar highlights the modern fascination with what is individual, its preoccupation with "the unmistakably distinct personality," and notes it as a potentially positive quality. It might be a sign of decadence, but it also "has its reverse side in an indisputably greater concreteness."[30] Catholic philosophy is thus "broadened" into the modern concern for concreteness, but not without permitting its former riches to direct its vulnerable opening-up into the modern era. Made vulnerable in this fashion, Catholic philosophy once again stands ready to despoil the riches of nature for the sake of the Church, since, "The more nature develops in fullness, the more material does supernature possess in nature to transform, elevate, and permeate like a yeast."[31] Though modernity has in many ways inverted the despoiling of riches, still philosophy's fruitful contact with nature is maintained though it is now more complex.

Synthesis: Foreshadowing *Herrlichkeit*

From before the Second World War to its close, von Balthasar's thought strafes across the same problematic midpoint at various angles. He struggles with the role of the past in the present (whether in the form of artistic tradition or theology's great eras), and with modernity's amnesiac individualism (in artists or in philosophers or theologians), all of which turns around a deeply theological concern to legitimate what is natural by preserving what is supernatural. The extremes of modernity, and indeed the extremes of past epochs, distort that concern. In this way, the themes of *Apokalypse* receive further expansion: the past in question is moved more fully into a concern for a "total history," which in theology must mean confronting the Patristic age (and its pagan inheritance) and the Scholastic age. The deification of death, narrowed to its tragic consequences in Rilke's Orpheus, is refined in the form of a disquiet over the place of the individual in the modern age: does modern individualism, undergirded by a distorted metaphysics, result in the lonely modern encounter with death? Von Balthasar answers in the affirmative, and yet with a radical hope that the modern concept of the isolated individual can be transfigured into a vivifying interest in what is personal.

Von Balthasar is optimistic in the sense that the modern age *does* have something positive to contribute, namely its keen sense of what is concrete and individual; he is pessimistic in the same sense that this strength always threatens to dismantle the fundamental Christian insight into the vast difference between God and the world, an insight revealed in fullness in the Incarnation. Von Balthasar bears a profound interest in the strengths of modern thought, especially its personalism, and a profound distrust of its fragmented sense of history. He is at once convinced that the Church can benefit by the modern age, and convinced that there is no more severe threat to the Church (its culture and its faith) than the modern age.

The most fundamental source of von Balthasar's hope is Christological, a continued theme of his early and later writings. Von Balthasar refers back to Christ as the "law" of his thought: inasmuch as personalism can reveal the unique "personality" of Christ—and thus of us—in new ways, it is good; inasmuch as art can reveal the fundamental qualities of our relationship with our Creator, it is also good. So von Balthasar lauds these positives and, following them, condemns their opposites: splitting the personal into a history-less individual leads to the fragmentation of Christ and his Church, and to the rejection of God's complete transcendence.

There is a more tangled contradiction buried beneath von Balthasar's work so far, and that is his sharp distinction between the realm of art and the realm of the religious. If he is to follow this distinction to its fullest conclusions, then it leaves art not only distinguished from religion as nature is distinguished from grace, but also it fissures the two so deeply that it is possible to wonder *why* von Balthasar is so concerned with art at all. That is, if art does not *in any respect* bear qualities of the religious (bearing instead an "abyssal difference"), then why should it be brought into conversation with what is religious, and with such care? Further, why should its errors be so thoroughly resisted? Finally, in a reflection that at last exposes the ragged edges of the contradiction, if this *abyssal difference* is really to be maintained so strictly, does it not work against von Balthasar's beloved law of the Incarnation? This law exalts what is natural as natural, without violating the distinction between created nature and divine nature, and it also describes the unity of creation and God. Is there not, after all, a communication of idioms in the Incarnation, and is it not fair to seek some analogous communication between art and religion? The abyssal difference between art and theology, left as von Balthasar has developed it, only partially accounts for such a law—only accounts for the difference.

Von Balthasar himself has not yet addressed this inner contradiction, and at the beginning of *Glory of the Lord* he councils us to a "constant vigilance required to keep the transcendental beauty of revelation from slipping back into equality with an inner-worldly natural beauty."[32] Von Balthasar maintains this position *and* nuances it, arriving at a fuller account of the "law" of the Incarnation and of the analogy of being.

HERRLICHKEIT: REDEEMING BEAUTY IN THE LIGHT OF GLORY

Given von Balthasar's profound struggles with the modern distortions of beauty, it is all the more impressive that he emerged with his theological aesthetics. It would have been logical, understandable, if he had relinquished hope for art's fitting use in the Church. After all the violence of another world war, compounded by the profound fragmentation of modern art before and during the spilling of blood,[33] coupled with von Balthasar's express bitterness, it would have been easier to retreat to the glories of a history long past. Yet this is precisely the response that von Balthasar is at pains to reject, and in 1961 he emerges with *The Glory of the Lord: A Theological Aesthetics*. He emerges, in other words, with a massive project that sets itself to the restoration of beauty in theology, which means he must restore metaphysics as much as beauty, and means as well that he must show how art is supported by (and supports) such a metaphysic. Von Balthasar sets about a project that *hopes* for a theological beauty that animates the past in the present. It is a hope that grows to fullness as its volumes are written.

Key in von Balthasar's interactions with modern art and philosophy—and their underlying, shared conceptions of beauty—have been three resounding themes: (1) metaphysics, especially the analogy of being;

(2) the question of authentic *personality*; (3) the Christocentric "law" of understanding the world, which is ultimately Chalcedonic in tone. All three themes work together to determine the contours of von Balthasar's critique of modernity and his hope for its riches. All three themes contribute to what emerges in *Glory of the Lord*.

The primary theme determining the others is von Balthasar's Christology. We have so far seen it operating only in nascent form, and we have also seen how von Balthasar makes it clear that Christology helps us to best understand both personality and metaphysics. Put another way, we might say that Christology governs our reception of medieval and classical thought (the broadly metaphysical, in von Balthasar's estimation) and of modern concerns (the personal). In this respect, a helpful reading of *Glory of the Lord* is as a Christological metaphysic of personality. That is, here we have a theological project that is out to restore beauty in both an ancient and a modern sense, which von Balthasar will claim can only be done through a theologically determined *glory*. What follows is von Balthasar's unique entwining of the personal and the metaphysical, in contradistinction to modernity and yet drawing from it. We will examine the aesthetic contours of von Balthasar's understanding of metaphysics and personality, and this is to be distinguished—though not divided—from the account of dramatic action that occurs in *Theo-Drama*.[34] While in many ways *Theo-Drama* is more explicitly concerned with "personality" than *Glory of the Lord*, the emphasis here is on von Balthasar's theological-aesthetic understanding and how it is metaphysically located.

The Beautiful Christology: Form and Metaphysic

Christ, as divine Person, is personal to the highest degree, and all other definitions of "personality" flow from him. The Christology presented in *Glory of the Lord* is fundamentally a Christology of *form* (gestalt). Christ is the *form* of God, the revelation of God's inner life through the flesh of the Incarnation. Everywhere, von Balthasar speaks of gestalt. It is a word of manifold meanings, a multilayered concept that brings together his theological aesthetics. Gestalt is not, however, meant in the sense that modern psychology has come to take it; instead, von Balthasar seeks other sources. The term draws upon classical philosophy as well as a more modern inflection, incorporating insights from Thomas Aquinas to Johann Wolfgang von Goethe to G. M. Hopkins.[35]

Von Balthasar draws on the medieval term *forma* (form) and its cognate *formosa* (beautiful), in order to adopt the medieval reflections on beauty, particularly that of Bonaventure, to whom von Balthasar devotes an essay in *Glory of the Lord*.[36] When he speaks of gestalt, he means to invoke medieval ideas. This medieval conception of beauty itself has pagan philosophical roots, the most important of which for Bonaventure and most medieval thinkers was Neo-Platonic thought, especially as Augustine and Pseudo-Dionysius adopted it. So when, at the height of the Middle Ages, Thomas Aquinas explains that beauty must involve proportion, integrity, and *claritas* (clarity/luminosity), he speaks from a broad and well-established tradition.[37] "Proportion" refers to a symmetry of parts, "integrity" to the unity of the object, and *claritas* to "the splendour which inheres in it."[38] Form, in the medieval sense, encapsulates what makes up the beautiful: proportion, integrity, and *claritas*. The beautiful thus draws together disparate parts into an inner unity, a unity that is always also *splendid*—that is, arresting and love-worthy. As von Balthasar explains in his own rendering of the old philosophy, "there is this fact: that the figure (*Gebild*) and what shines forth (*ausstrahlt*) from the figure make it worthy, make it love-worthy."[39]

To the classical definition von Balthasar adds the nuance of G. M. Hopkins's inscape. In an article commenting on some aspects of his project, von Balthasar explains Hopkins's concept of inscape as that in which "The mind sees an organized whole, with all the articulation of detail necessary for the comprehension of the basic idea manifest in its fullness."[40] Inscape is the way in which beauty, which always escapes the grasp of the knower, nevertheless appears in order to lend lucidity to what is observed. United to form, inscape emphasizes the way in which beauty in particular refers to wholeness. Or, as von Balthasar says of form, "It signifies a coherent, limited totality of parts and elements perceived as such, yet which demands for its existence not only 'a' context, but 'the' context of being in its totality."[41] In addition to the trifold medieval dictum of proportion, integrity, and *claritas*, von Balthasar uses Hopkins in order to emphasize the mysterious wholeness-quality of form.[42] While integrity accents the wholeness of the beautiful object, inscape accents the wholeness of our perception of the beautiful. Important for now is inscape's sensibly grasped *wholeness*, which von Balthasar means to incorporate in gestalt.

In a manner rather similar to his use of Hopkins, von Balthasar alloys Goethe's understanding of *Gestalt* and *Bild* (image) with the medieval sense of form.[43] Von Balthasar does this most expressly before the trilogy is written, in a 1952 article called "Persönlichkeit und Form."[44] This article foreshadows the achievements of *Glory of the Lord* with respect both to its metaphysical concerns and its concern with what is personal.

Von Balthasar begins with the ancient understanding of form (here he uses *Form*, not yet *Gestalt*), which is rooted in two Greek concepts: *eidos* (image, idea) and *morphe* (shape). The combination of these terms hones form into something at once organic—tangible, sensible—and technical, a perceptible idea able to be discerned and described.[45] Modern thought adds a psychological realism to form, concomitant with an interest in what is personal. For von Balthasar, both ancient and modern concepts are at play in Goethe's understanding of gestalt.[46] With Goethe, form possesses what von Balthasar calls a "distinct inner finitude" (*deutliche innere Endlichkeit*), which means that a form is shaped by an "inner law of self-realization" (*inneres Gesetz der Selbstverwirklichung*) that the form at once already possesses and is realizing; that is, form is characterized by entelechy.[47] For Goethe, the self-realizing form of nature is so immanent to it that "Life is an end in itself, and form is a means of preserving and increasing life."[48] Form is thus for Goethe, while limiting (it *shapes*), also infinite. This infinity of form is much too extreme in von Balthasar's eyes. After all, he asks, "Is the idea of an infinite form of worldly essence a contradiction in itself?"[49] Goethe cannot really assign finitude *and* infinity to worldly reality without straying into pantheism. So von Balthasar distances himself from what is, in Goethe, ultimately a complex though pantheistic notion of form, since worldly form acquires such infinity as to merge with God—or rather becomes, in Goethe's terminology, God-Nature.[50]

What von Balthasar wants to adopt from Goethe is the sense that form functions as an inner law of self-realization, which is a realization both of nature (broadly) and of subjectivity. In both "Persönlichkeit und Form" and *Glory of the Lord*, von Balthasar links Goethe to a *wholeness* construed through a modern sense of *personality*. "His aim," says von Balthasar of Goethe in *Glory of the Lord*, "was to combine the cool precision of scientific research with a constant awareness of the totality apparent only to the eye of reverence, the poetic-religious eye, the ancient sense for the cosmos."[51] If with Hopkins von Balthasar comes to emphasize a wholeness of perception in gestalt, then through Goethe that perception is redoubled and reinforced alongside a perception of the wonders of *all* nature, a perception that brings the perceiver to wholeness.

Yet for von Balthasar, form cannot serve a self-enclosed, self-realizing totality, a God-Nature. In the end, such a restricting understanding of form eliminates one of the most ancient qualities of the beautiful: its splendor, by which form, in von Balthasar's eyes, retains an ability to be "the real presence of the depths [of being], of the whole reality, *and* it is a real pointing beyond itself to these depths."[52] Form, then, must be characterized by openness to the transcendent God, which sets von Balthasar apart from Goethe.

Against Goethe, but with Hopkins, von Balthasar cleaves gestalt to Christ, who is the form of forms—concretely, historically—and yet who is also, as God, beyond form.[53] Form thus receives a real, rather than an illusory (as in Goethe), limit. It is through Christ that von Balthasar is able to unite the broadly objective speculation on beauty from the Middle Ages and the broadly subjective reflection from the modern era.

In "Persönlichkeit und Form," von Balthasar responds to Goethe with a Christological position that prefigures his theology in *Glory of the Lord*. Yet before he introduces Christ, von Balthasar explains some basic epistemological concerns when it comes to knowing. In correcting Goethe, von Balthasar begins with Thomas Aquinas's claim in *De veritate* that the human mind knows God implicitly in all it knows (*De ver.*, q. 22, a. 2, ad 1). This leaves knowing to be understood as part of the "orientation of one's existence to an alien, un-possessed (*unbesessner*) truth." Indeed, Thomas helps us to understand the "first truth" of knowing, and that is that "the subjective spirit is not its own truth."[54] In this way, von Balthasar both reinforces the openness that he sees lacking in Goethe—instead emphasizing how our every act of knowing is implicitly related to God—and in the same position argues for the creature's profound dependence on God for truth. Form must always be *splendid* form: expressing "depth" and pointing beyond itself.

Taking up this position allows von Balthasar to propose an important connection to Christ, who is form in the most supreme sense possible: he in his humanity reveals the fullness of the depths of God, while the finitude of his humanity is preserved. So von Balthasar calls Jesus Christ the Father's "temporal mirror in the flesh" (*zeitlicher Spiegel im Fleisch*), emphasizing that the Son in the unity of his divinity and humanity reveals the Father to us. This revelation happens *in* fleshly finitude—not against it, nor destroying it. Von Balthasar explains:

> In this two-one of the image (*Bildnatur*) of the Son, the paradoxes of man are solved: the finite image is exceeded, but not destroyed; the Incarnation is a function of the being of the Word (*Wortseins*); the creaturely image (*Bildnatur*) is an expression and conveyance of the eternal and infinite image (*Bildnatur*).[55]

The unusual term *Bildnatur*, more literally translated as "nature of the image," emphasizes the iconic, expressive qualities of the Incarnation. The flesh of the Son expresses (*Ausdruck*) the Father, and in doing so Christ in his flesh shows the way our fleshly nature is and ought to be open to God. Because of this focus on *flesh*, there is a sensual, visible quality to form.[56] Christ reveals the Father uniquely, both eternally and in the economy of salvation, and he does so as the archetype (*Urbild*) of creation and the only Son of the Father. In a play on German prefixes, von Balthasar calls the Son the "original image of the origin" (*Ur-abbild des Ur-sprungs*); that is, the original image of the Father.[57]

The Holy Spirit, perfecting human nature, shapes Christians according to the image of Jesus Christ. Von Balthasar thus links our fundamental, natural "openness" to God to a perfected, over-perfecting openness in grace. It is here that von Balthasar emphasizes self-gift; as God is eternal, Triune self-gift, so we must give ourselves in the Spirit. What constitutes an authentic "personality," for von Balthasar, is *surrender*. This is a surrender that imitates the Son's Eucharistic surrender on the cross. In von Balthasar's eyes such a stance undoes all the "self-making" and "self-realization" ideals of modern personality.[58] Christian life is, instead, an "Advent-like existence" (*adventische Existenz*) of expectation and of vocation, of calling instead of self-determination.[59]

"Persönlichkeit und Form" ends with a long footnote describing Erich Przywara's understanding of the *analogia entis*. The concept of gestalt that emerges from this 1952 article and in *Glory of the Lord* is based in a concern for "openness" that is at once personal or existential as well as metaphysical. Each must presuppose the other. The openness of the human person to God is based in the fundamental metaphysical openness of all created being to God, which Przywara calls "polarity." Gestalt must involve subjective and metaphysical polarity.

In *Glory of the Lord*, von Balthasar takes care to explain the objective qualities of the Christ-form alongside our subjective response. Christ reveals the Father to us. What Christ illuminates comes, not from some other source (not even the faithful subject who observes), but from himself: he is the divine Son, and only he can reveal the Father to us. Yet this enables subjective response instead of omitting it:

> If the form of Christ is to be what it is in itself, then no age, no culture of itself can be privileged over the phenomenon. The determining Illumination (*entscheidend Enleuchtende*) is, then, up to him, in a double sense: that the form of Christ has in itself an inner rightness (*Richtigkeit*) and evidence—as in another, worldly area there is also this in a piece of art or a mathematical theorem. Second, that this accuracy that lies in the circumstances of the case also has the power to illuminate the perceiver, in a manner not only intellectual, but also existentially transforming.[60]

This "illumination" is at once the form itself and the splendor of that form, that splendor that draws the perceiver to itself.

That beauty has form and splendor prevents it from becoming sheer subjective delight. Instead, beauty is ever and always inhered with meaning—with form—and this inner meaning escapes immediate grasp. The subject, then, experiences rapture in the face of beauty, a rapture consisting in self-emptying, a kind of kenosis of the heart in order to make room for the beautiful. These qualities are true of *all* beauty and not simply the glory of God. Though von Balthasar speaks specifically of the Christ-form in *Glory of the Lord*, "form" as a concept is not restricted to dogmatic considerations. Indeed, it is in the Christ-form that all other forms are ordered to their ultimate ground and end.

Chalcedonian Christology retains a strong influence on von Balthasar, and he often treads the line of the "unconfused union" in order to further his thought. There can be no attempt to flatten the natural and supernatural into a single reality, though the relationship between nature and grace remains deeply entwined. The natural has its own integrity, which the supernatural never violates: "The supernatural is not there in order to supply that part of our natural capacities we have failed to develop. *Gratia perficit naturam, non supplet.*"[61] Christ remains unique; the ever-greater quality of divinity removes him from us into the realm of mystery. In spite of this—even *because* of it—we are called to strive after him. We cannot grasp Christ, lay hold of him as an object to be controlled, and yet in faith we may grasp him through precisely this inability; that is, through another way: through loving receptivity.[62]

By acknowledging the legitimate place of earthly beauty and casting it in language of receptivity—that is, we perceive it by being receptive to it and not by laying hold of it—von Balthasar draws one of his first and most lasting analogies between earthly beauty and divine glory. Our attitude or response to each is similar: receptiveness, which then allows the beautiful to enrapture us. Yet the result of such a reception radically differs depending on the beautiful (or glorious) object in question. The reception itself is guided by the expression of beauty, by the form itself and not a secret character hidden within it. As Francesca Murphy says, "For von Balthasar, an expression is 'extroverted': the form it manifests is not behind or inside it."[63] Earthly beauty must, in order to remain earthly, retain its contingent qualities and thus remains marked by death; divine glory, which is eternal, never fades or dies.[64]

Von Balthasar stubbornly maintains his distinction between created beauty and theology, and yet with a most vital further intimacy, hinted at in various ways early in *Glory of the Lord* and finally sealed not in art *in itself*, but in art viewed from perspective of the Incarnation. That is, von Balthasar comes to a fuller consideration of the Incarnation and what it must mean for sacred art. Aidan Nichols, in his own book about art and theology, *Redeeming Beauty*, discusses this growth in von Balthasar's theology at length. He notes that the von Balthasar of the early volumes of *Glory of the Lord* (1961–63, volumes I–III in the English version) maintains a strict distinction between art and religion.[65] In 1965, Nichols claims von Balthasar nuances his position with the article "Christliche Kunst und Verkündigung" (Christian Art and Proclamation).[66]

In "Christliche Kunst," von Balthasar links art and revelation through their mutual relationship to *disclosure* (*Offenbarung*). Both art and revelation disclose reality to us. Here von Balthasar uses a Heideggerian phrase to begin relating art to theology, taking up concepts from the philosopher in something of a transfiguration, which will take a particularly strong role in von Balthasar's metaphysical project. Again, the next chapter will discuss the adaptation of Heidegger in more detail. For now, it is important to see how von Balthasar employs "disclosure" in a manner that breaks Heidegger from the self-enclosed entanglement with death that von Balthasar accused the philosopher of succumbing to in *Apokalypse*. He does so by recalling, with Thomas Aquinas as an aide, the transcendentals of being. These properties—he names the One, the True, the Good, and the Beautiful—are characteristics that all beings share. When we see that being, that all instantiations of being, shares universal properties, we are forced to ask how being can possess such unity, which for von Balthasar is defended particularly when we focus on the One and the Beautiful. But the transcendentals show us a unity of created being that created being does not possess in itself, pointing beyond created being to a source greater than itself.[67] Von Balthasar will make an identical argument, with greater expansion, in the *Epilogue* of his tryptich.[68]

So being, which discloses in the modes of its universal properties, also discloses that it is not its own ground for existence. For von Balthasar, this is an open end. Human reason can speculate after this ground, and even know it vaguely, but theology must step in to order further statements. Or, more properly speaking, revelation allows us to know the ground of being, which is the Triune God. The glory of the Trinity, expressed in the person of Christ, discloses both worldly and divine being.[69] More importantly, Christ "shapes" worldly being and brings it to fullness. Von Balthasar argues that "The interior design [of humanity and the world] is carried through by the formative power of the unique, distinctive, personal nature of Jesus Christ: he is the valid 'expression-image' (*Ausdrucks-Bild*) of the invisible God (Col 1:15)."[70]

In his uniqueness, Christ discloses to us the *analogy* between beauty and glory—von Balthasar has not lost this sensibility—and Christ's self-disclosure allows us then to see how artistic inspiration and the inspiration of the Spirit are related to one another. If, in Scripture, the "artist" who is the Gospel writer is permitted authentic freedom of expression and that freedom nevertheless serves to reveal God in the inspiration of the Holy Spirit, then the Christian artist can be permitted such freedom and is also enabled to express God in the Spirit in a way that, though not identical to Scripture, is marked deeply by analogy to it.[71] In other words, art really *can* express revelation. As Nichols says of von Balthasar after the 1965 article, "For *this* Balthasar, then, Christian art is essentially a 'form'—with the naturally aesthetic connotations of that word—in which divine revelation is presented."[72] Art thus can and must have a vital place in the life of faith, a vital location as that which can illuminate divine revelation. The "abyssal difference" between art and religion is not enough to bear the weight of this conclusion, and von Balthasar finally surpasses the rift by way of the Incarnation.

There is an earlier point in *Glory of the Lord* where von Balthasar foreshadows his own development. It is helpful in illustrating in what way the Incarnation can be said to play a role in von Balthasar's view of art. In the first volume, von Balthasar notes the tragic qualities of earthly beauty—its contingence, its continual evanescence. He juxtaposes earthly beauty's death with Christ's, and in that juxtaposition earthly beauty is given its final orientation:

> In the experience of the earthly beauty there is a moment of eternity (*Augenblick Ewigkeit*): because the eternity-bearing form (*ewigkeit-sahltige Gestalt*) of the beautiful object tells the onlooker who experiences it something of its timelessness. Still enveloped in the beautiful form is a "sorrow of the gods." It must die, and the state of blessed-engrossment (*Selig-entrückten*) includes a tragic contradiction: both act and object include in themselves their conflicting death. In John there is no question of such "sorrow of the gods," because the dying lover indeed died for love, his death was no limit, but the powerful statement of his love. (Jn 10:18)[73]

There can be no *sorrow of the gods*, properly speaking, in light of Christ. Earthly beauty's death receives its redemption, as it were, in the unique death of Christ experienced on the cross: here is a death of an entirely different kind than earthly beauty's tragic loss, and one that in its difference reveals that earthly beauty has integrity and purpose.[74] Christ, after all, *dies* (out of love), and (in love) lives again. By way of anticipation, it is possible to see in his death the possibility that earthly beauty does not always have to die in tragedy, so long as its death is a loving surrender to the Father in analogy to Christ's own surrender. What is true of the believing subject as described in *Glory of the Lord I* is, inchoately, true of earthly beauty *writ large*: receptivity and self-gift permit beauty to admit its own contingency, and yet in doing so to also rise above it by leaving room for what transcends it—by leaving room, that is, for divine glory.

Von Balthasar desires that the expressiveness of Jesus Christ and the expressiveness of art coincide with one another. There is to be a sympathy, as it were, between the expressive flesh of Christ and the expressiveness of works of art. An *attunement* of the former to the latter. As in the rest of von Balthasar's theology, the best manner of achieving such an attunement is through imitation. Earthly beauty, through surrender, is capable of revealing to us qualities of Christ's ultimate surrender on the cross. This theme of surrender echoes the early "Kunst und Religion." Beauty's surrender, contrary to the destruction of earthly beauty that is feared, will in fact invigorate it. The animation of beauty through surrender is no more clear than in the heart of the poet of the *Divine Comedy*, who von Balthasar raises up as an example of a theological aesthetic unparalleled in grandeur.

The Beautiful Art-Metaphysic: Dante

Von Balthasar chooses Dante Alighieri to open his *Glory of the Lord* volume on "lay styles," and for no arbitrary reason. With Dante, classical art shifts into the vernacular and never turns back, and it takes along with it the great riches of classical knowledge. "Synthesis," von Balthasar says, "that is just what Dante is: a synthesis of scholasticism and mysticism, of Antiquity and Christianity."[75] Dante's *Divina Commedia*, which von Balthasar uses to interpret Dante's earlier works (especially *Convivio* and *Vita Nuova*), employs the vast range of knowledge inherited over the ages in a brilliant and unprecedented artistic achievement. The *Commedia* is a lofty mirror of ages past, a summation and integration of philosophy and theology. Von Balthasar compares the ambition of Dante's synthesis to the *Secunda Pars* of Thomas Aquinas's *Summa Theologica*, "For Dante the poet, like Aquinas, makes the ethics of Antiquity in its abstractness the broad basis of Christian morality." Dante presses further, and through his art he adopts ancient historical and mythological tropes to conceive of them together alongside Christian moral and theological themes.[76] After all, it is Virgil who leads him through Hell and Purgatory, and the mythological gods still relate to their old planetary spheres in Heaven.

Dante is still more daring. Above Dominican and Franciscan scholastic theology, he posits a "third" theology.[77] Though Dante does not name the third theology, the one placed at the highest spheres, von Balthasar admits, "It is not inconceivable that Dante considered himself to be the originator of this new, third theology."[78] In any case, Dante was highly aware of his unique position, of a unique artistic-theological mission that would drive him to compose the *Commedia*.

Most of all, the uniqueness of Dante's work is derived from Dante himself. Von Balthasar is quick to emphasize the uniqueness of Dante's personality, and how the *Commedia* is bent around the highly personal journey of the poet. This is to be contrasted with Thomas Aquinas, who intentionally disappears behind his work. Yet the grand cosmic scale of the personality that journeys from Hell to the very heights of Heaven is achieved only through the deepest humiliation.[79] We are left, then, with a paradoxical personality: "His name only appears once in the *Divine Comedy*: at the climax of his meeting with Beatrice, when, still veiled she looks at him and calls him. . . . And yet the whole *Divine Comedy* is a poem written in the first person."[80] This paradoxically unique-humiliated personality is the key to the *Commedia*. By virtue of this paradox, personal and metaphysical heights work for each other rather than against each other, and richness of personality is only achieved through abyssal depths of suffering. At the opening of *Inferno*, Dante has lost hope in darkness. The poet's heart is repaired along the perilous steps of Hell and Purgatory, the latter of which rends him with the sharpest and harshest confessions.

Dante's unique personal note, the driving song that lifts him from the lowest place to the highest, is centered around the figure of Beatrice. It is his love for Beatrice that illuminates his breathtaking journey through the cosmos, stretching his heart to comprehend the cosmos (and ultimately, in mystery, the Trinity) and so make his heart worthy to love

Beatrice herself. Von Balthasar says of this unprecedented twin trans-figuration: "Only Claudel's *Le Soulier de Satin* again achieves Dante's dimension, in which personal love and the shaping of the universe are mutually conditioned."[81]

Dante's utterly unique achievement, the grandeur of his artistic work, rests in its bewildering dimension. Here he must, by necessity of eros, remain a unique personality striving upward in desire, otherwise his eros descends into a faceless longing identical to pantheism, akin to Goethe's "cosmogonic eros."[82] Yet this personality must also be purified, or else it will disintegrate in the face of divine glory—and indeed will shatter in the presence of Beatrice herself, who shines as a reflection of God's glory. He must even go so far as to leave behind any idea of love as an inextricable, imperious fate, allying love instead with humble freedom.[83] Dante's very understanding of love, as well as his desire *in actu*, is transfigured. In this way, every circle of Hell, every stage on the mountainous climb through Purgatory, every sphere of Heaven, serves to shape the poet's heart. Only thus is Dante able to render his unique achievement a reality, revealing how personal love and Christian charity need not be opposed. As von Balthasar explains:

> One can surround the real figure of Beatrice, as also Dante's real life of love, with as many question marks as one wishes. Nevertheless, the principle is established for the first time, and never again so magnificently: for the sake of infinite love, it is not necessary for the Christian to renounce finite love. On the contrary, in a positive spirit, he can incorporate his finite love into that which is infinite—but at the cost of terrible sufferings, of course, as Dante shows us.[84]

What proceeds through the *Divina Commedia* is an ingenious artistic marriage between the personal and the metaphysical. The poetic union at work in Dante helps us to see, in the realm of beauty centuries before von Balthasar lived and wrote, a similar concern for cosmic and personal verity. For von Balthasar, the union achieved in Dante—a union he is also after—is only possible in light of Christ. Von Balthasar himself argues, in *Glory of the Lord I*, that love for the particular and love for all things (for being itself) are incompatible until they—the unique and the universal—are united in the hypostatic union without their destruction.

Such a unified and unifying love can only be Christian love, "which is founded on Christ's hypostatic union and which joins together what in human terms is eternally incompatible: love for one existent is conjoined with love for Being itself."[85] In so arguing, he recalls a major theme from his interpretation of Maximus the Confessor in *Cosmic Liturgy*. In the same moment, von Balthasar also recalls Dante's poetic theme in the *Divina Commedia*. Both Dante and Maximus are after the same incomprehensible union, one through art and the other through theology. Unlike Maximus—or rather, unlike the Scholastics—Dante gives concrete personal existence primacy over essence, and *this* for von Balthasar is Dante's new (and modern) way.[86]

Von Balthasar shows a similar sense of primacy of "personality" in *Glory of the Lord*. While by no means abandoning metaphysics—indeed, metaphysics is a dominant theme and retains a specific, almost heuristic primacy in von Balthasar's theology—the *personality* that governs his theological aesthetic is the Incarnate Son. In Christ, created being is employed at a

> new depth as a language and a means of expression for the divine Being and essence. . . . it is not Sacred Scripture which is God's original language and self-expression, but rather Jesus Christ. As One and Unique (*Eine und Einzige*), and yet as one who is to be understood only in the context of humankind's entire history and in the context of the whole created cosmos, Jesus is the Word, the Image, the Expression and the Exegesis of God (*das Wort, das Bild, der Ausdruck und die Exegese Gottes*).[87]

Christ is incomparable and unique, the only Son, the ultimate personality, yet that uniqueness is only to be understood within the created being that he adopts when he takes human nature upon himself. In other words, the exegesis of God the Father that the Son accomplishes for our sake in the Incarnation is realized *through* created being. His unique status as Son—his unique "personality," as it were, his incomparable and concrete identity—shows us not only himself and the Father, but also gives new light to metaphysics. With God's self-revelation, von Balthasar argues, "Being itself here unveils its final countenance, which for us receives the name of Trinitarian love."[88] With divine being revealed so, we can comprehend created being "as having an interior structure likewise founded on love, as Augustine tried to demonstrate in the second part of his *De Trinitate*."[89]

Jesus Christ's unique primacy as divine Person thus helps us to understand metaphysics anew, so that we can finally perceive in the very finitude of created being not its destruction, but its fulfillment through its own finitude. Angelo Scola, drawing from von Balthasar's self-summary in *My Work*, calls the Christological-metaphysical perspective we see here a "meta-anthropology."[90] A meta-anthropology raises metaphysical concerns into questions about the disposition of human beings. It helps to respond to the problem of finitude anew, yet without the loss of metaphysics. This problem of finitude and yearning, so much the urgent concern of von Balthasar's interlocutors in *Apokalypse*, receives a response neither through the elimination of transcendent infinity—the eternal, ever-greater God—nor through the elimination of finitude. The *greater* uniqueness of God himself, instead of suffocating us, enables our real fulfillment: "when Being is confronted as love the threat which infinity poses to finitude vanishes."[91] Particularity and universality are no longer adversaries in Trinitarian love. "Meta-anthropology," though von Balthasar's own phrase, is thus inadequate to describe the primacy of "personality" at work in his theology and metaphysics. It is not, in the last analysis, any human being who is raised to synthesize metaphysics and subjectivity; it is Christ, whose unique identity is Trinitarian. He enables authentic *personality*.

Yet such a revelation about personality is not without its demands. Neither von Balthasar nor Dante can give the personal any sort of primacy without a concomitant dedication to the purification of personality, indeed a purification shaped not merely in *personal* (or existential) terms, but also in cosmic terms. For Dante, such a concurrence is wrought through his confession to Beatrice at the end of *Purgatiorio*, where he meets her for the first time after many years and must admit his heart's infidelity. In von Balthasar's eyes, this meeting is the one toward which both *Inferno* and *Purgatorio* drive, and in which *Paradiso* is to be understood.[92] It would do us well to recall its central events.

The two meet at the border between Purgatory and Heaven, shot through by the River Lethe, which in ancient mythology causes forgetfulness. Dante has not yet crossed the river, and he sees Beatrice arrive on the other side in a chariot—this von Balthasar also interprets as the procession of the Church[93]—in a shower of songs and flowers:

> within a cloud of flowers
> that rose upward from the angels' hands and then
> fell again, within and without the chariot
>
> appeared a lady, who wore an olive crown
> over a white veil and, under her green mantle,
> a gown the color of living flame.
>
> And my spirit, already accustomed
> in her living presence to being filled
> with awe, trembling, exhausted—
>
> now my spirit, though I could not see her in full,
> succumbed to her mysterious virtue
> and felt the strength of its ancient love.[94]

Stern yet veiled, Beatrice commands Dante to look at her. The encounter thus takes on the shape of a confrontation, with Dante standing as the shivering guilty party.

> "Look well! Look, I am indeed Beatrice.
> Indeed you have deigned to climb the mountain?
> Did you not know that human happiness is here?"[95]

Beatrice asks of Dante an explanation for his abandonment of hope, which was where we had found him at the beginning of *Inferno* and which is now unveiled before Beatrice's light as infidelity to her.[96] Crying, Dante confesses his fall:

> I said, weeping: "Those things
> with their false pleasures turned my steps
> at once when I no longer saw your face."[97]

Now the confrontation melts into the framework of an apology and a plea for healing. The charged personal encounter, it should be noted, has at the same time adopted the contours of a much more universal experience of blindness and forgiveness. Dante and Beatrice are themselves, and yet more than themselves: they are individuals and also types. After this extended confession, the angels beg Beatrice to unveil her face. Her beauty surpasses its former beauty, and Dante's poetic powers splinter:

> "Turn, Beatrice, turn your sacred eyes,"
> was their song, "to your faithful one who
> took so many steps in a journey to see you!
>
> By your grace do us the grace of unveiling
> your mouth, he may behold in you
> the further beauty that you hide."
>
> O splendor of eternal living light!
> Who, growing pale under Parnassus,
> or, drinking from its well,
>
> would not find his mind overburdened
> to describe the way you appeared,
> the way your features were in harmony with heaven,
>
> when I saw your face fully unveiled?[98]

For von Balthasar, the confession to Beatrice is a personal and an ecclesial reality: it is a description of the Sacrament of Penance, where personal love must "grow" to objectivity and where the "sacramental, ecclesial form [is] unveiled and justified and convincingly shown to be love" and thus to be quite personal.[99] Dante must speak his guilt, and he must see the beauty he abandoned; yet Love is cruel for the sake of teaching the Beloved how yet to love, and Beatrice's harshness is unveiled as a greater beauty. The "death" of Dante's preconceived notions of his beautiful reunion with Beatrice permits an intensification of the beauty that stands before him, beyond which he had imagined. The scene mimics von Balthasar's own convictions that earthly beauty, to be rescued, must be open to divine glory: at first this seems like a threat to what is earthly, but this threat is in fact earthly beauty's source of life.

Dante's confession makes him ready to experience a new intimacy with Beatrice as they journey through Paradise together, as she teaches him of its heightening spheres. Beatrice's heavenly joy, indeed her laugh (*riso*), lifts Dante ever-closer to God.[100] Von Balthasar is at pains to explain this heavenly intimacy as one of freedom, and not of slavery. No, says von Balthasar, "The beloved does not imprison the poet within herself; on the contrary, she opens up for him the perception of all reality."[101] Again, this purified, personal love is not an eschewal of the cosmos; it is the means by which Dante better perceives it. The metaphysical hierarchies of the universe, stretched out from the depths into the stars, receive more clarity the higher Dante's love raises him.

In *Glory of the Lord*, von Balthasar discusses a resonant concept of personal and metaphysical purification through love. Christ, argues von Balthasar, along with being

> the archetype of man, represents in himself the archetype of the entire cosmos as well. The only thing that can correspond to his (literally) 'trans-porting' beauty, a beauty, moreover, which exacts imitation, is a pliancy of the whole man which places one's entire existence at his disposal as malleable material to be shaped into his image.[102]

The "pliancy" of the human person—alternately discussed as receptivity, docility (teach-ability), and attunement—is a graced transformation of the whole human being. *Love* is the summation of this personal encounter, a personal encounter that also perfects nature. Love is, again, not to the detriment of metaphysics in its account of the personal, so much so that we must ask again whether von Balthasar's self-styled "meta-anthropology" sufficiently describes his project. Being continues to play such a constitutive role, that the phrase *anthropology* is increasingly misleading. Here we have an anthropology so rooted in concerns of being, especially in its Triune structure, that old tropes pitting anthropology (or existential concerns) and metaphysics against one another simply exhaust themselves.[103]

Love thwarts the divisive either-or. It is the Triune God who loves us in Christ, and whom we love in Christ. In the Incarnation, we approach the "contemplation of Being in the beloved Thou, which is at once God and man and which is worthy of all possible believing and adoring love."[104] It is grace, grace given to us by the eminently personal God in Christ, which enables us to love and adore to the perfection of our nature and of being itself.

As high as Dante reaches, his poetry is increasingly stretched to its breaking point. The masterful union of the personal and the metaphysical wavers under the weight of beauty when he sees the Triune God. Here, both Dante and Beatrice are subordinated to the Triune mystery and to the Church. Says von Balthasar: "Mary, not Beatrice, is the final image; Bernard, not Dante, speaks the last word of prayer."[105] Even the "third theology" must acquiesce in all obedience to the mysteries that overpower it.

> O eternal light persisting in yourself alone,
> knowing and understanding in yourself alone,
> intending in yourself alone, you inwardly love and rejoice!
>
> That cyclic turning which, so conceived, seemed
> to shine in you like reflected light
> as my eyes looked on attentively,
>
> the light seemed in itself and its own color
> to be painted with our effigy:
> so that my gaze was drawn to it.
>
> As the geometer tries with care
> to square a circle, but cannot find,
> thinking through the puzzle, the right principle,
>
> such was I at this new sight:
> I wanted to see how our effigy could fit
> into that circle, how it could persist there;

but the wings of my understanding could not reach
until my mind was struck
to a blaze with its desire for light.

Here my high fantasy failed me,
but already my desire and will turned,
like a wheel revolving in time

with the love that moves the sun and the other stars.[106]

In our extended encounter with Dante, we are confronted with a vision of life and death that, while bearing markers of modernity, is of an entirely different sort than the one von Balthasar diagnoses in *Apokalypse*. Here death is not conceived of chiefly as an end to life, nor even as the ground and determination of life. Death is instead part of a radically cosmic sensibility, contextualized in the face of a universe that is even more dynamic and comprehensive after death. Could Rilke, with his elegies that lead into a shapeless landscape of pain, imagine Dante's vertiginous journey?

The *Commedia* presents us with a view of eternity and of earth's participation in eternity. Death is not a caesura; the saints (especially Beatrice) intercede with such care that death is indeed barely a barrier at all. For Dante, von Balthasar explains, "The possibility of man's fulfillment existentially demands eternal life."[107] *Eternal life*, not death, is Dante's preoccupation; God's grace is the ground and determination of life. Finitude is no longer to be overcome as a detriment; through Christian love, finitude is rendered able to encounter eternity without its own destruction. In the Florentine poet's vision, Rilke's fears are not only inverted but also transfigured and overcome.

What von Balthasar's interpretation of Dante helps us to see is an alternative theological aesthetic, taking flesh in the form of the reeling journey in the *Commedia*. It is not only possible to move against Rilke's narrow transcendental vision, it has already been accomplished. The very breadth of Dante's work throws into relief Rilke's thin understanding of both life and death.

Dante also helps us understand von Balthasar's own unique integration of theology and beauty, an integration achieved through the unique Person of Christ. Christology helps von Balthasar in two ways: it is concrete and specific. The two natures are united in the single and unique Person of the Son. Metaphysics becomes "meta-anthropology." Mark McIntosh describes von Balthasar's anthropological-theological move in *Christology from Within*. "One of the most fundamental methodological impulses in von Balthasar," McIntosh explains, "is his preference for concrete historical event and encounter over more universal metaphysical claims."[108] By virtue of this preference, the particular experiences of the saints and mystics are allowed to contribute to von Balthasar's Christology. Dante, almost allegorically, attains a similar concreteness and specificity with respect to his account of his love for Beatrice. We see, then, that a heart can love the cosmos and a particular person without rending itself in pieces.

In Dante, we also observe the ways such a "meta-anthropology" fails to be an adequate description of what is occurring in von Balthasar's theological aesthetic. Given what we have observed in this chapter with respect to *personality* and *being*, we must ask—and have not yet answered—how the specific and the universal relate to one another in von Balthasar's aesthetic thought. Is it sufficient to describe von Balthasar's work as a work *from* metaphysics *to* personality (or the concrete, existential, etc.)?[109] As we have observed, metaphysics abides even in these categories, much as Dante's heart in his encounter with the Trinity is made to move in time with the love that moves the cosmos. What, then, *is* happening? For now, the question has developed into an open-end. We will address it more concertedly in the next chapter.

Yet Dante does not escape von Balthasar's critical eye. There is yet a weakness in the *Commedia*, one that von Balthasar argues on primarily theological grounds, since Dante is metaphysically of a similar mind to von Balthasar and conceives of transcendence in a concordant fashion. Metaphysics alone is not enough to support a theological aesthetic. When it comes to *Inferno*, von Balthasar wonders if—to follow Dante's logic to its full—a poem about Hell is in fact possible.[110] "Nothing can happen in Dante's Hell," von Balthasar points out, "because love is absent. And according to his own doctrine, as well as that of Antiquity, of

Augustine and of Thomas, love is the interior motive force of all living things."[111] So the conversations with the souls in Hell are at best illusory, built on the necessity of the narrative and not animated by the inner theological motives of the *Commedia*.

What Dante is missing, according to von Balthasar, is "the Cross, the substitutionary death of Christ."[112] It is both a Christological insufficiency and a Trinitarian one. Dante essentially fails to consider the nature of Trinitarian love to its last ends, a love that for von Balthasar must extend even into the depths of Hell and that for Dante cannot (for Hell is the absence of God's love). Von Balthasar continues:

> For this reason the *Comedy's* image of God is not really Trinitarian but an extraordinarily intensified, Christian version of the Eros of Antiquity. And it is quite clear that the relationship of Dante and Beatrice, of Gabriel and Mary, of earthly and heavenly love, of Eros and Agape within an Eros that is regarded as embracing all, is the last word of the poet.[113]

Dante's theological aesthetic falters in this last dimension, and in the final analysis has not brought the fullness of Christian uniqueness into its synthesis. Here von Balthasar critiques Dante on the grounds of the theology he himself develops in *Mysterium Paschale* and *Theo-Drama*, and the theological correction to be found there posits an understanding of Trinitarian love that also embraces Hell through Holy Saturday.

Whether von Balthasar is correct to critique Dante depends on the rightness of the theology he presents counter to it. Or it is perhaps Dante who critiques von Balthasar, offering a more accurate cosmic vision than von Balthasar's own. That question I leave aside for the sake of a more pertinent insight: that von Balthasar's assessment of art is both metaphysical and theological, and so his critiques extend beyond whether a work of art is overtly Christian. A deeply Christian work such as Dante's is subject to error should its interior development of Trinitarian, Christological love fail or falter. That is to say, a theological aesthetic does not acquire rightness in being theological (even governed theologically) by itself. Just as metaphysics must receive new light, theology, too, must stand in the light of revelation and receive correction. This makes von

Balthasar's theological aesthetic more than it might seem at first, providing a view of the world that—like Dante's—extends from the very depths to the very heights and attempts to embrace all.

The rightness or wrongness of von Balthasar's theology of Holy Saturday aside, he himself perhaps underestimates Dante's vivid Christological sensibilities. After all, the *Commedia* closes with the mysterious image of man in the center of the Trinity, the Incarnation. That love that "moves the sun and other stars" is thus a Trinitarian and Christological love, and it just as surely moves all of Dante's cantos as it does the spheres.

REFRAIN: RILKE IN *HERRLICHKEIT*

As we have seen, Dante's vision of the cosmos is radically distinct from that of Rilke's. The poet Rilke returns again in von Balthasar's triptych, though—significantly—not as an example of a good (literary) theological aesthetics as happens with Dante, Hopkins, Péguy, and others in *Glory of the Lord III*. Instead, Rilke appears buried in von Balthasar's volumes about metaphysics, emerging as a figure to be countenanced in *Glory of the Lord V: Metaphysics in the Modern Age*. Such a placement immediately allies Rilke to the unraveling of metaphysics rehearsed in its pages, and echoes many of the same notes to be found in *Apokalypse*. He is still placed alongside Heidegger, who follows him as the final gasp of the "classical mediation," and von Balthasar points his reader to his original analysis of Rilke in the third volume of *Apokalypse*. In many ways, von Balthasar's critique of Rilke is more of the same—and yet its context in *Glory of the Lord* renders it remarkably different.

Von Balthasar views Thomas Aquinas's real distinction between essence (*ens*) and existence (*esse*) as the height of metaphysical inquiry.[114] This real distinction is, in von Balthasar's eyes, a delicate balance, and where it is forgotten or skewed, being is either made into a "comprehensive concept of reason" (as in Scotus), or made to "identify it (once again) with God" (as in Eckhart).[115] The various threads of the modern decline of metaphysics form a narrative in which no single figure can receive most of the blame for the loss of Thomas's real distinction, though Scotus receives a good deal of scorn.[116] In all cases, the two "options" von

Balthasar lays out emerge as the end points of many modern, philosophical considerations of being: either being becomes an empty holding-place for reason or being becomes an empty holding-place for God. Either way, both being and God are bereft of real meaning, serving instead as variables in an equation—blank and dead tools for a conclusion.

There is no single form that such a divestiture of meaning takes, but all share a sort of forgetfulness of the past. To be clear, they all share a forgetfulness of the peculiar *Christian inheritance* to the modern age, which unites (but does not identify) pagan philosophy and revelation. This inheritance is a relationship that is "indissoluble, because the transcendental claim of reason and the universal claim of revelation will always sit uneasily together." Von Balthasar calls the relationship between Platonic (and Aristotelian) and Christian thought the "double inheritance" of the current age, and insists it "will not cease to fascinate the human mind."[117] Indeed, in "The Classical Mediation," the section of von Balthasar's narrative in which Rilke appears, von Balthasar notes the desire in these particular philosophers and artists to reach back to the classical age in order to somehow rescue worldly being from the Christian inheritance. But there is no real going back behind Christianity, not now that Christianity has illuminated (personal) freedom alongside being, and so now those who seek to avoid Christianity face a "moment of decision," standing as they do "before the yawning abyss of reason and freedom." In their encounter with this abyss, with what is apparently irreconcilable, there is an extended attempt to seek the glory of antiquity again as a way to reconcile reason and freedom. But this attempt fails, and the decision emerges—the decision for (or against)—"self-surrender to the sign, in all its purity, of the glory of God's love revealed in Christ."[118] Once again, there is no avoiding the Christian inheritance.

Von Balthasar's review of modern metaphysics focuses on its shift to the human person as the center of its reflection, a shift that at its most extravagant conclusions places the human person in the center to such a degree that nothing beyond the human person can be imagined any longer. Founded in Kant yet stretching far afield from him, everything (for Kant and for others) begins with the narrow vision of the ethical person. The religious is excised from the question of being, and— incapable of imagining a transcendence that does not encompass the myopia of the human condition as its measure—God is rendered a symptom of this philosophical nearsightedness. So God must be "immanent in the world," leading to a relationship between God and the world that is "necessarily one of identity. Negative theology completely vanishes."[119] God and the world are one, and so God can be known as the world is known—an epistemological rupture only heightened by rational materialism.

While Rilke will resist this latter epistemology, especially in its technological forms, he nevertheless succumbs to the total immanence of God in the world. In many ways, Goethe is the groundwork for Rilke's poetry, especially with respect to Goethe's understanding of *nature*. For Goethe as von Balthasar reads him, nature "possesses its own unity, and thus its own glory, in itself, and the *eros*, which does not seek to penetrate beyond it, remains an anti-Christian 'cosmogonic *eros*.'"[120] Goethe in this way disintegrates glory and beauty, and the longing of human eros strives after created being into the night of its limits. Von Balthasar notes a section from Goethe's poem "Vermächtnis" (Legacy) as an illustration:

> In being let yourself be blessed!
> Being is eternal: for laws
> perpetuate the treasures of living things,
> in which the All adorned itself.[121]

Being, von Balthasar notes with no small amount of sadness, may as well be a word for God. There is, for Goethe, no real imagining of a nature open to something other than itself; nature is all.[122] Von Balthasar calls this phenomenon elsewhere in the fifth volume the "eternal God-nature kenotically among men."

So Rilke, like other poets (von Balthasar also identifies Hölderlin as the precursor to both Rilke and Goethe), takes the basic premise of God's immanence to its radical conclusion.[123] The *Sonnets to Orpheus*, with their torn and fragmented poet-god, in this way form the crowning artistic achievement of the classical mediation: the modern effort to reach back behind Christianity to a lost and loved pagan joy finds vindication in Rilke and tragedy. There can be no real going back, and so—quite unlike the pagans—terror looms behind beauty as that which never can be mastered.[124] Though the myths for Rilke and those like him preserve a certain power to express, and indeed though Rilke employs them with skill unparalleled in his era or after it, still he has not revived them.

In von Balthasar's words, "They remain at best 'names' with which we designate our universal fate, well aware all the while that this in its occurrence transcends all names."[125]

Von Balthasar notes, with a certain sympathy, the way Rilke's efforts to work consciously against Christianity have him grazing against its heart almost despite himself. Because the "classical mediation" increasingly breaks down, unable to bear the weight of the questions asked of it, modern philosophies "must increasingly live from Christian material, despite their contradiction and rejection of it."[126] Rilke in his own striving after Orpheus brushes close to the chalice Christ must drink, and sees in his way how death has been made into a foundation for new life.

> Silent friend of many distances—feel—
> how your breath still increases this space.
> In the frames of the shadowed belfry
> let yourself ring. That what feeds on you
>
> becomes a strength beyond nourishment.
> Go from and go on in transformation.
> What is the experience you suffer?
> The drink is bitter—become wine.
>
> From the endlessness of night, be
> the spellcraft at the crossway of the senses,
> the meaning of their strange meeting.
>
> And when the earthly forgets you,
> say to the still earth: I flow.
> Speak to the rapid waters: I am.[127]

He sees how love must give itself away. And, half-seeing, he like his panther turns away in weary frustration—as if he perceives that he must give up his beloved counter against Christianity, and cannot make himself do it. In any case, he gives to Orpheus God's privileged words ("I am") and renders their eternity only through eternal passing away ("I flow").

At the center of von Balthasar's review of Rilke is a poised assessment of Rilke's understanding of love. Von Balthasar's assessment reflects the original given in *Apokalypse*, but now it is more pronounced, more obvious. In the light of a Christian theological aesthetic, love becomes more profoundly what is *at risk*. Von Balthasar pits the classical Christian insistence on the absolutely transcendent God, who is love and makes love possible, against Rilke's desire for a love without an object. Here most of all von Balthasar notes the tragic way Rilke nearly approaches the Christian position in the midst of his rejection of it.

According to von Balthasar, Rilke desires more than anything an "intransitive love" that lacks a Thou, transcendent in the sense that it rises up and reaches, but in a manner wholly distinct from either Christianity or Platonism.[128] Rilke's love has no object, placing it at a sharp divide with ideas of the past. "What is rigorously excluded," says von Balthasar, ". . . is the element of dialogue, the sense of community which takes lovers captive, the fidelity."[129] This is a wholly narcissistic love and, for Rilke, Narcissus is a hero and not a tragic figure.[130] In other words, Narcissus finally succeeds in achieving a love that is not wounded by the tragedy of its need for another. There is no other at all. That Narcissus is made a flower is no loss, especially in Rilke's use of the image: a rose has neither an inner space nor an outer, and so illumines for the poet the possibility of such an existence for his own heart.[131]

Rilke sees *poverty* as the answer to love, a state of emptiness by which he like Narcissus may be set free—not for others, but rather so that he might freely love on his own (solitary) terms. He perceives that he must give himself away, and his youthful *Book of Hours* praises figures like St. Francis for their poverty. The poet understands that there *is* a link between being poor and being free. In this, von Balthasar sees Rilke stepping close to Christianity and its emphasis on kenotic poverty, yet turning away from Christianity in the same moment with his rejection of what Christianity presupposes in Trinitarian love.[132] Poverty must, after all, be a poverty *for* others—a *kenosis* with a *telos*.

Rilke's intransient love is the presupposition for, or rather the matrix of, the collapse of real transcendence—that is, a transcendence that has an object that it itself does not possess. Now there is no glory by which beauty might be understood, and so beauty itself becomes terrifying. Von Balthasar notes that in Rilke the chain of being has been shattered, and "Therefore there is no longer any continuity between the beautiful and the glorious, which can now appear only as the terrifying."[133] Now contingent desire has become Absolute, and there can be no hope of a responding Thou.[134]

So Rilke's poetry becomes inextricably tragic, since every limitation it runs up against thwarts the drive toward fulfilled love, instead of, as with Thomas Aquinas, serving as the presupposition for what sets it free.[135] This is the "mystery of the fragmented God," which for Rilke enables poetry.[136] Von Balthasar thus notes, with *Duino Elegies* and *Sonnets to Orpheus*, that "praise and lament are everywhere inseparable" for Rilke. Here again, with more emphasis than anywhere else, von Balthasar notes that in this inseparability Rilke manages to reach the heart of Christianity without knowing it.[137] In Christianity, it is possible to lament and to praise at the same time, since in sorrow there is yet the hope of the resurrection. Yet this is what Rilke has set himself against, because this is not the intransitive love he so thoroughly desires.

Still, Rilke despite himself yearns for what he has rejected in Christianity. Or rather, he longs for what Christians in faith receive as their inheritance, revealed in and through Christ: Rilke longs at last for human love to find purpose and peace. Though his poetry in general labors intensively against such a conclusion, still in his *Duino Elegies* he betrays himself for the secret possibility that human love—which, of itself, can only end in death—is not in the end futile. Von Balthasar notes the Fifth Elegy:

> Angel!: suppose there's a place we know nothing about, and there,
> on some indescribable carpet, lovers showed all that here
> they're for ever unable to manage—their daring
> lofty figures of heart-flight,
> their towers of pleasure, their ladders,
> long since, where ground never was, just quaveringly
> propped by each other, —suppose they *could* manage it there,
> before the spectators ringed round, the countless unmurmuring
>   dead.[138]

Rilke hopes for someplace where love at last might tower in victory, some impossible height by which its temporary ecstasies might no longer be temporary. He dashes his own hopes in the next, Sixth, elegy and more thoroughly in the Seventh. Still von Balthasar does not let this moment of weakness slip away unnoticed: for von Balthasar, here is the poet's inchoate yearning for what only the Trinitarian God can provide. It is what von Balthasar spends the length of *Glory of the Lord* attempting to explain: that these various contingencies, tragically made absolute in various ways in modern thought, can indeed find fulfillment—if only they were willing, in their poverty, to embrace the poverty of the cross.

Von Balthasar both praises and condemns modern thought. He praises its lively sense of what is *personal*, of that dimension of human existence that is particular and experienced. He condemns its history-less individual (a fragmentation of what is personal), its nihilistic overcoming of the past for the sake of an atomized human being. In both theological and artistic circles, von Balthasar struggles to find what purpose the modern age might have for the Church and for art. He is convinced that there is such a purpose, and that it has to do with this heightened understanding of the personal. Von Balthasar consistently reassures us, over and against his bitter evaluations of art's anarchism and theology's narrowed rationalism, that Christ—the ultimate personality, in a positive and quite modern sense—can help the artist to again express with vitality and can help the Church again know the fullness of theology.

The volumes of *The Glory of the Lord* in many ways serve to respond to these problems that haunted him in the past. Despite showing himself fully capable of bitterness over the status of art, *Glory of the Lord* is filled with optimism. Von Balthasar sets himself to the task out of confidence that a theological aesthetic formed according to the shape of Christ is not only possible but also necessary. It is Christ who will vindicate created beauty through divine glory, precisely because the former needs the latter in order to be properly understood. Our understanding of beauty has degenerated because we have forgotten God. Von Balthasar responds with a reminder of God's glory, and then proceeds to show the continued presence of this glory in almost exhaustive detail: from philosophers to theologians to saints to poets. Even if, as he himself claims, theology has forgotten beauty—it ultimately cannot, because the Word has become flesh, and demands to be known as beautiful.

As von Balthasar writes his theological aesthetic, his thought develops with more thorough nuances to aid his own consistency. His caesura between art and theology is softened for the sake of finally acknowledging the ways in which art (especially Christian art) can express the form of Christ and for the sake of accounting for the ways in which he already goes about using artists in his own project. Art and theology still are not collapsed, but a sort of intimacy is permitted to develop between them—an intimacy of analogy, which affirms the breathing space of difference while at the same time allowing for profound similarity. In this way, von Balthasar can finally show himself to be a most thorough theologian of a theological aesthetic: Christ drives him to acknowledge art anew, and with this growing acknowledgement old wounds are in their way healed and there is hope again that art can serve a vitalizing role in the life of the Church. Beauty and glory: both have a place in the Church, and art employs beauty for the sake of glory.

In this new context, Rilke appears as a figure that sets himself against what von Balthasar strives to draw together in his theological aesthetics. Rilke views God as thoroughly immanent, and not even divine in the strictest sense. He desires an intransitive love without a Thou, directly opposing the Christian and Trinitarian understanding of love. In these two primary ways, among others, Rilke's poetry is a symbol of the metaphysical loss experienced in the modern age. His is an aesthetic built from the font of being-as-nothing, a welling song of despair. Against him, von Balthasar emphasizes a reaffirmation of the Trinity—and shows, in a poignant manner, how Rilke himself yearns for this.

Against Rilke stands the medieval figure of Dante. For Rilke's every doubt that love is possible without destroying the lover and the beloved, Dante bears the unwavering conviction that love redeems what is personal as well as what is universal. Dante's poetry is an art-metaphysic of the highest degree, taking advantage of art's most unique qualities—that is, as Rilke himself would say, its *thing-ness* and *specificity* (Rilke's *Dingedichte*)—for the sake of shaping a poem that knows no threat between a lover's specificity and the world-embracing love of God. The difference between the two poets could not be greater, and in it we see the possibilities of authentic transcendence contrasted against narrow, immanent transcendence. Incarnate in each art, as it were, is a radically different understanding of what the world is and where it is going. Von Balthasar affirms Dante's vision because he sees the truth of Christian revelation in it and also critiques Dante on the grounds of Christian revelation. The two agree metaphysically, but not Christologically—which von Balthasar then uses to turn back and ask whether Dante's cosmos (especially Hell) in fact bears the proper dimensions of reality. Metaphysics is open to Christology, and Christology illumines metaphysics.

It is to this metaphysic that we must now turn. From this chapter, an urgent question has emerged: With what metaphysic does von Balthasar respond to the modern age, and how does that metaphysic play a constitutive role in his theological aesthetic? How can metaphysical categories allow for what is personal, in von Balthasar's sense, without succumbing to Karl Barth's critique of the analogy of being as more determinative of truth than Christology? These are the questions we ask in the subsequent chapter.

THREE

Measuring Metaphysics

Being, Language, and Christology

The Vision of St. Francis

My prayer rose like incense
in the dead of night,
curling upward against the sky.
Sweet smoke coiled, gray shaped by the night.
Shaped and held by the dark,
which was itself alive.

I saw the darkness move.
I saw the living night.
It caught the thin silver of my prayer and spun,
flared out like wings—dark and light,
woven close and feathered soft.
Stretching sudden, reaching out.

And I reached back, narrow arms open wide.
I reached for the whirling fire-night, the burning
silver-shadow wings shining dark.

We did not touch, the fire that flung itself out
across the globe, and I—
with my featherless wings.

Featherless me, a bony reflection of the spreading
wings, the spanning fire, whose tongues of light
extended in the crossways of shadow and splendor,
bent together and unblent.
And in the wreathe of silver and dark—
I saw the face of Christ.

In the previous chapter, we uncovered von Balthasar's continued interest in classical metaphysics—that is, in being as the foundation of reality and our thinking about reality—alongside his consistent interaction with modern thought, especially modern *aesthetic* thought. Von Balthasar's work is at once to be understood in contradistinction to what is characteristically modern, which for von Balthasar is atomized and a-historical, and as an unusual appropriation of what is modern, which for von Balthasar means attention to what is personal and concrete. What makes von Balthasar's theological aesthetic distinctive, or we might even say *strange*, is that *Glory of the Lord* operates neither as a rejection of modernity, nor as an annexation of modernity. It is both and neither.

Von Balthasar critiques modernity on ancient grounds, on those metaphysical presuppositions that both the Patristic and Scholastic eras bore as the ground of their thought. The theological aesthetic is in many ways a project bent on resuscitating these lost presuppositions, and it works counter to modernity inasmuch as such presuppositions cripple certain basic tenets of modern thought. The poet Rilke, for example, receives sharp critique because von Balthasar discerns in Rilke's work the ultimate collapse of immanence and transcendence; the ultimate collapse, that is, of the analogy of being. Von Balthasar detects its poison everywhere in Rilke's work, and the poet becomes representative of a larger disaster in Western thought as a whole.

This larger disaster is the destruction of metaphysics and the loss of beauty. In his theological aesthetics, von Balthasar constructs an expansive historical-theological narrative in which the development of metaphysical and theological thinking advances and collapses together.

After reaching the metaphysical heights of Thomas Aquinas, theology fractures—splintering the unity of the transcendentals—in several locatable moments. Duns Scotus, Martin Luther, René Descartes, and Immanuel Kant serve as central, though not exclusive, figures. We will examine von Balthasar's answer to this disaster in this chapter.

All is not lost in the modern age, and von Balthasar traces the thread of God's glory into modernity, an era that both illuminates and conceals the aesthetic. His work here involves pronounced forays into literary authors, many quite modern, who preserve the aesthetic despite its problematic loss in other areas of the Church. Von Balthasar's task, it becomes clear, is not so much to review the hopeless death of beauty in a sort of historical tragicalism, but rather to show how beauty not only can be (and needs to be) resuscitated but also to show how beauty can be further illuminated in the modern era. This resuscitation is to be accomplished at both the theological and philosophical levels, and for von Balthasar the theological will guide the philosophical.

With this task in mind, von Balthasar strives to found his theology on a metaphysic of being *and* a thoroughgoing Christology. The language of being suffuses his work, always operating as the backdrop to his theology, including his aesthetics. The reinvigoration of the aesthetic in theology is not meant to surpass or supplement traditional metaphysics, but to operate within its development. As we observed in the last chapter, beauty can be subjected to the laws of being,[1] and the Incarnation "uses created Being at a new depth as a language and a means of expression for the divine Being and essence."[2] Beauty is a metaphysical category and the Incarnation uses metaphysical categories in unexpected ways in order to express God's fullness.

What von Balthasar presents in his trilogy is a theology that rests on the principles of being, and yet that also extends beyond them to include a concern for personality, especially Christological personality. That such a project is possible at all is, for von Balthasar, an expression of Christian revelation's place amid other forms of human knowledge: it stands above them and incorporates them.[3] Theology makes the philosophical questions of being—of the real and its qualities—*more* urgent instead of less so.[4] What is more, the personal expression of the Son in the Incarnation nuances von Balthasar's thought with an emphasis on what is unique and concrete: on what is personal. The last chapter established that von Balthasar's emphasis on "personality" is not an eschewal of metaphysics, nor even an attempt to surpass it, but rather it abides in his metaphysics. It is left to us now to uncover what von Balthasar imagines metaphysics to be, and is to become, in the face of his modern, Christologically determined use of personality. We also need to uncover what it is that he means by *personality*.

As in *Glory of the Lord*, we will find that von Balthasar links philosophy with the concerns of theology, emerging with a theological-philosophical account of the analogy of being, an account wherein the singular Incarnate One governs theology. It is, in other words, possible to *distinguish* his philosophical moves, but impossible to *separate* them from theology. This chapter will be spent in an effort to discern von Balthasar's basic metaphysical principles such as he himself describes them, and such as they can be extrapolated from his theological effort. The analogy of being dominates his metaphysical account, and with a nuance at first deceptive, making it appear as if analogy is perhaps the only metaphysical principle of great interest to von Balthasar. We will see that, to the contrary, the analogy of being touches the surface of an intricate account of created being's inner dynamism of expression, which must be understood in its ultimate relationship to—and distinction from—divine being, a relationship guided in its definitive contours by the Incarnation of the divine Logos. In sum, von Balthasar possesses what by all rights should be called a Christological metaphysics. It is this characteristic Christocentrism that makes von Balthasar's theological inquiry into poetry and poetic language possible.

THE EXPRESSIVE STRUCTURE OF CREATED BEING

Modern Foundations: Heidegger's *Aletheia* and Przywara's Polarity

One of von Balthasar's most important descriptions of his metaphysics, worked out alongside an epistemology, occurs in *Theo-logic I*. Originally written in 1947 as *Wahrheit Bund I: Wahrheit der Welt*, the volume would become the first of the trilogy's last section, even though chronologically it is the first of the entire trilogy to be published. The only change von Balthasar made to the work, after putting it aside and writing the volumes for *Herrlichkeit* and *Theodramatik*, takes place in the introduction. It is possible to read in *Theo-logic* some future indicators of massive sections in his trilogy: the passages on truth and mystery, with their focus on images and beauty, are a primordial gloss on *Glory of the Lord*; and the passages on the freedom of the subject serve as a backdrop to *Theo-Drama*. With the book essentially untouched from its first publishing in 1947 to its republishing in 1985, it lends foundational consistency to von Balthasar's project.

The work itself is, in Peter Henrici's words, "a phenomenology of truth."[5] *Theo-logic I* is that: it presents a view of metaphysical truth that consistently refers back to the fundamental experiences of the subject encountering its own truth and the truth of others, and places a strong accent on the subject's relationship to others as a central epistemological-ontological foothold. *Theo-logic I* is also much more, as David Schindler suggests.[6] Eschewing phenomenology's ultimate rejection of metaphysical categories, von Balthasar instead defends being and makes of it the foundation of his work: "being, precisely *as* being, can be unveiled and apprehended."[7]

The opening volume of *Theo-logic* presents a *dynamic* portrait of created being, and "dynamism" here is meant to encapsulate the multiple and simultaneous ways in which created being *expresses* itself (von Balthasar's preferred word for "expression" is *Ausdruck*). Created being is not static; rather, created being with its varied relationships—within the subject, between subject and object, between mystery and truth, and so on—is in a constant state of being expressed. For example, von Balthasar describes how the subject "awakens" by expressing itself and how the object, too, comes to fullness in its expression in the sensorium of the subject.[8] So "dynamism" in von Balthasar's sense is not meant to prop up a sagging account of traditional metaphysics, wherein the classical understanding of being is accused of ossification and useless abstraction and so stands in needs of correction.[9] Instead, it is more helpful to think of created being as already quite dynamic in itself, and thus to think of von Balthasar's interest in the varied relationships between being and beings as based in that dynamism and as an amplification of it. To presume otherwise—to presume that von Balthasar intends to work against classical being—makes nonsense of his interest in being's inherent expressiveness. This is what he imagines Thomas to be driving at already in the thirteenth century, and von Balthasar finds in this Thomist idea a sympathetic correlate in Heidegger's idea of truth as unconcealment or unveiling.[10] Thomist being and Heideggerian unveiling are brought together when von Balthasar describes truth itself as the *unveiling* of being, the expression of being's inward depths.[11]

Von Balthasar knits together a basically Thomist metaphysics and epistemology with the Heideggerian *aletheia*, forming what Fergus Kerr calls a "Heideggerian Thomism."[12] Truth as an "unveiling" is developed alongside more familiar Thomist interests in the transcendentals, the freedom of the knowing subject and the sensory qualities of knowing. The most important Heideggerian theme in *Theo-logic* is *aletheia*, "unveiling," which is for von Balthasar a concept closely allied with "expression" (*Ausdruck*).

A helpful place to start is with Heidegger's essay "On the Origin of the Work of Art," written somewhere between 1935 and 1937. In this essay, Heidegger discusses how beauty—especially the work of art—is suited to the unveiling of truth. A work of art is created in order to "shine" or illuminate being, and this illumination is the unveiling or unconcealment of being and thus of truth. "This shining, joined in the work, is the beautiful," writes Heidegger. "*Beauty is one way in which truth essentially occurs as unconcealedness.*"[13] Yet it is not the illumination of being alone that orients art to truth; it is also art's concrete particularity, its "thing-ness," and in a related respect it is also art's historicity that gives art its unveiling character.[14] Thing-ness, or particularity, and historicity mean that art's unveiling of being takes place not in the abstract, but in time through concrete beings.

It should be noted with great care that not all of von Balthasar's interest in the "expression" of being is rooted in Heidegger. Bonaventure's theology of the word has a profound influence on von Balthasar in this respect.[15] One of the dominant concerns here is to show the various layers of continuity and discontinuity between von Balthasar's beginning in *Apokalypse* and his later trilogy. Heidegger plays a key role in both works, and so the emphasis here is on the Heideggerian qualities of being's expressiveness and unveiling, though von Balthasar's use of those concepts is enriched by his knowledge of Bonaventure.

The two qualities of art that Heidegger highlights, particularity and historicity, are characteristics that von Balthasar invests himself in when writing both *Glory of the Lord*, as we have seen, and *Theo-logic*. Heidegger links beauty with the unveiledness of being and so with truth, and in *Theo-logic* von Balthasar makes a similar move when he attributes an inherent unveiledness, expressiveness, or manifestness to being: "Unveiledness is, first of all, an absolute property inherent in being as such."[16] Unlike Heidegger, von Balthasar relates created being's expressiveness to divine being, since the Trinitarian God is not only the self-knowing knower, but is also—as it were—the "self-expressing expresser" to a degree impossible to created being yet imitated by created being.[17] The Son is the expression of the Father, and in this essential, perfect, eternal relationship, created being's basic structure as self-expressing is intimated and surpassed. In allying himself with Heidegger's *aletheia*, von Balthasar shows the usefulness of the concept while also transfiguring it at the most fundamental of levels. This makes von Balthasar deeply Heideggerian, and yet anti-Heideggerian. We will continue to see how expression in particular serves von Balthasar in exactly this contradictory way.

Von Balthasar's further conversion of *aletheia* takes place in his interaction with the concept of polarity as Erich Przywara develops it. Here the analogy of being plays a fundamental constitutive role in von Balthasar's understanding of created being, a role worked out in terms of "polarity." He expands Przywara in order to fill out his own account of created truth and being. Ultimately, the analogy of being allows von Balthasar to give to the truth of the world an inner coherence, even an integrity of its own; an integrity that does not rest in itself, but rather rests in God.

The young von Balthasar studied metaphysics under the tutelage of Przywara, whose works *Analogia entis: Metaphysik* and *Polarity* help to form a view of the world and a view of God that remained with von Balthasar throughout his life.[18] The important concepts to understand with respect to von Balthasar's appropriation of Przywara are "similarity within greater difference," "polarity," and "openness." All three terms comprise the over-arching meaning of the analogy of being.

Believing he has retrieved Thomas Aquinas, Przywara characterizes the relationship between God and the world as a similarity within an ever-greater difference, which is language drawn from the Fourth Lateran Council.[19] For Przywara, this difference is not simply a negation—making it a statement about what God is *not*—but rather a positive quality, a "polarity" that constitutes a positive "relationship" with the world in the dissimilarity between the two. James Zeitz describes Przywara's polarity as an "alterity to alterity," a qualitative difference between two poles that, by virtue of that difference, places the two in reference to one another.[20] This is for Przywara a "tension," and in a manner similar to two ends of a rope held taut, the distinctive poles held at odds from one another in fact hold the link together. Analogy, vivified by the *maior dissimiltudo* of polarity, does not consist in less and more, but in a relationship of incomparables.[21]

Przywara describes creation as "open upwards,"[22] and at the same time indicates that its fulfillment can only occur "from above downwards."[23] He here works a basic exposition of the traditional *potentia oebedientialis* in terms of his favored "polarity" in order to emphasize creation's *openness* to God. Openness, for Przywara, more adequately expresses creation's complete and objective dependence on God for its being and its fulfillment in such a way that neither are made necessary to God. Von Balthasar, writing in *Theology of Karl Barth*, characterizes Przywara's analogy of being as "the destruction of every system in favor of a totally objective availability of the creature for God and for the divine measure of the creature."[24]

Von Balthasar's *Theo-logic I* adopts Przywara's interpretation of the analogy of being, but more importantly, it applies and amplifies Przywara's concepts *within* the structure of created being. *Theo-logic I* operates through a *series of polarities*. A review of the book's major sections reveals each successive positive tension (polarity): the polarity between the subject and the object, the polarity within the subject due to the subject's freedom to express itself, the polarity between being's self-expression and being's abiding mystery. Finally, all of the polarities that suffuse worldly being are undergirded by the primary polarity: the distinction between God and the world.[25] The major relationships described in *Theo-logic I* are polarities to the degree that qualities of otherness are positively related to one another by virtue of their otherness. The subject and the object do not absorb one another; neither do mystery and truth. They remain *other*, and are "polarities" in the sense that their otherness constitutes them positively.

The various relationships that inhere in created being in *Theo-logic* are *not* polarities as if created being were a series of junctures between absolute difference, since the only absolute difference is that between God and the world, which is the first and final polarity. The final "polarity" lends meaning to all intra-worldly tensions, especially inasmuch as these polarities are to be found analogously in God. The God-world relationship is at the same time quite unlike those to be discovered in the world.[26] The world is not intrinsic to God. There is, rather, an infinite difference between God and the world. In *Theo-Drama*, this will become an "infinite distance."[27]

The most unique expansion of Przywara's thought occurs in *Glory of the Lord V* with von Balthasar's "Fourfold Distinction."[28] The Fourfold Distinction takes the polarities latent in *Theo-logic I*, drawing them in the main from Thomas Aquinas and filtering them through Przywara's positive assessment of difference (polarity), and expands them to four real distinctions to be found in created being. These four are (1) inter-subjective difference, (2) the difference between the becoming of contingent beings and beings themselves, (3) the difference of beings from being itself, (4) the over-arching difference between created being and its trifold difference, and God.[29] The Fourfold Distinction closely allies Przywara's polarity with Heidegger's conception of being, to the transfiguring of each.

With the Fourfold Distinction, von Balthasar is expressly involved in making concrete the chief differences he discussed decades earlier in *Theo-logic I*. As before, the analogy of being—distinction number four—governs the proper understanding of the other distinctions. D. C. Schindler insists that what makes the Fourfold Distinction unique is that "it fully embraces the anthropological turn of modern thought without surrendering the great classical metaphysical tradition."[30] It should be added that the distinctions are in many ways designed to *defend* classical metaphysics instead of overturning it. The Fourfold Distinction is the crystallization of von Balthasar's "purely metaphysical" thought, a thought that is governed in its foundations by the concerns of theology.[31]

The analogy of being, considered through von Balthasar's development of Przywara, serves as the foundation of von Balthasar's metaphysics. It is at once simple and complex. In the words of Michael Murphy, "A simple description of the *anolgia entis*, therefore, comes with ambivalence: on the one hand, the concept is simple. . . . We understand one thing in terms of something else. On the other hand, the analogy of being has a complexity about it that no language can access."[32] It is here, in analogy, where most accounts of von Balthasar's metaphysical thought begin. Through Przywara, created being's very finitude is a positive characteristic of created being, making it what it is, rather than a deficiency. It is possible to see von Balthasar's adoption of the complexities of polarity as a further nuance of being's expressiveness. The expression of the object in the mind of the subject, and the subject's unfolding or self-expression in the encounter with the object, take place in the context of being's essential polarity. In other words, it is not possible to understand von Balthasar's use of Heidegger's *aletheia* outside of a concomitant understanding of Przywara's polarity. The two modern metaphysical claims condition one another: *aletheia* cannot be grasped, in the way von Balthasar uses it, without also always referencing the analogy of being and thus being's fundamental "openness" to God. This works against many of the flaws von Balthasar identifies in Heidegger as early as *Apokalypse*, particularly Heidegger's inability to understand contingency in the context of a transcendent and eternal God. Przywara's polarities are, meanwhile, explained further through the proposition that "openness" must also mean the "expression" of being, particularly in the primordial intersubjective relationship of beings to other beings. In other words, Przywara's metaphysical concerns are allied with a Heideggerian aesthetic insight into being's expressivity.

Classical Metaphysics: Thomas Aquinas, The Real Distinction, and Wonder

Von Balthasar's metaphysics thus far is essentially composed of an expressive account of the analogy of being; that is to say, the accent is almost entirely on various analogies (viewed positively as polarities). This lends his work a narrowed sense of the metaphysical, restricting it to the vast realms of "being" and "analogy" without considering, say, causality.[33] His metaphysics also possesses an emphatic interest in "expression." This is a "dynamism" framed in terms of created being's tendency toward expression and self-realization. If we are to continue building toward a better understanding of von Balthasar's Christological metaphysics, there is one further theme in particular to add: Thomas Aquinas's real distinction between essence and existence.

One of the rare places in his trilogy where von Balthasar discusses metaphysics itself instead of operating on its presumption occurs in two of the middle volumes of *Glory of the Lord*: the fourth volume, "Metaphysics in Antiquity"; and the fifth volume, "Metaphysics in the Modern Age."[34] The fourth volume, while spent in reflections on both pagan and Christian philosophers, receives its dominant perspective from Thomas Aquinas. As far as von Balthasar is concerned, the greatest heights of metaphysics are reached in the thought of Thomas Aquinas. This height is nothing else than the real distinction between *esse* and *essentia*, which he calls "a philosophical thesis" that "enables us once again to make a clear differentiation between the 'glory' of God and the beauty of the world; indeed . . . it enables us to recover the true meaning of that glory."[35] This differentiation recalls the analogy of being in general, since in God *esse* and *essentia* are identical, and in creatures the two are distinct. Glory can be recovered because the metaphysical distinction between God and the world is here so firmly established and related, and the right contemplation of God's glory must draw from this basic distinction. Looking behind Pzrywara, von Balthasar sees the fundamental outlines of the analogy of being affirmed in Thomas Aquinas, and this despite Thomas never using the term.

Thomas's contribution to metaphysics is not reducible to the *analogia entis* alone. For von Balthasar, there is also an urgent anthropological question to be asked alongside general metaphysics: it is not just, "why is there anything at all?", which is Heidegger's question, but also, "what is the human person's place in creation?"[36] So Thomas "sees man, to whom it has been given to reflect on being, in a peculiar state of suspension between nature and supernature: he is disposed by nature for the revelation of God in grace; and although he can make no claim to grace, without it he can never be fulfilled or complete."[37] The philosophical distinction between essence and existence has profound effects on theological anthropology: the doctrine, which permits us to imagine an essence that still must *become*—a nature that has an end toward which it tends— provides the grounds for also imagining human nature as possessing an end that it itself cannot achieve, and that is beatitude. The distinction between essence and existence does not *prove* that the human being "is disposed by nature for the revelation of God in grace," but it does lend insight into how the human being can be so disposed at all, because human nature tends toward an end. Von Balthasar is arguing, in other words, that human nature is in its most fundamental structure an openness tended toward God, as Przywara tried to argue, and that Thomas's distinction crystalizes and illuminates this fundamental structure.[38] Thomas's distinction, because it defends the openness of human nature, thus also illuminates the human orientation toward *wonder*: we are capable of wonder because we have ends toward which we are drawn, and because we are fundamentally not-God. Wonder is an expression of our transcendence and of the mystery of being.[39]

But Aquinas's achievement is, according to von Balthasar, a delicate balance of tensions that successive ages are unable to maintain.[40] The unity of beauty and truth, of aesthetics and metaphysics, falls apart with thinkers such as Descartes, Kant, Hegel, and others. Knowing, "real knowing," truncates to a skeletal definition of truth verified through epistemological doubt and finally disintegrates into sheer relativism with the expulsion of metaphysics from philosophy. Now theology and philosophy can barely distinguish between God and the world, and von Balthasar understands this as a poverty that results in the strangeness of Hegel (among others), who must now always have one truth die for the sake of another, with God himself somehow "becoming." Wonder is certainly no longer possible, let alone metaphysics.[41]

This is a rather depressing narrative of developments. Nevertheless, von Balthasar's volume on metaphysics in the modern age is neither short nor dark. Instead, he moves forward to discuss a rather strange and new category: the metaphysics of the saint. Here, he covers a lengthy succession of saints and the varying degrees to which their insights—in mystical writings, for the most part—reveal the truth of metaphysics, that is, the extent to which their descriptions of God and the world conform to the way the world really *is*. Not every mystic achieves the proper balance of insight, as they in their ecstasy often tend to collapse God and creation into a single sought-for unity. Meister Eckhart receives sharp criticism for this.[42] Figures like Nicolas of Cusa receive attention as admirable appropriators of reality, since for Nicolas the central forming idea is, according to von Balthasar, that "God is all (otherwise he would not be God), and yet the world exists, and this real world cannot be added to God's reality as an increment."[43]

With the saints, wonder at the world and at God is once again possible because the distinction between the two in the analogy of being has been preserved. The Christian saint grasps the distinction and unity between God and the world through the life of faith, and in doing so grasps it better and unreservedly. This is why the saint can be said to preserve a true philosophical insight, despite not being a philosopher.[44] Since the insight is grasped in the light of faith, the wonder of the saints is different in kind than that of the philosopher. Though analogous, this saintly *wonder* is really *worship*.[45] The whole analogy of being is ordered toward worship, not in itself, but in the sheer openness of created being. *It cannot answer the question that it itself is.*[46] By this very fact (this immutable *fact* that creation is *not God*), created being is ordered toward—made for, intended for, finds its fulfillment in—worship.

What can be observed in von Balthasar's metaphysic of the saint is a creative unity between the life of grace and the intellectual life, between the order of redemption and the created order. With such a unity, it is possible for him to argue that revelation reveals the meaning of the world, and that the world finds the fullness of its meaning in revelation. In von Balthasar's own words, "If in this manner biblical revelation rests on the basis of the primal God-world distinction, and thus on metaphysics, and radiates from this point, then metaphysics correspondingly attains fulfillment in the event of revelation."[47] Thus, all the intra-worldly distinctions of created being find resonance in the Incarnation of the Word, who bears in himself the insurmountable distinction between God and the world, as well as the distinctions present within creation, while at the same time uniting them. Revelation, though "at odds ... to all that is foreseeable ... must nevertheless enter into the distinctions [of the world] as a form of completion: the word of God must be written into the word of Being, the word of Being into the words of creatures which are exchanged as comprehensible words among existent creatures."[48]

The Christian is for von Balthasar the "the guardian of that metaphysical wonderment which is the point of origin for philosophy."[49] Philosophy (and theology) finds its authentic self again through the storehouse preserved in the Christian saint. The saint has preserved what Thomas understood best. This is not to say that philosophy will dissolve into theology so much as to say that the saint has kept philosophy's original and best attitude, which is the disposition of *wonder*. The saint keeps this disposition not necessarily because the saint is the perfect philosopher, but because it is Christ's own disposition; that is, it is an attitude ultimately expressed in unrestricted openness, for wonder consists in delight over what it receives and perceives. The saint imitates Christ himself, and in this way the point upon which von Balthasar's "metaphysics of the saint" revolves is really Christological.

Preliminary Synthesis: The Expression of Being

With the metaphysic of the saint, we have Thomas Aquinas being employed in a manner that is once again quite modern; that is, we have a theological move based on an interest in personality and personal dispositions, namely the attitude of worship. Yet what the saints preserve through their prayerful attitude is not, as far as von Balthasar is concerned, something new. Their success is not a success over-against the past, but rather a contemplative preservation of it: in their posture of worship, the saints show us in their subjectivity what is objectively the case in classical metaphysics. Worship is only possible if the real distinction between essence and existence is maintained. In this way, it is possible for us to see how von Balthasar's move toward modernity is rooted in a concern to preserve what he considers the heights of metaphysical insight as it was achieved in Thomas Aquinas.

Von Balthasar's emphasis on what is concrete and personal—or rather, what is concretely, and thus personally, experienced by the believing Church—is attended by a concomitant commitment to "classical" metaphysics. He is beholden to Thomas Aquinas's metaphysical assessments, and this despite great reticence toward Thomas as a theologian of beauty.[50] If von Balthasar's self-professed commitment to Thomas Aquinas is taken seriously, then it must also be said—perhaps in irony—that von Balthasar's theological aesthetic does not work without Thomas. The theologian who fails beauty ultimately upholds it.[51] Whether or not von Balthasar's critique of Thomas's aesthetics withstands investigation, and there is evidence that it does not,[52] the metaphysical underpinnings that Thomas provides continue to bear the weight of von Balthasar's aesthetic project.

As we observed in Dante, von Balthasar's assessment of Dante, and in an inquiry into von Balthasar's theological aesthetics in the light of the *Divina Commedia*, personality is not opposed to metaphysics. Each conditions the other. Concreteness and personality are ordered toward and ordered by more "general" categories such as being, even as more authentic personality or personalities (such as a saint or a humbled Dante) better grasp being.[53] What we are better equipped to understand now is *how* this claim can be made. Since being is, for von Balthasar, inherently expressive, then what relates being in general and personal beings in particular is *expressiveness*. Both bear the structure of expression: the subject must express itself to be an authentic subject, and being is always in the midst of unveiling in truth and superabundant goodness. What is more, both persons (through worship) and created being (through its very structure) express the fundamental polarity of the analogy of being; in order for either being or beings to be properly understood, we must also acknowledge the *analogia entis*.

Here Heidegger, used against himself, helps von Balthasar to make the case for classical metaphysics's perduring relevance, and this in opposition to Heidegger's onto-theology critique.[54] The expressiveness of being, rightly grasped, enhances or enriches classical metaphysics by reinforcing its essential contours (especially the analogy of being), and by revealing the metaphysical relationship to personality. Heidegger's *Dasein* has been turned on its head. *Dasein* is no longer being-toward-death or being held out over the nothing, which in von Balthasar's mind exposes the nihilism at the heart of Heidegger's thought. Instead, *Dasein* is better understood as being toward the *analogia entis*, and ultimately *Dasein* means being held in existence by the Trinitarian God.[55] If in von Balthasar's assessment Heidegger makes finitude a transcendental, and thus eternal, then von Balthasar's response to Heidegger is to show how finitude can only be understood when it is *not* identified with eternity. Von Balthasar's response is a classical one with respect to Thomas Aquinas, since the distinction between essence and existence helps us to understand how we are not like God and yet like God. Classical metaphysics redeems the modern interest in the personal, and in this sense it retains heuristic primacy even in the face of von Balthasar's preference for the personal and concrete.[56]

Von Balthasar's marriage of a broadly classical metaphysics with broadly modern concerns for what is personal occurs in his Christology. Here his theological interests complexify the relationship between personality and metaphysics. In the first place, the concept *personality* itself has so far remained rather vague, excepting an emphasis on what is existential and concrete. Second, rather than viewing existence (what is personal) and essence (and other metaphysical considerations of being) as opposed to one another, competing for primacy, it is more helpful in von Balthasar's case to see the relationship between the two as an "oscillating midpoint."[57] Metaphysics anchors personality, and personality renders metaphysics more urgent. Von Balthasar's explicit preference for what he calls the *analogia personalitatis* over the *analogia entis*, as in his book *Prayer*, is not to be understood as a stance against the latter.[58] Personality cannot be grasped authentically without first presupposing the analogy of being, and in this restricted sense metaphysics continues to govern concepts of what is personal—as in von Balthasar's inversion of Heidegger.

So the heart or midpoint of von Balthasar's theology refers constantly to both metaphysics and personality, with the emphasis shifting according to the question at hand. Each is brought together in a complex fashion in the Person of the Incarnate Word, whose hypostatic union transcends and orders both. We must now examine von Balthasar's unique Christology here, and in doing so clarify both his use of the analogy of being and his understanding of personality.

CHRISTOLOGICAL METAPHYSICS

Christology and the *Analogia Entis*

A major development in the expression of von Balthasar's metaphysics—a *theological* metaphysics—is his book *Theology of Karl Barth*.[59] Here von Balthasar places himself in lengthy dialogue with the Protestant Barth, who explicitly rejected the analogy of being. In this work, von Balthasar insists that Catholic theology must by its nature remain "open,"[60] and that "The Church as such cannot possess a rigid, enclosed metaphysics."[61] He thus rejects what Barth desires to reject, which is a self-sufficing "principle" that governs theology in the place of Christ. But the openness of the Church, according to von Balthasar, does not *eliminate* metaphysics as Barth thought—replacing it with *event*—since "Vatican I defended the *duplex ordo* and therefore the totality of reality in God."[62] Metaphysics is still necessary in theology.

Authors such as Steven A. Long have expressed suspicion toward von Balthasar's interaction with Karl Barth, especially as it is depicted in von Balthasar's explication of nature and analogy in *Theology of Karl Barth*. Long is concerned that von Balthasar is so focused on relating nature to grace that "nature becomes the equivalent of a theological vacuole or empty Newtonian space, a placeholder for grace."[63] Von Balthasar's metaphysics as a whole would also fall under this critique, at least inasmuch as von Balthasar acknowledges its necessity but threatens to render that necessity into empty speech for a prelude to the Incarnation. A point-for-point response to Long's exegesis of *Theology of Karl Barth* has no room here, but already it should be clear from the wider context offered in this chapter so far that von Balthasar's concept of nature is more robust than Long imagines. Still, his concern is a healthy one and apropos to bring forward now as we delve more deeply into this book of von Balthasar's in particular.

In *Theology of Karl Barth*, von Balthasar characterizes the argument over nature—and thus categories like being, natural theology, philosophy, and so forth—as a "Janus-faced" question in the Catholic Church, one that always presses two almost dialectical possibilities.[64] One "face" is the consistent insistence on the priority of grace and on the fact that grace perfects nature. The other "face" is the consistent insistence on nature's integrity outside of grace. Von Balthasar weighs these two concerns by contending that "a natural order without grace is both meaningful and possible,"[65] and that "everything touched by grace retains its natural side: grace is always a grace in a nature and for a nature."[66] This is a careful line to walk, one that von Balthasar admits remains a problem even in Catholic theology. He further problematizes the question by suggesting that "our only option is to recognize a certain kind of *analogy* between the two uses of the concept of nature."[67] That is, depending on whether nature is being used in a philosophical context or a theological one, its meaning analogously shifts. Theology never simply imports philosophical terms as if acquiring a new garment; the term itself, irradiated by grace, shifts to a new horizon of meaning. This irradiation includes the term "nature."[68]

Von Balthasar's insistence on an *analogy* between uses of "nature" is central to his argument, both against Karl Barth's rejection of the *analogia entis* and against Thomist critics like Steven A. Long, although perhaps not to the complete satisfaction of either. Long does not take note of von Balthasar's argument in this respect, and it would have soothed his concerns over von Balthasar's eschewal of "abstraction." As Long notes, "Balthasar argues that nature cannot be abstracted in its essential intelligibility from the complex in which it will be found, and from its mode of existence," which means it cannot be abstracted from salvation history and grace.[69] What Long should also note, in view of von Balthasar's claims for analogous uses of the word "nature," is the context of von Balthasar's statements. Von Balthasar makes the argument against abstraction in the context of a dialogue with Karl Barth, a Protestant who is deeply disturbed at a Catholic imagination that seems capable of removing salvation history from its speculative landscape—a worry that von Balthasar is anxious to refute. He wants to show that Catholic theology is always also *Christian* theology, indebted to and concerned with Christ. This tilts his comments on nature in this book especially, and his reticence toward abstraction elsewhere occurs as well in a *theological* context. Von Balthasar's use of "nature" shifts in more explicit philosophical contexts, as in "On the Tasks of Catholic Philosophy in Our Time," reviewed in the last chapter.[70] Here von Balthasar shows himself to be more amenable to "abstraction" in the way Long means it, which is to say to a point of view that theoretically brackets Christology for the sake of further understanding.[71] In *Theology of Karl Barth*, von Balthasar desires to defend the necessity of nature outside of grace. It makes more sense, then, to understand von Balthasar's position as one Long himself suggests, yet appears to distrust: "If Balthasar meant only that, concretely speaking, there is no pure nature in the sense of a nature *existentially unaffected* by sin and grace, that is true."[72]

In his dialogue with Karl Barth, von Balthasar rests his attention not only on preserving the concept of nature—and of the analogy of being—in the face of Barth's critiques, but also on Barth's more positive contributions to theology, particularly his profound Christocentrism. Von Balthasar argues that Christocentrism is also a feature of Catholic theology.[73]

He does not oppose the analogy of being and Christocentrism since the analogy itself is, as he says in a passage on Przywara, "nothing other than the provisional and abstract expression for this ultimate truth [of the Incarnation]."[74] Moreover, he argues, "one of the presuppositions of the Incarnation is that there must be a true priority of nature and reason!"[75] The analogy of being serves the Incarnation, not as a controlling idea, but rather as the philosophical expression of that obedient openness by which God redeems all of creation. If von Balthasar finds in the Virgin Mary that "flesh" that utters its agreement to the Incarnation of the Word by "letting it be done," then in the *analogia entis* he finds that universal created reality that echoes the subjective, creaturely *fiat*. What Barth wants—a theocentric, Christocentric universe—can only be achieved in fullness *with* the analogy of being, not without it.[76] Even in the case of von Balthasar's theological considerations, natural concepts must retain their integrity or else grace is no longer gratuitous.

Much of von Balthasar's Christocentrism is rooted in his work on Maximus the Confessor, *Cosmic Liturgy*, originally published in 1941, before *Wahrheit*, with a substantially revised version appearing in 1961.[77] The book focuses on Maximus's eloquent defense of Christ's human will, for which Maximus was exiled. In his introduction, von Balthasar insists that Maximus's position, while certainly serving as a defense of human freedom, in fact draws from a far-reaching view of the entire cosmos.[78] Maximus's comprehensive theology is first of all the fruit of the Council of Chalcedon, which von Balthasar believes Maximus brings to its fullest theological consequences.[79] The unconfused union between Christ's two natures, as expressed in Chalcedon, becomes for Maximus the rule for the unity between God and the entire cosmos accomplished in Christ. The free response of the human person to God's self-revelation in Christ, which would become the theme of *Theo-Drama*, is made possible by Christ and brought to fullness in Christ, and in Christ the various internal divisions of the human being are brought into synthesis.[80]

Cosmic Liturgy displays frequent interactions with Thomas Aquinas, despite the fact that little historical evidence links Maximus with Thomas. When critiquing Maximus, for example, von Balthasar recalls the vital importance of the real distinction between essence and existence as presented in Thomism,[81] and compares Maximus and Thomas's presentations of a natural desire for God.[82] One is presented with, as it were, a

Thomist Maximus. Brian Daley notes this as a problem in his retrospective introduction to the translation.[83] Given how von Balthasar would later describe metaphysics in his trilogy, however, the move is systematically fortuitous even if far from historically accurate. Maximus the Confessor describes the Incarnation as the synthesis of God and creation: the careful interweaving of every created distinction into a real unity that nevertheless does not destroy what is distinct. Chalcedon, through the eyes of Maximus, is in von Balthasar's view the guiding light for every subsequent theological construal of God and the world: "unconfused union." Thomas Aquinas's work reaches a similar graceful synthesis, and von Balthasar freely relates the two: Thomas's scholasticism meets Maximus's patristic synthesis.[84] The distance of history does not destroy the theological kinship of either figure in von Balthasar's mind. For the theologian to examine the analogy of being, Chalcedon must serve as the primary lens. Both Thomas and Maximus incorporate Chalcedon in their work to exemplary degrees and become for von Balthasar his twin guiding lights for a Christological metaphysics.[85]

Von Balthasar must now retain the careful distinctions of both Maximus and Thomas, else he will fall into pantheism or panentheism. The Incarnation cannot be made identical with the analogy of being, or God and the world are collapsed into a single horizon. Nor can the analogy of being serve as the necessary foundation for the Incarnation, or Barth was right all along: the analogy of being is really the single principle upon which Catholicism rests regardless of Christ. The Incarnation can *fulfill* the analogy of being, but not in such a way that the Incarnation is made necessary to created being or created being made necessary to the Incarnation. We are left with von Balthasar's answer, as expressed in his *Epilogue* to the trilogy: the *analogia entis* is "made present (*gegenwärtigende*) in Christ."[86] In other words, the Incarnation makes explicit the analogy of being with a clarity impossible to philosophy, yet without the *analogia entis* being made identical with the Incarnation. Thus, "the essential polarity of worldly Being, whose poles can only be understood through each other," that is, the polarity that characterizes the analogy of being and every analogous relationship immanent to creation, "inevitably points to an identity as ground—which however . . . cannot be constructed from the poles themselves."[87] The Incarnation illuminates the analogy of being *because* the two are not the same.

Here is where von Balthasar responds to Barth's concerns while at the same time inverting them—insisting as he does on the integrity of the *analogia entis* even as he gives it a Christological light—and where it is possible to see how the two thinkers part ways in their concepts of transcendence. Barth, especially the early Barth, insists on a divine transcendence so absolute that, in von Balthasar's eyes, there threatens to be no commensurability or comprehensibility between the creature and God. Von Balthasar worries over Barth's destructive dialectic as early as *Apokalypse*, and repeats that concern in *Theology of Karl Barth*.[88] Much as God's transcendence—indeed, an absolute transcendence—is necessary in theology and philosophy, von Balthasar prefers analogy to dialectic. The absolute difference between God and the world cannot be grasped without the similarity it supports. Here von Balthasar thinks he is being both more philosophically and theologically consistent than (at least the early) Barth. Christ speaks to us through our shared humanity, and this speaking presupposes not only his infinite superiority over creation, but also a likeness between Creator and created.[89] Von Balthasar's Christocentrism is distinguishable from Barth's inasmuch as the former's is always concerned to protect the integrity of creation vis-à-vis the Creator, emphasizing their likeness amid their greater difference. This, for von Balthasar, reinforces God's transcendence because the likeness shared between creature and Creator allows us to recognize the difference between the two more radically: analogy is the expression (*Ausdruck*) of the difference.[90]

The Christocentrism expressed throughout the trilogy is for the most part drawn from the Christocentrism of Maximus the Confessor. Von Balthasar stresses Christ as the synthesis of the cosmos in his trilogy much as he does in *Cosmic Liturgy*. In language that resonates with Barth's concerns, von Balthasar highlights the way Christ unites all of the various distinctions of creation, and finally the distinction between God and the world, in himself. The Incarnation is the key to the fulfillment of creation, a fulfillment achieved along the lines of Chalcedon's proclamation: unconfused, undivided unity. The manner in which Christ's humanity and divinity are united is, analogously, the manner in which all of creation is brought into unity with God. Przywara's polarity is recognizable here as well, but greatly modified. Now even the openness of creation, which for Przywara the *analogia entis* defends, is a Christological openness. The relationship between God and creation is not determined by the analogical principle, but rather through Christ himself. Von Balthasar can then radicalize that basic relationship, positing a much greater level of intimacy, such that the creature can offer a graced response to God. This *graced response* transcends Przywara's abstract openness. Von Balthasar is enabled to radicalize the analogy of being because he examines it through the light of Christology.

Yet being is also, as we have observed, more than analogy. Being is also expressive. So if von Balthasar is to be thorough within his theological use of metaphysics, then he must also relate the expressiveness of being with his Christology. It is to this problem that we now turn, and which will enable us finally to introduce theological language to our complex of themes alongside metaphysics.

Christology and the Expression of Being

For von Balthasar, Christology is deeply invested in metaphysical questions of the analogy of being. This is at the same time a Christology entwined with the Church's dogmatic pronouncements on Christ. In this way, Chalcedon's pronouncements are not to be understood as against or entirely other than the laws of created being; rather, Chalcedon gives to created being, and thus to the analogy of being, a new light. We have thus far observed von Balthasar's Chalcedonic construal of the analogy of being, which serves as one of the primary characteristics of his Christological metaphysics. Here, the analogy of being is illuminated in light of its concrete expression in the two natures of Christ.

The harmony between the *analogia entis* and the hypostatic union is not a relationship of absolute identity, or else Karl Barth's critique of Catholicism is rendered accurate and devastating. Instead, von Balthasar's response shows us how prior metaphysical speculation—that of the Greeks, as appropriated by Christians—can receive further development in the encounter with revelation. Christ is not the conclusion to be arrived at with the close of metaphysical speculation; he is the unanticipated fulfillment and thus development of that speculation. Being is open, but cannot anticipate the exact contours of that to which it stands open. So Christ is at once recognized as an anticipated fulfillment, and understood to shatter the bounds of anticipation.

This Christological revelation of being is, most of all, a development into further concreteness, since for von Balthasar the ultimate illumination of the analogy of being occurs in the Incarnate Son. General laws of being are married with personal specificity, and abstraction is no longer to be opposed to the concrete and historical, though von Balthasar's preference remains with the latter. Still, von Balthasar's Christological metaphysics extends beyond the concretization of the analogy of being in Christ, beyond an analysis of created nature in the light of Chalcedon essentially derived from a Thomist-hued Maximus the Confessor. With the emphasis on the *personal* union of natures in Christ, von Balthasar has reintroduced his preference for what is personal, and it is possible for us to better understand what he means by it.

When von Balthasar refers to the *personal*, his primary frame for its possible constellation of meanings is the Person of Christ. The definition of a Person is, first, Trinitarian: a Person in this case is one who receives divine being uniquely, entirely, and eternally through the mutual indwelling of the Trinity. To speak in terms of the economy: a person is one whose identity is entirely one with a received mission, a statement that is only true in the strictest sense in the cases of the Son and of the Spirit. Here an analogy is at work between the Son's eternal reception of his identity and being from the Father in absolute unity of essence, and the economic expression of that reception in the Cross and Eucharist. Human personhood is a further analogy, related to the economic mission of Christ: a *theological* person—to be carefully distinguished from general human subjectivity, which von Balthasar is anxious to affirm—is one who has received an ecclesial mission and lives out that mission in the Spirit in imitation of the Son. Most of *Theo-Drama III* is dedicated to describing these basic qualities of personhood.[91]

The theo-dramatics is concerned for the most part with a theology of history as it is expressed in the "drama" of salvation. Personality, in the case of the middle-part of von Balthasar's trilogy, is construed in terms of its historical specificity. *Person* has to do with *mission*. Yet what has *person* to do with *expression*? This is the aesthetic question, and the one with which we are at the moment most concerned. Positing a person as expressive, as we have already done in the "Preliminary Synthesis" of this chapter only opens the door to an answer. How might we interpret personality with respect to the theological aesthetics?

In a perhaps roundabout way, two smaller books outside the trilogy, two books pertaining primarily to history, help us to understand the aesthetic importance of Christological personhood: *A Theology of History* and *A Theological Anthropology*.[92] The first of these works to be an outline or "nucleus" of a theology of history, while the second—with a rather misleading English title—attempts to consider some of the same problems of the earlier book in a more focused review of the *wholeness* Christ brings to human experience and history. Examining specific qualities of these two works together will help us grasp how personality and the expression of being relate to one another in von Balthasar's thought.

A Theology of History concerns itself with the various ways that what is abstract and universal stands opposed to what is singular and concrete, with each threatening to subsume the other: essentialism and historicism are each capable of reductivism.[93] Being and history seem to persist at odds with one another. There is no resolution to this opposition either within created being or creaturely history; this would eviscerate the createdness of each. The only resolution is "a miracle undiscoverable and unguessable by philosophical thought," and that is the Incarnation.[94] In Christ, "without being nullified, the abstract laws are, in him, integrated and subordinated within his Christological uniqueness"[95] and it is through his absolute uniqueness that the uniqueness of historical human experience—as well as of history in general—are finally related to essentiality without abolishing either.[96] The union is achieved by virtue of Christ's uniqueness because he, as unique Son, is in himself a total identity between loving receptivity (the receptivity of his being from the Father) and adoring act (of thanksgiving to the Father): "between being and the act in which the whole of one's being is lovingly received."[97] Thus the one who eternally knows no opposition between essence and existence, between being and act, gives to the world an analogous unity through the hypostatic union. *A Theology of History*, written before *Theo-Drama*, thus helps us to understand how dramatic categories are not to be opposed to essential categories. Each are united in the life of Christ, who is man and who is God, and whose historical life is the wellspring of the eternal life of the Church.[98]

A Theological Anthropology, better titled *The Whole in the Fragment*, helps us to more clearly understand how Christ's whole life draws together the contingency of creation—the fragmentary qualities of created being and of creaturely history—into a wholeness united to divine life. Here von Balthasar repeats the basic tension between essential and historical categories as in the other work, and in terms we should by now recognize from both *Apokalypse* and *Herrlichkeit*:

> Either the human being is again redeemed to spirit (from matter) by the surrender of one's unique personality (so Hegel and his predecessors and successors), or tragic dualism remains the last word, heroically seeing imperfectability (as the eternal return) as absolute (so Nietzsche), or else the fragment undergoes its "failure" (Jaspers) and its "determination unto death" (Heidegger) within which is a flash of wholeness that one sees only in forgoing it.[99]

There persists here the same tragic either/or between essence and existence, being and history, which petrifies either at the cost of one. Here personal concreteness and uniqueness are sacrificed for the sake of a synthesis, resulting in the death of the personal and (ultimately) of the historical, or else personality is redeemed in the lonely confrontation with death and thus with nonbeing.

Von Balthasar rejects the premises of this tragic either/or. The fragments of created existence are, instead, adopted by the Son, in whose image temporality was created.[100] It is not the open-ended contingency of creation that must be destroyed; it is the false presupposition that this inherently fragmented being stands opposed to fulfillment at all. The contingency of created being, affirmed most of all in the basic notion of the analogy of being, is instead exactly the way it stands open to fulfillment. In other words, the *wholeness* of creation—considered either ontologically or historically—does not rest in itself, even as (and especially as) we affirm its immanent goodness. That wholeness is only to be found in God, in the God who becomes man and thus brings created being and history to the fulfillment to which it stands open but cannot immanently achieve.

Christ's full humanity is key here, since it is through that humanity that the redemption and fulfillment of contingency is accomplished. It is here, too, that we are finally able to understand the link between not only essence and history—as in *Theo-Drama*—but also that between essence and expression—as in *Glory of the Lord*. The hypostatic union brings cre-

ation to its fulfillment in a highly developed historical sense, since it is
the historical life of Christ that brings about that fulfillment in the Spirit.
Yet it is also through the union of the Second Person to a humanity like
ours that God expresses himself to us, and also expresses us to ourselves.
The Word *speaks* to us through his humanity. Here, in a move toward
language, we can in a much fuller way grasp the union of being and of
aesthetic expressiveness that von Balthasar is attempting to describe.
Here the speaking is personal, since it is the Word who speaks, but in
speaking he uses the language of created being in his humanity. "The
ways the Word makes himself comprehensible to us are infinitely varied,"
writes von Balthasar.

> His humanity is an instrument from which every melody can be
> drawn; even silence, the pause, can be an effective mode of commu-
> nication (*Art der Mitteilung*). Likewise as varied are the ways of in-
> terpreting that the Word gives us.[101]

The expressiveness of being is, in von Balthasar's unique construal
of language, brought into contact with classical metaphysics in a highly
personal and concrete fashion. It allows us to understand how all three
themes of this book—metaphysics, Christology, and language—are married to one another without an opposition that forces a choice between
them. It is to this theology of language that we now move in order to
provide the final major characteristic of von Balthasar's Christological
metaphysic.

CHRISTOLOGICAL LANGUAGE: CHRISTOLOGY, METAPHYSICS, AND EXPRESSION

Christological Language and Metaphysics

The heart of von Balthasar's reflections on language can be found in
Theo-Logic II. The book spends itself exhaustively in the quest to respond
to the following problem: how is it that the fullness of divine truth,
which the God-man is, can be expressed within the limits of earthly
being? Further, how can this be so without destroying earthly being,

disfiguring it under the burden of divine truth? Early in the text, von Balthasar discloses a guiding statement:

> The man Jesus is the truth as the expression (*Ausdruck*) of the Father, and he is interpreted (*ausgelegt*) by the Holy Spirit as such truth. However, since this man Jesus is simultaneously the expression (*Ausdruck*) of the whole God (the Father and the Spirit are in him), the human logic in which he expresses God is itself nothing other than an "image and likeness" (*Bild und Gleichnis*) of the triune God.[102]

Many of his themes are already familiar. Divine truth—the truth of the Triune God—and worldly truth are both related and unrelated, and it is key to understand once again that this is not merely a comparison between the two. They cannot be compared at all. This sounds very much like his refrain for the analogy of being. What von Balthasar develops is the Christological location of the incomparability of God and humanity, and he does so by applying it to Jesus's "otherness." Jesus is distinctive, set apart, and at the same time exists in a radically intimate relationship with humanity, particularly on the cross.[103] He is "other" because he is divine, and because that divinity is expressed in his humanity. He is "set apart" even in the Gospels. So Jesus's otherness lends to him a paradoxical strangeness with respect to humanity despite sharing fully in humanity: "Jesus possesses a human nature that is complete in every respect, and yet he appears before his fellowmen as wholly other."[104]

The concepts of distance and similarity, already so familiar in von Balthasar's philosophy of the analogy of being, are expressed in Christ; now it is rendered in terms of a fully theological insight, one that von Balthasar finds in the Council of Chalcedon as both caution and positive affirmation.[105] Chalcedon defends Christ's specificity as a single human being, one divine *hypostasis*, and at the same time as a human being like us in all things except sin. Von Balthasar thinks Chalcedon's essential outlook has a bearing on the *totality* of the Incarnation: the unity of the Head with his Body, by which all of creation is united to him, is in Chalcedon rendered as a unity that is at once restrictive and expansive. Christ is, in other words, *specific* and *universal*. In von Balthasar's trilogy, this means that the Incarnation has bearing on *all* created truth, just as in *Glory of the Lord* he is the "measure," and that this universality does not in itself validate all *possible* ideas. Only that which is conformed to the Christ-form is, in fact, true and beautiful.[106]

Yet none of these reflections resolves the question as to the way the Christ-form illuminates and informs created truth; these reflections only state that it does. To answer the "way" of the problem, von Balthasar avers to the relationship between Christ's humanity and his divinity. In *Theo-logic II*, he locates the interplay between divine and created truth within the broad and flexible category of the "image," which is ultimately a Christological category. An image, in its heuristic definition at least, expresses something that it is not. Von Balthasar stresses the character of "image" in three senses: (1) the Son as the "image of the invisible God" (Col 1:15), which is the primary or highest sense, (2) human nature as an image of God, a fact that is affirmed and transformed by the Incarnation, and (3) the prohibition of images in the Old Testament, which will by virtue of the Incarnate Son continue to place *limits* on images.[107]

All three senses coexist, governed by the primacy of the Son's identity vis-à-vis the Father: he is, first and always, the exegesis—the expression and image—of the Father.[108] Peter J. Casarella, in his essay on von Balthasar's theology of language, focuses on this Trinitarian center: the Son as Exegesis, Word, and Expression of the Father.[109] His emphasis is on the theology of words themselves and their sacramental reflectiveness. My focus here, a complementary one, is on how this Trinitarian center is employed in the justification of the use of sensible images.

The Son is primordial image. When the Son unites himself to a human nature in the Spirit, he becomes an "image" in a further sense because now he *visibly* expresses in his humanity what is invisible and mysterious. Here it is important not to conflate the two senses of image functioning simultaneously in the Incarnation: the Son as the eternal image of the Father and the Incarnate Son continuing to serve as the Father's eternal image now united to a human nature. To confuse the two would amount to positing an eternally incarnate Word. Von Balthasar instead insists on the priority of the Son's eternal relationship to the Father, and it is this eternal relationship that determines his self-expression in the Incarnation.

As the image of the invisible God, the Son in his humanity and in the fullness of his human life expresses the divine life. That he does so *in his humanity* means that the original image (*Urbild*), the Word, speaks through the humanity that is already an image of himself. God speaks first of all through human nature itself, through a human nature hypostatically united to the Second Person of the Trinity. At the same time, God speaks through the whole complex of human thought and gesture. Von Balthasar focuses, for example, on Jesus's parables. These draw on normal human experience and are often deliberately about the ordinary. For von Balthasar, the use of parables indicates the ways in which human nature is *already* prepared to receive divine truth because it is *already* an image of that divine truth.[110] The images that Christ uses in his parables are already ordered toward him, and his use of created images affirms creation's integrity as his image; that is, the parables affirm creation's "preparedness" to be used as Christ's instrument.

Von Balthasar desires to understand the *multiplicity* of ways God speaks, which means approaching more explicitly what might be called the "language" of the Incarnation. This *language* is an expansive one, with the parables serving as but one mode, and von Balthasar's use of the term "language" is deliberately malleable. There is not one definition to be kept in mind, since he does not mean "language" in any restrictive sense. He means to describe the whole field in which God communicates himself, and in the Incarnation God takes advantage of every possible field. The "language" of the Incarnation for von Balthasar is in fact *created being itself*:

> creaturely logic sustains the weight of divine logic, thanks to the art of divine logic: God has made the creature according to his own image and likeness (*Bild und Gleichnis*), so that through his grace, the creature might become able to speak from within as a body of sound (*Klangkörper*) through which God is able to express himself and be understood. [He expresses himself] therefore no longer merely within the structures of human language but within the "language" residing in the structure of worldly being in itself.[111]

Von Balthasar stretches the term "language" to include every possible quality of created being, so that the grammar of the Incarnation—governed in its use from the outset by divine truth or "logic"—is the grammar of the totality of creation. Human nature, the appropriate "loudspeaker" of God's artistry, is exhaustively employed to communicate

God's own self, and all of creation is employed through the human nature of Christ. No quality of created being is left untouched by God's self-expression in the Incarnation.

Since every quality of worldly being forms the language through which God speaks, then the "greater dissimilitude" of the analogy of being partakes in God's self-expression, alongside the very weakness of human flesh.[112] Von Balthasar must be cautious, else the loudspeaker will become the originating voice. That is, if all of creation is permitted to so totally express God in the Incarnation to the degree von Balthasar claims, then it is but one more step to collapse the difference between God and the world and thereby make God completely comprehensible. Augustine's warning is appropriate here: "If you have comprehended it, it is not God."

Von Balthasar shows awareness of this problem. So for von Balthasar the act of *expression*, as creation expresses God in the Incarnate Son, does not mean to *exhaust* God, but rather the reception of the "super-word" of the Son occurs through humble *fiat*. The fullness of divine truth remains mysterious even as it is fully expressed in the Incarnate One because it is characterized by surrender.[113]

Surrender is where Christological "language"—the grammar of being as it is used in the Son's humanity to express his divinity—and von Balthasar's emphasis on Christological personality coincide. That is, surrender is both a defining characteristic of ontic language and of authentic personality. Through surrender, the two are brought together analogously, and in Christ we can say that they are the same inasmuch as his cruciform surrender always expresses both his eternal disposition and the disposition of the world.

Christological Language and Personality

Surrender is a "plasticity," an "openness," permitting itself to be molded according to the form of Christ. Von Balthasar elaborates the language of the Incarnation while also elaborating the meaning of surrender, developing them in tandem. The human body itself is thus a major grammatical foothold because it is a *flexible* instrument; it is a "versatile set of instruments" for understanding, so much so that concepts and words must "rely on the senses in their openness to the world and on the images the senses convey."[114] All the while, it is the spirit that grasps essences.[115] Human physicality bears a profound ability to surrender to being, to be formed by it.

Images are physical, involving the senses, and the depth of our physicality as human beings gives images a powerful place in human knowing. Von Balthasar continually returns to certain primary "images" of human experience, such as romantic love or a mother's smile. This last image is especially significant in the way it reveals the flexible expressiveness of human images. A mother's smile is, for von Balthasar, a "'word' as image" since it is received as meaningful speech despite containing no speech at all.[116]

So von Balthasar's use of the term "image," like his use of the term "language," is flexible and multi-layered. An image presents us with meaning, which also means it presents us with the illumination of being. An image can be like speech inasmuch as it is meaningful to us in an analogous fashion, yet an image also stresses our physicality as well as our openness to truth in ways that words alone do not. This is because the images of creation, which together form a sort of composite image-language, are effective only inasmuch as they "become transparent to the self-emptying love of God and are drawn into it."[117] Surrender is, ultimately, *transparency* to the Triune God, and so is language. Only thus can language express truth and mystery, can language express being, without violating it.

To recall *Theo-logic I*, truth is the unconcealment of being. This "unconcealment" is generally mediated by images—classically speaking, by the senses—and it is through images that we come to know the truth, indeed the truth of all being. Yet, even when the subject knows created truth, let alone divine truth, there is still *mystery*. Truth and mystery coincide, and it becomes clear that von Balthasar does not consider "mystery" to be a truth to be known at a later date, but is rather *the transcendence of truth*, in fact an abiding quality of the truth we know. In *Theo-logic I*, von Balthasar calls on beauty to mediate between truth and mystery, serving as their unity, since the truth expressed is at the same time inexpressible. Beauty is associated with *images*—since beauty is in part sensory expression—and in *Theo-logic II*, images receive further expansion. An image, while not identical with what it expresses, must be transparent to what it expresses. The humanity of Jesus Christ is the ultimate example of an image that is transparent to what is expressed, namely the divinity of Christ, which is why von Balthasar stresses that even Jesus's humiliation expresses the divine.[118]

Images achieve transparency to the divine only when their limitations are also acknowledged. This, too, is a quality of surrender since "Man realizes that he cannot and must not capture the divine in images . . . and that he nevertheless cannot renounce his sense-bound, bodily nature."[119] The images employed by language cannot do all things, cannot grasp God as totally understood, and yet language can operate in no other way. This may serve as some response to Francesca Murphy's critique of von Balthasar's emphasis on the experience of holiness, which always threatens to become a harsh ideal.[120] Language, after all, unveils being. In response, von Balthasar calls for a consistent return to the expression of being in images, and not only their abstraction. The *verbum mentis* must "constantly turn back to the image" from which it has been abstracted in an endless epistemological loop.[121] This is why, for von Balthasar, images (and here it would be helpful to recall his expansive use of the term) retain their relevance in theological discourse. Images are an inextricable quality of the human encounter with God in faith inasmuch as they are governed by Christ, the superabundant image.[122] This superabundance is expressed in an abiding silence in the speaking Word, "one that marks the (for man, unguessable) distance between God and the creature,"[123] so that in his words there are silences that "are handed over to an ongoing, never to be ended hermeneutic of the Holy Spirit within the history of the Church."[124]

Word and silence stand together in images, which are both expressive and mysterious. It is here, after a prodigious journey through von Balthasar's foundational metaphysics, into his Christological metaphysics, and finally into his views of language, that we are now capable of seeing just how deep his aesthetic interests run. Images—one of the primary themes of the aesthetics, with its focus on "seeing" the form—retain relevance from the expressiveness of being into the expressiveness of language. Von Balthasar's use of metaphysics and language together, without opposing them to one another, is what makes his theology a theo-poetic. His fascination with art, and the expression of truth in poetry among the other arts, is not simply ancillary. It is necessary to it, because images themselves are necessary to theology. We are now able to turn back on

his assessments of art and ask how they might be understood as pro-
grammatic to his theology.

By looking to the Incarnation, von Balthasar can outline how God
through the Incarnation employs the qualities of created being's basic
structure discussed in this chapter—expression, polarity, openness, and
the distinction between essence and existence—in order to express *himself*. Indeed, the analogy of being, which governs von Balthasar's understanding of the terms listed above, is itself "made present" in Christ. The
Son is for all eternity the expression, the image, of the Father. In his use
of image in *Theo-logic II*, von Balthasar recalls yet another complex term
to be found throughout his trilogy. In this context, "image" means that
which expresses something else. The Son, who is not the Father, nevertheless fully expresses who the Father is. Von Balthasar layers this basic
definition of "image" with another *composite of definitions* when the Son
takes on human flesh. This means that images are sensory, much as
human flesh is physical. It also means that the images the Son uses to
express his divinity are *human* images: every complex of human relationships and human signs—from words to deeds to physical gestures—are
also part of the "grammar" of the Incarnation. They are the order by
which the Incarnate One communicates himself. All of the various characteristics above serve to show that images, taken in the most expansive
sense von Balthasar employs, remain necessary—and not only *relevant*—
to theological speech. Christology must govern this speech. Further-
more, images do not make expression of the truth *easier*, but rather
emphasize the abiding mystery of truth even in the midst of real, and in
the case of Christ total, self-expression. So von Balthasar's theological
aesthetic, bolstered by this theological logic, makes expansive use of
images and of art—especially poets such as Dante—in order to argue
its case.

But these two positions listed above are not the same as justifying poetry, or the poetic use of images, in theology. Justifying the use
of poets and poetic language in theological discourse is not as simple
as equating poetry's use of images with poetry's worth. It is not enough
to say that poetry uses images and therefore must also be relevant to
theology. Nor is it enough, indeed, to indicate that poetry is capable

of agreeing with Christian theology. Finally, it is not enough to reveal the ways in which poetry can perform theology, that is, the way it accomplishes its own poetic ends while at the same time reinforcing and expanding theological concepts. This last we have already seen in von Balthasar's critiques of Rilke, since he sees the theology performed in Rilke's poetry and critiques it on theological grounds in *Glory of the Lord* and philosophical grounds in *Apokalypse*. All three possible justifications of poetic language—its use of images, theological agreement, theological performance—are insufficient arguments for the use of poetry in theology because all three unite poetry and theology only superficially. They present the *likenesses* of theology and poetry, but do not express either a possible link or—more vitally—governing critiques.

Von Balthasar's Christological metaphysic, as highlighted in this chapter, provides a much more thoroughgoing manner for appropriating the poetic and the metaphysical. First, poetry imitates in its creative forms the basic structure of created being. Its verses and stanzas exist alongside one another in relationships of varying *polarities*, presenting apparently opposed ideas that are only understood together. But their oppositions are neither perfect nor absolute and must be interpreted according to the central ideas that the poet establishes to govern every series of polarities. Poetry uses sensory landscapes of sight and sound (meter, rhyming, assonance, etc.) in order to *express* and *unveil* reality, analogously resembling von Balthasar's discussion of Heidegger's *aletheia* and indeed Heidegger's own discussions of art. As far as poetic language is concerned, all of creation may be used in order to express the truth. All of creation has a specific and unique expression that may be brought into human language. In von Balthasar's words:

> The form of a tree, of a butterfly, of a landscape expresses something very precise, although different in each case. . . . From time immemorial, fairy tales have attributed to some specially chosen persons the grace of being able to understand the speech of, for example, beasts. The poet, too, has been credited with the gift of translating this expressive language into the words of man.[125]

Poetry cannot be presented as an *alternative* to metaphysics, because it in its very thought structures affirms and inchoately employs basic principles of metaphysics. Indeed, poetry's explicit desire for transcendence and fulfillment—whether or not fulfillment is found—is another manner of affirming Thomas's distinction between essence and existence, since this distinction is the grounds for positing human nature's transcendence and the limits of that transcendence according to that nature's powers. Rilke's poetry strives for some place beyond the angels, beyond even death, in which peace may be found; Dante's poetry reaches from Hell to Heaven for the very sight of God. In each case, poetry works for some sense of transcendence, though each case is markedly different. Rilke imagines life in death and struggles against limitation until the only destruction of limitation is to embrace death; Dante must experience humiliation and purification—a constant recognition of who he really is and who he really has been—so that he can really see.

So poetry, like metaphysics, must recognize its limitations. These limitations can be described along both metaphysical and Christological lines, but it is most appropriate to unite both limiting agents. When von Balthasar approaches poetry, he comes to it with a firmly Christocentric perspective. Poetry must vindicate the dynamic self-expression of created being, searching out its inward polarities, while acknowledging the limitations of creation's tendency toward expression: it cannot reach its own fullness. The collapse of God and the world amounts to the destruction of the unconfused union achieved in Christ, which will only distort the truth toward which poetry tries to orient itself. Poetry is obviously governed by Christ in this respect, so that von Balthasar's *metaphysical* critiques of Rilke are also *Christological*.

Von Balthasar's Christological metaphysics permits poetry to be employed in theology from its very roots upward, as it were, and at the same time limits it: poetry must coincide with the Christ-form, must preserve the mystery of that form, and must serve that form. In the next chapter, we will explore further the ways in which Christology governs the use of poetry in theology and the purpose of poetic language in theological discourse. Poetry's role in theology will be both expanded and limited, finally giving way to Scriptural-sacramental language. This will begin the constructive half of the book, where von Balthasar's use of metaphysics and poetry will be extrapolated into a theo-poetic that helps to explain his theology.

FOUR

A Theological Poetic

Conversio Ad Phantasmata

The light burned low in the dark.
Golden-red quivered against black,
heating the night. Lit you soft and stark,
fired against angles that faded into lack.
You burned in outline.

Edges flickered scarlet and shadow,
shaped against your jaw, your neck.
Light curved along your face—you glowed.
Eyes closed. You slept, stretched
out in traces of fire.

And I watched you, memorized each turn
of light and night. Received the form
of you, a silhouetted impress that burned
its way from sense to thought—borne
away to dreams.

By "dreams," I mean desire,
awakening at your essential stress,
your imparted shape. Much as fire
readies wax to acquire a likeness,
so you were both heat and seal.

In knowing you I longed for you,
heart fashioned in a sympathetic scape,
a likened light. So I bent to
be near you, reflecting back your shape.
And I, anxious to give what I had received,
closed my eyes to kiss you awake.

The previous chapter reviewed the contours of von Balthasar's metaphysics. What emerged from this exploration was anything but an overcoming of metaphysics, or a dry digression away from the question of beauty. It revealed instead von Balthasar's thoroughgoing engagement with the analogy of being, which persists in his theology according to his Christology. This indicates that von Balthasar's theological project is a retrieval of the Christian tradition and an unusual one. While it is evident that he presumes and employs metaphysical concepts in order to lay the groundwork for his theology, his metaphysical emphases revolve around the loci of *analogy*, *expression*, and *polarity*. These, while not nonmetaphysical of themselves, are not typical metaphysical terms and concepts.

From von Balthasar's constellation of metaphysical terms, one in particular surfaced in order to draw them together: that of *image*. Three different and simultaneous qualities of von Balthasar's use of the concept of image are: (1) the Son as the image of the Father, (2) human nature as an image of God, and (3) the limits of images. The first of these governs the application of the rest, and so it was possible to observe how von Balthasar's Christocentrism controlled his use of concepts without submerging them into a flattened Christological logic (a "pan-Christ," as it were). Because von Balthasar does not obfuscate nature and grace despite constantly averring to them together, his Christological control permits him to elevate the role *nature* plays in theology. His use of images—in the knowing subject, in the realm of belief, and so on—indicates that here, in the image, what is natural is permitted to become an expression of the supernatural without their conflation.

Images are the avenue by which important characteristics of von Balthasar's theological project can be understood, namely the poetic qualities of his project. By "poetic," I mean von Balthasar's constant use of images to describe his theological position as well as his references to art and artists. In contrast to other attempts to somehow incorporate art into theology, von Balthasar's metaphysical use of images allows his theology (1) to bear poetic qualities from its ground to its height, and (2) to nevertheless govern his use of those poetic qualities without straying into either overly rigid rationalism or sheer agnosticism.

The reason von Balthasar's theology can bear the "weight," as it were, of a constructive use of images—instead of stripping his statements down to their logical content—is both methodological and metaphysical. Methodologically, he sets out to consistently employ poetic concepts according to their own logic (as they are used in the art of poetry), but also employs these concepts according to the primacy of the Incarnation. This "systematic arrangement" or "style,"[1] though it provides no sheer *system*, works because von Balthasar does not incorporate poetic reasoning into theology without transforming it. Instead, he allows his Christology to help him gather his poetic reasoning and order it. This makes von Balthasar's theology amenable to the more ordered, Scholastic theologies of the past while also differentiating him from them. Metaphysically, von Balthasar's founding philosophical positions permit him to adopt poetic forms of expression while also grounding his use of those forms in a thorough account of the expression of truth. In other words, von Balthasar's work is just as beholden to dogmatic accounts of revelation as any other theology; poetic forms are not a manner of obfuscating either tradition or logic.

This chapter turns back to von Balthasar's trilogy in order to discuss his poetic logic, or rather, his theo-poetics: an expressive use of images in theology governed by God's self-revelation in Christ. We will see how language and metaphysics are not two opposed concerns, but rather deeply interrelated. The relationship is made explicit in D. Stephen Long's *Speaking of God*, which in turn helps us to understand how von Balthasar's unique reflections on metaphysics allow us to link traditional metaphysical concerns with a rather modern theo-poetic. Finally, we review major characteristics of a theological poetic: those principles that can be observed in poetry, and which operate analogously in theology.

SPEAKING OF GOD: LANGUAGE AND METAPHYSICAL EXPRESSION

What we have in von Balthasar's theology of language is not, as such, a theology of language: it is a theology of the Incarnation, out of which his assessment of language emerges. Words are not von Balthasar's first concern; *the* Word is. That emphasis, which inverts modern lines of thought, is not a mere semantic investment in the priority of revelation within theology. It is a specific investment in the nature of truth, one that conceives of truth along both immanent and transcendent lines—as the *Truth of the World*, and the *Truth of God*. The nature of truth, and the nature of theological language, is guided by classical metaphysics invested with modern concerns. We observed in the last chapter how von Balthasar, using and overturning Heidegger, was able to link metaphysics and language through the expression of being. This, united with the Incarnation, gave us a beginning for a theology of language.

The priority of the Word made flesh neither violates nor overcomes human nature; it explicates human nature and brings that nature to a fullness that it desires but cannot achieve. Because of what he thinks Christ illuminates about human nature, von Balthasar is pressed to incorporate an elastic use of language in his theology: he employs images, for example, but not at the cost of metaphysics. We now move to explore how the simultaneous defense of metaphysics and expansion of theological language is possible. Because von Balthasar himself does not discuss how he makes this possible, it is helpful to begin elsewhere.

D. Stephen Long and *Speaking of God*

D. Stephen Long, forging his own recovery of metaphysics in the book *Speaking of God*, explains the link between the Incarnation, truth, and language: "The incarnation is true. Truth is the incarnation. These basic theological propositions offer insight into how we speak of God, relate faith and reason, pursue theology within a common and publically accessible language, and can recover truth, even the truth of politics."[2] Long's project is a helpful launching point for a discussion of von Balthasar's unique weaving of poetics and metaphysics, not merely because Long uses von Balthasar to contend that we cannot lose metaphysics, but also because Long perceives the vital connection between Christology, language, metaphysics, and ultimately politics.[3] Long's navigation of the relationship between metaphysics and politics is accomplished through a careful linguistic assessment of truth, guided by a theology of the Incarnation. How he makes this assessment opens the door for us to see how von Balthasar does it, and to see how a theo-poetic is an affirmation of metaphysical reality and not an avoidance of it.

Early in his book, Long seeks out the primary characteristics of both Karl Barth and Hans Urs von Balthasar's theologies to set the stage for his project. He adopts Barth's distrust of theological thought that does not place the absolutely transcendent God at the center of all its affirmations and negations, and he adopts von Balthasar's optimistic evaluation of the analogy of being that gives human statements about God a weight without making them determinative of God. These two positions, which might be summarized as a Barthian affirmation of God's transcendence and a Balthasarian affirmation of analogy, guide the contours of Long's progress through the vexed arguments over truth.[4] He is thus able to avoid Feuerbach's contention that "God" is simply a designation for what is in reality human—Long is defending, in other words, God as God—and able to explain human language's participation in the transcendent realities of which it speaks.

Long begins, first, with the fact that knowledge of God is *given* to us by God and that this enables real speech about God using human reason.[5] Because of the priority of this gift, theology should not eschew metaphysics in favor of a "gift" that prescinds human reason, as if the gift-nature of theological language enabled it to avoid what is human. Theology should, rather, look to metaphysics and "recognize its legitimate role in theology," as opposed to false views that either avoid it or reify it.[6]

To enable the proper placement of metaphysics in theology, Long engages with a broad range of modern philosophers and theologians, tracing their troubled relationship with metaphysical and theological language. Major modern interlocutors include Immanuel Kant, John

Milbank, Ludwig Wittgenstein, Henri de Lubac, and others. He places these thinkers alongside traditional voices such as Augustine and Thomas Aquinas and asks whether metaphysics has disintegrated into irrelevance or retains its central place in theology. Long answers with an affirmation of metaphysics, which partially conceals his efforts to give due credit to modern concerns. He takes these seriously and considers them with care. After all, his final account of metaphysics works to show its *political* importance, a quite modern move that upholds metaphysics in an innovative fashion.[7]

Much of Long's own position with respect to language turns on a unique interpretation of the work of Charles Taylor, who lays out the groundwork for an expressive view of human language that overcomes the modern impasse with language and meaning. In Taylor's account, there have been multiple linguistic turns, one of which in particular has been useful to modern thought: he calls it the "expressive"[8] turn, or alternately "expressive-constitutive."[9] By expressive-constitutive language, Taylor means to describe a theory of language in which Heidegger plays a decisive role and where language "makes possible" new meaning.[10] With care, Taylor opposes this linguistic turn to what he calls a "designative" theory of language, where language is "conceived as an instrument."[11] Instead, an expressive theory of language accounts for how knowledge and language are vitally linked, indeed to such a degree that *language enables meaning*. It also permits "language" to include things such as gestures and other symbolic communications.[12]

For Taylor, the expressivist turn is closely allied with art. Figures such as Heidegger and his predecessor Herder develop an expressive concept of language alongside the development of Romantic art. With Romanticism, Taylor argues, "Art is now seen not as imitation, but as creative expression."[13] Indeed, art demands the plurality of expression that expressive theories attempt to explain, and art presumes a complexity of human speech in a manner similar to expressive theories.[14] Heidegger has a key role to play in the emergence of these theories, and Taylor notes Heidegger's concept of *expression* in particular: here expression does not simply make meaning possible; it also completes it.[15]

For Heidegger and for Taylor, the fact that language enables and completes meaning does not render it a tool of sheer subjectivity, incapable of meaning discernable beyond the specific speaker. Language has a telos or end that, in Taylor's words, "dictates a certain mode of expression, a way of formulating matters which can help to restore thingness," in other words, to restore the vital knowledge of things—a major concern of Heidegger's.[16] Taylor's concern is that meaning is not merely indicated, but embodied in the expression; this relates language and meaning more intimately.[17]

Long adopts Taylor's account of expressivist language, and expands it along theological lines. When discussing Taylor and the linguistic turns, Long explains how such a position can be expanded theologically: "A Marian theology will help us make sense of this; it requires a place for human participation and contribution even in the incarnation."[18] So, a view of language that perceives language as expressive shows us how the human contribution to truth has an authentic place. Saying that language is constitutive is not, in this respect, the same as saying that human beings *create* truth. It means that human language participates in and contributes to the manifestation of truth. To draw out the Marian qualities of such a statement: it must mean that human language is constitutive of truth's expression, but only if it is first determined by the truth. Mary is, particularly in view of the Catholic dogma of the Immaculate Conception, always graced in preparation for her role in salvation. Grace enables her vital contribution and sustains it, not to the detriment of her humanity but to her ultimate fulfillment. So Long argues that all human language operates in some analogy to Mary and the Incarnation: we really contribute to the speaking of truth, yet in such a way that we are already sustained by it and drawn toward it. In other words, our relationship to truth and language is not merely horizontal—effected on the same plane—but also *vertical*, so that the truth governs us even as we contribute to its expression.[19]

This vertical relationship does not rob human language of its immanent reason, but rather enables it. Long summarizes such a position by saying, "Truth is the condition in which we live; it is not a tool we use. It conditions speech; speech does not condition it."[20] The Marian parallels thus continue, since she is conditioned by her Son. Von Balthasar describes such a prior conditioning when he explains Mary's *fiat*: "She is not the Word but the adequate response awaited by God from the created sphere and produced in it by his grace through the Word."[21] Her word is in this way given a profound place in the Incarnation, but always in a fashion secondary to the Word: she is *graced response*. Long argues that this is not only a Marian doctrine but also a linguistic one.

Since the truth conditions speech—since we are *constituted* even as we *constitute*—this affirmation also opens the way for a thorough relationship between truth and love. That is, for a strong connection between metaphysics and morality. Long brings forward a Marian theology to once again direct his insight: "In saying yes to the Holy Spirit, Mary gives birth to God, and therefore of course—she makes truth appear. Truth invites a human contribution." Here, Long has repeated what he has already explained with respect to expressivist language. But he goes further: "because truth emerges through Mary's holiness, these two concepts—holiness and truth—must, like love and truth, be thought and performed together."[22] Holiness and love are not quite identifiable terms, but they are intimately related. To posit the possibility of one as necessary to the expression of truth is immediately to posit the other.

In this way, Long, drawing from von Balthasar's Mariology and his account of the transcendentals, gives language a central place in the theological discussion without letting it force the discussion into the impasse of relativism or agnosticism. Truth is placed firmly in the middle of theological discourse, and not truth without metaphysics—which would be, as far as Long is concerned, a contradiction—but a truth that affirms and locates metaphysics. Long thus develops an account of truth whose contours are more thoroughly aesthetic and moral without surrendering metaphysics for the sake of either, as has been the case in the past. "Truth," says Long, "emerges as the interplay between receiving the glory of God (aesthetics) and performing that glory in our own lives (dramatics)."[23]

If this is so, then Long has already made quite explicit the qualities of von Balthasar's triptych that are necessary for a theo-poetic. That is, those qualities of von Balthasar's theological project that make possible the theo-poetic he already employs throughout the trilogy.

Von Balthasar and Language: Metaphysical Presuppositions

In many ways, von Balthasar follows Heidegger and the other expressivists, as Long and Taylor identify them, inasmuch as he lends to language a constitutive rather than merely designative function. Indeed, von Balthasar's adoption of Heidegger's concept of truth as *aletheia* lends profoundly expressive qualities to his hybridized metaphysics: from its very foundations, created being is meant to *express*. Being expresses both its own qualities and, in virtue of its openness to expression, is able to express who God is.

But there is a nettled problem within expressive theories of language, one that—if not perceptible from within the field—is evident from the point of view of theology. That problem is how to navigate the difference, or perhaps distance, between the expression and the truth. To say that language constitutes meaning does not in fact overcome this divide. There is a difference between what is known and what is expressed, as seen no more clearly than in Bernard Lonergan's simple dictum: "men can lie."[24] The argument is simple and effective. In the case of a lie, there is no sharper divide between truth and expression. A lie is even, as Paul J. Griffiths notes in Augustine's theology, a much more deliberative form of expression: "Lies require effort; truth none."[25] What the individual has said constitutes a lie, but what was said does not constitute an alternate reality in which the lie is no longer false. In other words, the truth persists despite its *lack* of expression. Charles Taylor notes a similar weakness in Heidegger, a serious inability to account for sin or evil.[26] Lies reinforce objective truth through a kind of inversion.

The problem expressivism here endures is the same problem that designative theories have, though in a different mode. Neither can capably account for our navigation, or judgment, between what is meant and what is expressed—between the truth and what appears. In designative theories of language, the difference is hopelessly reified, and the mode of expression has little to do with what is expressed. In expressive theories of language, the difference threatens to disintegrate so that the mode of expression and what is expressed are virtually identical. So expressivism overcomes the devastating weaknesses of designative theories of language without resolving the fundamental problem of the relationship between language and truth.

Heidegger posits a telos for language, as in Taylor's review above, but that does not enable Heidegger to escape the problem. A telos does not automatically rescue language theory from the problem of the "distance" between what is meant and what is expressed. The resolution would depend on the kind of telos described in the theory itself, and for a thinker such as von Balthasar a purely immanent telos is insufficient. As has been discussed in the three previous chapters, the problem von Balthasar perceived in modern German thought was precisely a problem of proper metaphysical ends. German thought, in absolutizing what is immanent, destroys transcendence and thus authentic teleological thought. To answer the problem of a lie, we must return to authentic teleological metaphysics.

In *Speaking of God*, Long anticipates a "Balthasarian" response to this problem. Or rather, in following both von Balthasar and Barth, Long hints at the solution without himself describing it. Because Long, von Balthasar, and Barth begin their accounts of theology and of existence by positing the absolutely transcendent God, all of them have already provided the means by which contingent truth (let alone divine truth) might be navigated without either the hopeless divide of designative theory or the collapse of expressive theory. That is, by acknowledging God, Long, von Balthasar, and Barth are all capable of orienting and explaining contingent reality. Though in Barth such a position often—at least on the surface—endangers the integrity of created or contingent truth, in Long and von Balthasar the position operates to defend the integrity of contingent truth.

As early as *Apokalypse*, von Balthasar argues that a loss of real transcendence and openness results not simply in the loss of God, but also results in a fundamental inability to account for contingent reality. Death, in this case, becomes absolute and absolutely determinative of existence. In *Theo-Logic* and *Glory of the Lord*, von Balthasar more precisely describes the problem as the loss of a vigorous understanding of the analogy of being and the grave rupture of authentic metaphysics. Without a meaningful account of metaphysics, which Christology makes more central and not less, there can be no proper explanation either of anthropology or epistemology. Authentic metaphysics is able to posit a notion of transcendence that does not surrender the immanent powers of the creature into the hands of death. It is capable, instead, of describing transcendence in terms of an end (telos) toward which nature intends, but that is not in fact a potency in nature as such. This is a telos distinctive from Heidegger's, whose metaphysical descriptions are, in von Balthasar's view, too immanent to admit of an end not to be found in the powers of a nature itself.

To put the problem another way: understanding that God is beyond created existence in such a way that the two are incomparable—God is not merely "higher" or "more than," but absolutely other—gives to the concept of transcendence an entirely different set of values compared with its modern use. We as human beings stand in relationship to the God who is wholly other than ourselves, and to say that we exist in relationship to such a One gives a new shape and direction to our existence. Here is a perspective that cannot be explained solely according to what is immanent to us. This is von Balthasar's extended argument throughout *Apokalypse*, one that receives more concise form in articles such as "The Fathers, Scholastics, and Ourselves" and "The Task of Catholic Philosophy Today."

By arguing in this way, von Balthasar is not simply positing the possibility of eternal life. This would be a mere superficiality: a mere extension of human life as if drawing a line farther along on a page, or making God a stop-gap for what is lacking in human knowledge (in this case, why it is that we die). If this were what a transcendent God helped us to achieve, then we would have no use for him. Transcendence would subsist along flat horizontal lines that we could draw ourselves. The analogy of being, understood in terms of Thomas's real distinction between essence and existence, demands a counter supposition. It demands a concept of transcendence that maintains the analogy of being *in order to* acknowledge God's difference from us, even as we are lifted into life with God. Here the modern metaphysic is revealed to be the flat world that it is, and classical metaphysics is shown for its roundness and depth.

What von Balthasar argues for is, in the language of *Glory of the Lord*, a metaphysical "attunement" to the God who is entirely incomparable to us, and yet toward whom all of creation tends. This is von Balthasar's contribution to our understanding of transcendence, a contribution that is itself a retrieval of the classical understanding:

> It [the creature] is ontologically resonant to God and for God; it is so in its wholeness and capacities, before any differentiation of these into spiritual and sensitive, active and passive. Because God is not to be considered a creature at any level, and because he does not possess a common Being with creatures, their original attunement (*ursprüngliche Einstimmung*) to him is not an intuition in the

epistemological sense, and it is not the result of a merely logical "conclusion" drawn from the finite to the infinite. The un-fixability (*Unfixierbarkeit*) of this original experience is only the noetic reflection of the ontological incomprehensibility (*Unfestlegbarkeit*) of Being as a whole over against God. Being as such refers in itself to the inaccessible Source.[27]

Arguing for *this* form of transcendence, as opposed to the narrowed versions he finds in Heidegger and Rilke, sets von Balthasar far apart from these despite all three figures being ostensibly concerned with "transcendence." They are not, however, concerned with the *same* transcendence.[28] Von Balthasar's position is a complete transfiguration of existence and its transcendent end, as transformative as the addition of symphony to a simple melody. A melody can be played alone, and with an integrity of its own; a symphony incorporates a melody, and also involves varying times and interpolating notes to such a degree that the melody itself is transfigured while remaining the "same" melody.

The defense of God's transcendence from other forms of transcendence—von Balthasar is here defending the traditional Christian understanding against modern ones—is a *theological* position for von Balthasar. But it is also an anthropological one, and in this way von Balthasar attempts to address quite *modern* concerns through his use of a traditional point of view. At its broadest, to say that God is absolutely transcendent is at once to say something about God, but also to say something about creation and the creature. The position intimates that creation in its very being tends toward God and is supported by him, and in a fashion much more radicalized than simple immanence (as in pantheism or pan-en-theism) or simple transcendence (as in the strictest deism). Analogy intensifies both immanence and transcendence. This intensification is at its most pronounced in human beings, who are *rational* creatures, and it is at this point that von Balthasar helps us to see the profound link between his metaphysical position and his epistemological-linguistic one.

First, we move to the epistemological attunement. We are "attuned" to God, von Balthasar argues, in our every faculty. What is more, Thomas Aquinas understood this best and incorporated it into his theology most thoroughly.[29] Thus, in *Theo-Logic*, von Balthasar argues alongside

Thomas for the sake of a profoundly intimate relationship between God and what we know—indeed, everything we know.[30] Aquinas achieves this through a careful union and distinction between Creator and creature, founded first of all on God's profound difference from the world. According to von Balthasar, because Aquinas first posits such a difference and maintains it, he is enabled to say with great daring, "All cognitive beings also know God implicitly in any object of knowledge."[31]

This statement from Aquinas's *Questiones disputate de veritate* (often simply called "De veritate") occurs in an article asking, "Do all things tend to God himself?" Aquinas answers in the affirmative, but is careful to indicate that all things "naturally tend to God implicitly, but not explicitly." By "implicit," Aquinas means to describe a notion wherein we are directed to God in our origin and our end but not without possessing agency of our own. Here, Aquinas focuses on how all our proximate ends are related to a single remote end, namely God. This does not eliminate what is proximate to us, but it does give each of our proximate ends a final orientation or end to order them. Moreover, because our appetites always seek what is good, all of our decisions tend us toward God, who is Goodness itself. This is the way in which we *implicitly* tend toward God. What is implicit in all of creation can, in the rational creature, become an explicit tendency—for we are able to know and love God explicitly. In this way Aquinas's position is at once metaphysical and epistemological. He presupposes a metaphysical teleology that at the same time supports an epistemological teleology: he argues for the ability to know God implicitly in all things, in a manner analogous to the way being itself always implicitly tends toward God. As von Balthasar argues in *Theo-Logic I*, "only a theocentric epistemology can make sense of the truth of worldly knowledge."[32]

If all being is "attuned" to God, then this favorite phrase from Aquinas has allowed us to see how our knowing faculties are also so attuned. This leads us to further surmise that language bears an attunement to God similar to the metaphysical and the epistemological, a case made all the more urgently given the intricate links we have already established between being and language. Von Balthasar's metaphysical position is naturally expanded into a linguistic one without a choice between the two, since the attunement characteristic to each is ultimately a shared attunement. Metaphysics, in order to be authentic, must be open—must be open to transcendence in the manner already discussed—in order for it to be expressive of reality and ultimately of God. Language, too, must admit an openness and humility before God in order for it to be authentically expressive of the truth, whether that truth is worldly or divine. Neither language nor metaphysics are closed off from one another, because it is proper to each to be open to what transcends it.

To continue the argument: if we can describe both metaphysics and language in terms of an attunement that allows us to explain how each resonates with truth—that is, how they are open to and able to express truth—then we can also explain how language (or metaphysics!) is capable of expressing a lie. We can do so because, while adopting and affirming certain tenets of constitutive theories of language, we cannot identify the expression and the expressed. If attunement, and not identity or self-enclosed constitution, is our primary concern, then we must admit that truth and language are not the same even as language conditions and makes possible the expression of truth. The expression is always outstripped by that which it expresses, and this is because what is expressed drives us to ask more deeply about what we have received.[33] If we can continue to ask questions about the "horizon" of truth opened to us in truth's expression, then we must admit a difference between the expression and what is expressed. We have known by anticipation, and not in fullness, and so we are able to ask further questions about it. This is not to say that we cannot know or speak with an identity between expression and expressed, only that there is not a necessary identity between them. Sacramental language, especially in the Eucharist, would thus constitute a hyper-speech in which expression and expressed are identical.

Because expression and expressed are not identical, we may also finally explain what a lie is, which is an expression meant to express something other than what it participates in and resembles. Inasmuch as expression and expressed are not the same, though they share a likeness, we are capable of introducing not only a difference between the two, but also a contradiction. Language constitutes what it expresses yet is not identical with it, so language is also able to constitute a lie. In the case of a lie, language is no longer attuned either to immanent truth or to the truth of God. We are thus capable of speaking what is not, speaking what has no being, and in doing so we express in dissonance rather than attunement.[34]

Further reading of Aquinas's *De veritate* helps us to understand what is happening with language here, and how the metaphysical crisis of modernity is at the same time a linguistic one—not because we must escape metaphysics but because we have tried to escape it and so distorted it. In *De veritate*, Aquinas reminds us what the truth is and what a lie is: "Just as truth consists in an equation of thing and intellect, so falsity consists in an inequality between them."[35] If the equation of thing and intellect—between known and knower—is akin to von Balthasar's attunement, then the inequality between the two is akin to dissonance. It would be anachronistic to consider the two ideas identical, and here I argue for a familial resemblance rather than a direct line of influence. Aquinas helps us to further understand a linguistic expansion of von Balthasar's basic metaphysical position.

In the same passage, Aquinas is quick to point out that a thing's relation to the divine intellect is essential to it, and inasmuch as God knows a thing, it is true. A lie is possible in the human intellect because the relationship between a created intellect and a thing is accidental, and not essential.[36] It is possible, then, for us to know a thing unequally—thus falsely, dissonantly. Because of his theocentric epistemology, Aquinas is able to describe lies without threatening to make lies constitutive of reality; a lie does not *express* reality; it expresses what has no reality.

Aquinas's statement that we know God implicitly in all that we know has a complex history in modern disputes over epistemological questions, quite apart from the disputes of Aquinas's day. It appears as a linchpin for the *nouvelle théologie*—and this contrary to their preference for patristic writings—particularly for Henri de Lubac. His book, *Discovery of God*, places this phrase alongside deeply modern figures such as Descartes and Leibniz.[37] Such a move is typical of de Lubac and his reinterpretation of Thomas Aquinas, one that sought to more closely ally nature and grace over-against the (Suarezian) Thomism de Lubac so openly loathed. Nature, he insisted, possessed a natural desire for the beatific vision—not that his move was taken well by Thomists.[38] The way de Lubac positions the phrase in *Discovery of God* emphasizes the *natural intimacy* between the creature and God, a move that closely follows his lengthy arguments over nature and grace in *Surnaturel*.

Von Balthasar was a friend and student of Henri de Lubac, and a close observer of the *nouvelle théologie*. He is often associated with it, both today and at the time of the movement's sharpest controversy. Von Balthasar, too, rejects *natura pura* except as a sometimes-helpful abstraction, and his use of Thomas's dictum in *Theo-Logic I* also means to place nature and grace in intimate relationship with one another, as with de Lubac. He does not, however, follow de Lubac and the *nouvelle théologie* without modifications of his own. His defenses against Karl Barth's critiques of "natural revelation" and the *analogia entis* lend a different quality to von Balthasar's assessment of Thomas Aquinas and the nature-grace problem. Here von Balthasar's use of Erich Przywara's polarity alongside a strong affirmation of God's absolute difference from creation makes his understanding of epistemology distinct from de Lubac's, since von Balthasar's move to give the intellect a most intimate relationship to the Creator in its every act of knowing occurs in conjunction with an effort to maintain sharp distinctions between the two.

What von Balthasar helps us to understand is the intimate relationship between language and metaphysics and how it is necessary to presuppose the analogy of being—for example—in order to understand language more appropriately. Presupposing a vigorous understanding of transcendence, which metaphysics is indispensible in helping us to do, allows us also to understand the way language (as well as being) is open to expressing what is greater than itself. Metaphysics allows for this because we need *not* suppose that what language expresses is identical with it. Transcendence, in the way von Balthasar understands it through Aquinas's real distinction, in fact demands that we *cannot* suppose that contingent reality is identical with what it is capable of expressing.

Instead of a mere identity, von Balthasar presses Aquinas further to help us argue for a *creative attunement* between what is and what is known and between what is and what is expressed. Just as we need not, and ultimately cannot, suppose that death is identical with created being, so we need not and cannot suppose that a lie is identical with created expression. The implicit linguistic threat of modernity mirrors the metaphysical one, and each problem cannot be answered through a totalized immanence. To grasp either, we must first know that to be contingent means being always already attuned to the God who is incomparable to us and yet who intimately grounds our being, our knowing, our speaking. Thus being and language stand and fall together.

We have, then, what we need to understand the way von Balthasar continues to stretch language to the limit point of its expressivity in his theology. One of the ways among many that he does so is through the creative use of images in his theological argumentation. This renders his metaphysical-linguistic position distinctive from Aquinas's, as we shall see, and yet von Balthasar also relies on Aquinas to make his position possible.

Transitioning into Theo-Poetics: The Index of a Mother's Smile

To argue for von Balthasar's distinctive position, we return again to the concept of a mother's smile. We must ask further questions of this favorite image of von Balthasar's, and it will help us to better understand the way von Balthasar expands both metaphysics and language together. The image of a mother's smile is, for von Balthasar, an organizing analogy for three separate and interrelated problems: (1) human epistemology, (2) metaphysical analogy, and (3) the governing role of love in both. The analogy of a mother's smile, in its broadest strokes, details how a mother smiles at her child before her child can smile back at her. She loves her child first, who then learns to love her. This occurrence is, in von Balthasar's mind, an almost primordial indicator of the nature of all reality. He does not argue so because all reality is somehow maternal—that is to miss the point—but because all reality is founded on an unconditional and prior love. The image of a mother and her child is a vivid human example of this fundamental reality.

Von Balthasar's analogy is, first, an epistemological statement. Because we are first loved by another, von Balthasar argues, we come to be knowing subjects. It is not *only* a mother's smile that does this, though von Balthasar focuses on that image in *Love Alone is Credible*. It is the fact of a prior love that is central to him epistemologically, of which a mother's smiling gaze is the greatest human illustration. A prior love operates in our awakening to every object we encounter. In *Theo-Logic I*, for example, von Balthasar recalls the fairy tale of Sleeping Beauty to reinforce his point:

> Unless an object announces itself in the space of the subject's receptivity, the subject is unable to transform its potential insights into

real knowledge. The opened stage remains empty, the drama of knowledge is not played. Only when the stranger enters the space of the subject does it like Sleeping Beauty awaken from its slumber: both to the world and to itself.[39]

This awakening is not simply an awakening of the subject as subject but also an awakening to the world—to contingent reality. Von Balthasar calls on both epistemology and ontology here, since neither excludes the other. The awakening here is, it must be stressed, to the *world* and to *self*.

Von Balthasar wants to see all knowing as an act of love, not as a "full, free, and spiritual love," but as an act akin to love. "In the creative mirror of the subject," he writes in *Theo-Logic*, "the object sees the image of what it is and of what it can and is meant to be."[40] It is not, then, facticity itself or alone that occurs in the knowing of a true thing; it is the loving acknowledgment of what is and what is meant to be. Knowing and loving, for von Balthasar, bear the same presupposing conditions for each to attain fullness: they require a creative obedience, a flexible openness, that permits the object or beloved the "space" to be what they are, and in permitting that space also gives object and beloved back to themselves in an act of free artistry. "Only the creative image of love," he says, "is able to measure the object with the measure, and hold before it the mirror, that contains its definitive and, therefore, objective truth."[41]

The "art" of knowing must, then, presuppose both an object or beloved that *is*—that has ontic attunement—and that can thus be known. Neither metaphysics nor epistemology are to be opposed. In *Love Alone Is Credible*, von Balthasar's epistemological-ontological position is rendered more obvious:

> After a mother has smiled at her child for many days and weeks, she finally receives her child's smile in response. She has awakened love in the heart of her child, and as the child awakens to love, it also awakens to knowledge: the initially empty-sense impressions gather meaningfully around the core of the Thou. Knowledge (with its whole complex of intuition and concept) comes into play, because the play of love has already begun beforehand, initiated by the mother, the transcendent. God interprets himself to man as love in the same way: he radiates love, which kindles the light of love in the

heart of man, and it is precisely this light that allows man to perceive this, the absolute Love. . . . In this face [of Christ], the primary foundation of being smiles at us as a mother and as a father. Insofar as we are his creatures, the seed of love lies dormant within us as the image of God (*imago*). But just as no child can be awakened to love without being loved, so too no human heart can come to an understanding of God without the free gift of his grace—in the image of his Son.[42]

The relationship between the I and the Thou, which von Balthasar is determined to make foundational to his epistemology and his metaphysics, is founded first of all in the primary, determining analogy between God and creation.[43] The light of knowledge that is kindled is cosmic in scope: in awakening to love, the creature awakens not merely to self but also to knowledge of the world. This is a knowledge that is itself founded by God's prior love for the whole world and for the creature.

In concentrating on a mother's smile, von Balthasar is out to make both a metaphysical and epistemological argument through our experience of maternal love. As children, we "awaken" to love only through a love that is greater than ours; a mother, after all, knows and feels love with a depth foreign to children and yet that awakens children to all the depths of responding love. In her loving gaze, a mother guards and bears an image of her child, an image held in the "creative mirror" of her loving knowledge, and in loving her child she gives her child that image. We must presuppose that she transcends her child for this to be so, transcending in a human and immanent manner. But this experiential image is itself an icon of God's loving gaze and an icon of the disposition of being itself. God holds all of creation before the creative mirror of his loving gaze, and we see how being awakens and lights up in love, how it is upheld in love, how its expressiveness is an imitation of the prior love that illuminates being. We see that our origin is not in ourselves, and we see in the loving gaze of grace an image of ourselves guarded, borne, and given to us.

We are reminded briefly of Dante, whose wild artistic achievement was to unite personal love and love for the cosmos, marrying the great philosophical inheritances of the Middle Ages and Antiquity with creative abandonment to the intimacy and specificity of love. "Beatrice," writes von Balthasar, "is nothing but blessed and eternal laughter (*riso*), an abyss of gaity, from which Dante sees his own happiness pouring down towards him."[44] This exchange of blessed happiness, in which Dante receives something of his beatitude from Beatrice's joy (indeed her own name is a play on the word *beatitudo*), is for von Balthasar the disposition of being itself. All being receives its beatitude from the joyful gaze of God, who transcends created being and also loves it—like a mother, or like Beatrice, who often represents Christ in *La Divina Commedia*.

In returning to a mother's smile, we can see again the ways von Balthasar is interested in uniting classical metaphysics with the personal through love. Yet there is also more at work here. By focusing on a mother's smile, von Balthasar has also presented us with an image, an analogy. It is an image that—in its flexibility—serves to make several cogent theological and philosophical points. He employs the analogy especially in the effort to show how love and truth are not opposed and how we are sustained by each even as we come to know each. With such an insight, von Balthasar works hard to describe our "vertical" relationship to the truth and to love, and in such a way that the transcendence of both is never a threat to our status as knowing subjects.[45] This is, as it were, a phenomenological reinforcement of the distinctive form of transcendence discussed above.

It is telling that von Balthasar seeks an image to describe a matrix of philosophical positions. He even uses the image of a mother's smile to explain our relationship to *images*. A mother's smile is a word-image—an image with meaning, understood as if it were a word.[46] By using such an image to present us with his argument, von Balthasar has deliberately stepped into a unique form of philosophical and theological logic without announcing that he is doing so. He here employs an aesthetic argument that, beyond simply proving itself to be "fitting," takes advantage of the fitting image to press his argument forward. Such an argument does not deny metaphysics its place in theology. The image of a mother's smile is not in spite of metaphysics, but alongside and within it. It is an image that reinforces a metaphysical and epistemological position, yet that also reinforces specificity and personality in a manner akin to modern art. Von Balthasar uses such a form of argumentation consistently, and it is what I am calling a "theo-poetic." "Theo-poetic" is my term, not used by von Balthasar at any point in his oeuvre. By using it, I am attempting to summarize a complex set of theological, metaphysical, and linguistic presuppositions that operate beneath von Balthasar's decision-making.

To improve our understanding of von Balthasar's unique form of theological expression, his theo-poetic, we will continue to look back on Thomas Aquinas's *De veritate* in order to compare and contrast the two. This will help us to grasp von Balthasar's alignment with and separation from a more "classical" position such as Thomas's, and in doing so will help us to grasp the strengths and dangers in a theological language such as von Balthasar's.

CONTOURS OF A THEO-POETIC

Many of von Balthasar's theological efforts, particularly his trilogy, can be understood methodologically as a *theological poetic*. This term bears with it several concomitant qualities. The first and most obvious characteristic is a preference for the use of images in theology, though this alone does not form a theological poetic. The second is that the theological poetic is ordered according to theological-metaphysical presuppositions—that is, it must fit together with these, and receive its shape from them even as it shapes our grasp of them. This is what makes von Balthasar's method a *theological* poetic and not simply a poetic. Finally, a theological poetic bears the markings of poetic "logic," which is poetry's peculiar manner of expressing its meaning. To understand the contours of von Balthasar's theological poetic, we begin with this last set of characteristics.

Poetic Logic

Poetry has a logic that is unique to it and that bears strong resemblance to the "logic" to be found in the other arts. This is because poetry, in a rather unusual fashion, is a hybridized art. It is capable of musicality, though it is not music; it is capable of narrative, though it is not a written story; it is capable of visual grandeur, though it is neither a painting nor a sculpture. Poetry relies on words to achieve its hybridized structure, fitting them together in an image-laden narrative that must *sound* beautiful as much as its imagery must be beautiful.

So poetry lives or dies according to words, and these are frail. Note, for example, the first two stanzas of the poem that opens this chapter:

> The light burned low in the dark.
> Golden-red quivered against black,
> heating the night. Lit you soft and stark,
> fired against angles that faded into lack.
> You burned in outline.
>
> Edges flickered scarlet and shadow,
> shaped against your jaw, your neck.
> Light curved along your face—you glowed.
> Eyes closed. You slept, stretched
> out in traces of fire.

The poem cannot make its point without first establishing the basic scene, which is that of a beloved lying asleep in the dark, outlined by the light of a fire. So the poem gives this sense, and yet gives no more than an impression of it. It is in fact the reader who supplies the rest of the scene, as the poem itself gives only a bare outline of the outline. The poem already presupposes its own fragility.

Words are closely linked to temporality, and this gives them their strength and their weakness. They move necessarily in time, a dynamism that gives them vitality, yet this means that words also threaten to decay with time. Yet it is exactly *this* strength and weakness (vitality and decay) that poetry exploits for the sake of its art, this precision and persisting ambiguity. Charles Taylor notes modern poetics' ability to take advantage of what he calls "an ontological indeterminacy," which must of its nature draw deeply from the past while forming a visceral present experience of the reality under discussion.[47] It is the nature of modern poetry to *resonate* instead of to dictate—which, for Taylor, means that poetry by a kind of performative act draws together new associations with what is familiar. Such an act makes poetry what it is and renders it almost impossibly fragile. Poetry lives under the "quintessentially modern worry" that language might die.[48] After all, "What reveals by resonation can cease to."[49] If we cease to know what it looks like to sit before a fire, then the stanzas above will cease to have meaning. This is to say nothing of the poem's references to epistemology, which we will explore in a later section: all of these do not resonate with a reader unfamiliar with them.

The logic of poetry—and here we still have yet to enter fully into the logic of a theological poetic—rests in its fragile and powerful ability to resonate. A poem will, as in the excerpt from *Conversio Ad Phantasmata*, press its point by its unusual comparison of images:

> And I watched you, memorized each turn
> of light and night. Received the form
> of you, a silhouetted impress that burned
> its way from sense to thought—borne
> away to dreams.

Now the poem takes its basic "outline" of a figure lit by fire, and compares that outline to a stamp or shape that can press its likeness onto another object. The logic here is implied—the poem does not say outright, "you stamped your likeness onto me"—and the implication is worked through the continuing use of light and dark contrastive images (light, night, silhouetted), which are now being furthered to more abstract themes (thought, dreams). The poem requires the earlier stanzas to make sense of its new uses of the previous images. The figure that "burned in outline," which is "traces of fire," now is the glowing outline of an impressible image of himself. So the meaning is not, as it were, in the bald words themselves; it is in their association together, and the central matrix of meanings is left implied instead of stated. It is in this way, among others, that poetry *resonates*.[50] This resonance is what helps to make poetry so profoundly experiential: the link of meanings happens markedly in the reader of poetry, more deeply than in prose, though prose too is effective only if it has been grasped and not merely read.[51]

The modern fear that language will die finds a response in von Balthasar's work. His poetic logic, while still acknowledging and employing fragile resonation, does not in the end rest in a horizon fraught with worry that language will disintegrate. Instead, von Balthasar sees in the very fragility of expression—its spider webs of meaning—a sign of our profound contingency, and this is a mark of our goodness and not our failure. To be a creature is to be different from God, is to be limited, and this difference is good—for God himself calls it good. So the very fragility of language is a virtue and need not be feared, since its fragility is upheld not in itself, but by the living God who took up the whole "language" of creation in the Incarnation and through it spoke to humanity. This is perhaps no more clear than in the last book in *Glory of the Lord*, in which von Balthasar discusses the New Testament. Here Christ, who is God, takes up the vulnerability and poverty of the world in order to proclaim himself as God: "he makes his absolute claim in equally absolute poverty and in the vulnerability which belongs to poverty, in the renunciation of all earthly power and every earthly possession."[52] Yet it is this fragile poverty that is open to his absolute proclamation and in which we see that it is possible for us to cease fearing the fragility of our own expression.

Charles Taylor notes that much of the modern concern for language's loss of resonance rests in the distinction (as in Heidegger) between creative and ordinary speech.[53] Creative speech resonates, echoes with "potentially world-making" power; idle or ordinary talk has little resonation beyond bare facts.[54] Von Balthasar is after something quite different from this distinction, as we saw in the last chapter through his comments on fairy tales. Even ordinary speech is, for von Balthasar, exalted to the level of expressive creativity through the Word. So von Balthasar characterizes even the very metaphysical qualities of the world (its bare facticity, as it were) as capable of lasting speech in Christ.[55] Poetry, then, need not be creative only in the sense of new world making; its primary creativity rests in its conviction that ordinary objects can become symbols for fragile meaning. This is poetry's logic, which is itself an echo of a much broader (Christo-) logic.

Von Balthasar roots all of creaturely logic—including poetry's fragile logic—in God's "artistry." Here is an artistry that, von Balthasar emphasizes, is infinitely different from the work it has created, yet the artist (God) and his work (creation) are at the same time intimately related. They are not related, von Balthasar insists, through the analogy of being alone but rather through God's free initiative to create and to confer his image on creation.[56] This makes the relationship between the two a primordial gift as much as it is metaphysical (metaphysics, then, is to be considered under the sign of "gift").

There are really two limits to language, one at the creaturely level and the other (a more complex one) at the level of the relationship between the world and God. The first limit refers to the paradoxical fashion in which human beings can grasp being, and yet in grasping being we are still left with an insurmountable mystery.[57] Truth, von Balthasar reminds us, is not simply what we understand, so that mystery is what we do not yet understand. Truth and mystery are instead concomitant qualities; the truth is *genuinely mysterious*, and this is a positive characteristic of truth and not its mere negation.[58] Further, what can be said of worldly truth is more profoundly the case with respect to God. This is the second limit. Worldly truth is made more mysterious—and is given, indeed, a much clearer sense of its limits—in the face of the truth of God. Yet the truth of God also anchors the truth of the world. This is because the truth of God is most mysterious of all; not in a merely agnostic sense, but rather as a positive statement about who God is. His surpassing absoluteness, and the mystery that abides in it, tells us something about the God who created us, and about ourselves.

As we observed in the section of this chapter discussing the metaphysical presuppositions of von Balthasar's understanding and use of language, von Balthasar presupposes a metaphysic that posits God's transcendence over the world in order to make sense of the world. He is, moreover, not interested in defending the bare facticity of truth so much as he is interested in defending the objectivity of ontological truth in love. So Taylor's "ontological indeterminacy" is, in the thought of von Balthasar, an ontological mystery, or rather, an ontological superabundance. The "indeterminacy" of human knowledge, particularly the careful inexactness of art, is not an expression of negative limitation but rather an affirmation of the self-diffusive goodness of being.[59] Because of this indeterminacy, a lack of conformity between what is known and what is expressed is possible, and so a lie is possible. Yet also because of this indeterminacy, it is possible to grasp why truth is capable of expression in more than one way.

The word "indeterminacy" itself begins to fail now, and *analogy* rises to take its place. So analogy runs through every level of von Balthasar's thought, not for the sake of a recoiling vagueness, but in order to more exactly express the way the world is and who God is. Analogical thinking, even at the creaturely level, tells us both that we *really know* and that our knowing remains *permeated by mystery*. Being itself is permeated by mystery because it is beautiful, good, and true; and the beauty of being's mystery draws us to it:

> Seen with the surface of the appearance (*Erscheinung*) is the perception of the non-appearing (*nicht erscheinende*) depth: only in this is the phenomenon of the beautiful given its enrapturing and overwhelming character, as it is only in this that the truth and goodness and being are ensured. This applies as much to the beauty of nature as to the beauty of art.[60]

Poetry's resonance is, then, an expression of the resonance of *all* language—the "language," that is, of all of creation. Even bare facts—questions about what *is*, the questions of metaphysics—bear a similar ability to resonate, which for von Balthasar is an ability to operate analogically.

If we return briefly to the image of a mother and her child, we see now why it is capable of performing so many functions at once: epistemological, ontological, phenomenological, and so on. It is an experiential typology of the resonance of being itself, since we experience being in multifarious ways, and yet being is that which is most common to all things. We live in the midst of an ontic attunement, as it were, that is always harmonized with the being of God—and because it is a harmony, the forms of worldly resonance are many, but not infinite, because the One to whom being is attuned remains the same. Even a mother is many things to her child inasmuch as her child relates to her in a hundred different ways with different delights and needs, but she herself is one. Her child's relationship to her is singular inasmuch as she herself is: though the tune may be played differently, still it is the same attunement.

To the degree that von Balthasar is able to relate the multitudinous character of created truth to the one Truth, which is God, he is in agreement with Thomas Aquinas's basic position in *De veritate*. Here we are able to see why Aquinas is anything but a naïve realist or designative linguist, since his grasp of language presumes a complex and creative relationship between the Word and the truth of human words. Both Aquinas and von Balthasar tend to imagine truth theocentrically: truth is singular because, as Aquinas says, "all things are true by means of one truth, the truth of the divine intellect." Yet in a second sense, the sense in which a thing is true to the human intellect, truth is many things, for "there are many truths about many true things, and even many truths in different minds about one true thing."[61] It is by this second sense that we may say language, and the truth it expresses, *resonates*.

Poetic Imagery

Poetry lives according to its use of images. This fact, though self-evident enough, does not describe the art usefully or indeed any theology that would try to adopt its qualities. The use of images of itself does not render a work poetic. It could just as well make it perplexing, opaque, chaotic—not to mention sentimental to the point of distraction. This potential hazard is perhaps what is most feared about a theological poetic in any sense of the word: any theology that would eschew careful thought for the sake of free poeticisms or mask lazy thinking with the use of beautiful words. Such a hazard threatens not only what we might call the objectivity of truth—our ability to know and discuss it—but also what we might call simple clarity of speech. Resistance to poetic ways of speaking and thinking thus reaches into the very heart of poetry and its fragility, opposing it in an attempt to affirm some manner of persistent truth or in an attempt to doubt any highly temporal expression of truth. However, the mere use of images is not enough for well-executed poetry, and certainly not enough for well-formed theology.

Still, we would do well to acknowledge the danger here, in the use of images. In *De veritate*, Aquinas begins to explain why images ought not be used in the "divine sciences," by which he means theology properly speaking. "Sense and imagination know only external accidents," he writes, "but the intellect alone penetrates to the interior and to the essence of a thing."[62] The penetration of the intellect to the essence of a thing demands, for a Scholastic like Aquinas, its abstraction from the sensible, which the imagination assists us in doing.[63] Ultimately, this must mean that the sensible impression on the mind (the phantasm, which the imagination is able to recall) must be abstracted away from as well. This is why the study of essences is called meta-physics: because it is beyond physics. Aquinas argues in this way not because he is against imagination in general, but because knowing the essence of a thing requires being able to know beyond its sensible impressions, especially in the case of God, who is not sensible because he has no body to sense. This argument is clearer in *The Divisions and Methods of the Sciences*, where Aquinas explains that we do know some things through imagination, but not all knowledge ends there. In the case of God, imagination and the senses are starting points, but not terminations: this is because God transcends both and because the human intellect is also capable (in a lesser fashion) of transcending both in its knowledge.[64]

Our caution, then, is not to confuse imagination—and thus the imaginative use of images—with knowledge of God, who transcends imagination. Though a simple caution, it is vital to remember at all times in the case of imagery-rich theology. Because God transcends the world, we cannot claim that imaginative works somehow grasp God better than—say—philosophical prose. This cannot be the case if we are to be consistent about God's transcendence. In arguing for the sake of von Balthasar's "poetics," it is important to recall that his use of images bears the weaknesses of all images, which is to say that they are not points of termination, but rather beginnings. Though Aquinas is more apt to leave behind these beginnings at earlier points in his theological reasoning, and von Balthasar much more apt to remain with them deep into his reasoning; still for neither man are these images points of theological rest.

Von Balthasar's crossway of disagreement with Aquinas is here, with the role of imagination and images in theology. He prefers their use, but we must ask: how are they to be used? Images must be used well, while acknowledging their limits—as in their prohibition in the Old Testament. Though it may seem unrelated, in asking this question it is possible for us to explore how poetry and theology are capable of *specificity*, as much as in the last section it became necessary to discuss abiding mystery. Specificity helps us to grasp a thing's usefulness, as well as its limits. Thus if in the last section, we emphasized analogy, fragility, and resonance—and so abiding mystery—here, with images, we will emphasize concreteness and specificity.

The Incarnation itself helps us to see how an immense mystery need not be vague at all, but rather quite specific: Christ comes to us as a specific person in a specific time, and the lives of the Christians who imitate him gain a similar specificity because they, too, live in a specific place and time. All the various moments of Christ's life, recorded in the Gospels in multiple (even contradictory) ways, are all specific mysteries. Specific in the sense that we remember how Christ did *this*—not how he could have, or might have, done something else—and recall the depth of meaning in what he did.[65] The rosary is in this way but a particular expression of Christian memory in general.

Christian memory consists in, among other things, images. Not disconnected images without content but images woven together and filled with inexhaustible content. Liturgical art, with its saints and biblical scenes and symbolic tropes, hyper-realizes such a basic reality. This quality of Christian images in particular helps us to see what is true about well-used images in general: they must be *specific*, and they must *express something*. The first is ordered toward a desire for visceral concreteness, not for the sake of excluding others but rather for including them; the second is ordered toward the conviction that speech (or expression) ought to contain something to be heard.[66]

Poetry of the last century has shown special interest in specificity, often to the point of maddening obscurity.[67] Modern poems are highly invested in the mundane, often with a fixity that brings its scenes to the point of an esotericism beyond relevance. This need not always be the case. Note how *Conversio Ad Phantasmata* continues its movement from where we last left it. The beloved is now "pressed" onto the lover, the speaker, who seeks to describe the desire that rises up as a result:

By "dreams," I mean desire,
awakening at your essential stress,
your imparted shape. Much as fire
readies wax to acquire a likeness,
so you were both heat and seal.

The central image is that which has guided the poem: the outline of fire. Now the image—the beloved figure, profiled by fire—is repeated in terms of desire for the beloved. Here that desire is understood as a heat that readies wax to receive an impressed shape and also as the impressed shape itself. The theme is reviewed not for the sake of repetition alone, but rather to expand the basic theme. We see an outlined figure not for the sake of an outline, but for the sake of describing love for someone. In this way, the poem's specificity with images—always returning to the outline of fire—*permits* this thematic expansion rather than obstructing it.

Desire as readiness and reception: that is the point of the stanza—but not in so many words. The poem gives us multiple implied meanings, not infinite in number, but still flexible and varied. It does *not* mean, for example, to imply that desire and hate are the same. That is the opposite of the poem's intent. Yet within its intent, we can see that there are multiple fields of meaning: dreams are sensible expressions of desire, similar to the outlined figure; desire awakens at an encounter with someone; desire directs the nature of the one "dreaming"; and so on. So we can see that an image *expresses*, but it does not express with univocity of meaning. Because images are beginnings, they tend to reflect Aquinas's "secondary" way of viewing truth—the human intellect's grasp of truth—rather than the primary, which is God, since God knows all things.

The lack of univocal expression in poetry, and thus in poetic language, could run the gamut from helpful to destructive. We could leap into fierce relativism or permit intolerable contradictions. Here von Balthasar responds with his understanding of form (gestalt), and it is here that we can see von Balthasar taking up the specificity and ambiguity of poetry once again and reordering it. Or rather, he bolsters its qualities with reflections that prevent it from descending into mere uncertainty without violating what is good about an image.

Modern art and philosophy, in von Balthasar's estimation, is always threatening to lose form. This destroys its ability to express, though the effort against form is made in order to try and achieve expression.

> Let us not forget that "form" (*Gestalt*) is primarily ordered toward art. But in the Hegelian system, art had its classical moment with the Greeks and for the present is actually passé. . . . Here rests the crucial challenge for Christianity.[68]

In this way, von Balthasar argues that modern philosophy and poetry—his discussion takes place in the context of a review of Hegel, Schiller, and Goethe—desire formlessness. They desire a rather specific form of abstraction: an expression that somehow gives shape to the profound indeterminacy of our existence.

Von Balthasar sees this modern moment as an opportunity for Christianity, its worthy (that is to say, good and urgent) challenge. Christianity and Christian art are not only unafraid of form—that is not enough to face the challenge, except to differentiate it from the modern—but Christianity and Christian art also know the flexibility of form, which is specific yet multifaceted. Form is concrete, even singular (especially in the case of Christ), yet known in multiplicity. For von Balthasar, the Christian imagination is capable of navigating between the various poles of existence, metaphysically and existentially, in a singular fashion—which is to say in a fashion charged with the fullness of grace, which knows the infinity of love in the most personal of ways: in the Person of Christ. As he argues in "Revelation and the Beautiful,"

> The beautiful, then, will only return to us if the power of the Christian heart intervenes so strongly between the other world salvation of theology and the present world lost in positivism as to experience the cosmos as the revelation of an infinity of grace and love—not merely to believe but to experience it.[69]

The Christian is capable of perceiving the relationship between the being of the world and the (surpassing) being of God. By doing so in grace, Christianity is able to testify to God's grandeur and to testify to the beauty of the world. Von Balthasar names the "Christian heart" as the epicenter of such testimony because it is the heart of believers transformed by grace that can respond to the modern world not only intellectually (as theology is charged with doing) but also with the response of living experience. It is a response, in other words, fraught with the weight of logic and of action.

So Christians can "see" the visceral relationship between one truth of God and the images that are used to embody the one truth revealed to us. Christians can traverse the complex relationship between meaning and mystery. Not for the sake of a lack of clarity, but for the sake of a "thicker" or more substantive witness to the fullness of truth, which is specific yet flexible, concrete yet mysterious. Images continue to be used in theology not out of failure, but out of necessity. Well-used images correspond to the fullness of truth, which is mysterious, complex, and lasting. This is why, in this life at least, Aquinas tells us that, "An image is the starting point of our knowledge, for it is that from which the operation of the intellect begins; not that it passes away, but it remains as the foundation of intellectual activity," and yet as foundation it cannot provide the terminus of our knowledge.[70]

A mother's smile summarizes who she is in a word-image, and in that word-image she gives herself to her child. Yet stopping there, and failing to fill the word-image with the fullness of an active and loving relationship, would empty it of its meaning. Aesthetics compels us forward, enraptures us, and does not permit us to rest. A mother's word-image to her child is not an end, but a beginning. Still, her smile remains with her child inasmuch as she continues to give it, as it continues to express the riches of her relationship with her child.

Von Balthasar would have images remain with us through the heights of theological inquiry, even into discussions of Trinitarian "distance" and the darkness of redemption on the cross. While both Aquinas and von Balthasar are highly biblical, the distinctiveness of biblical speech abides in von Balthasar's reflections with more strength the more abstract he becomes, as in *Mysterium Paschale*, for example, which is a book of soteriology soaked in biblical language. In such a decision to remain with images, he parts ways with Aquinas, though we are also able to see how neither theologian would claim that images somehow encircle our knowledge of God and so can rest in them. Von Balthasar's preference for images leaves him able to fixate on theological problems with the flexible specificity images allow, a preference that leaves him able to symphonically reason through questions of God and redemption. Yet his biblically informed flexibility, his gestalt of pictures taken at various angles, leaves him forever open to the accusation of muddled thinking or of anthropomorphism. If the secondary analogous place of truth's multiplicity—and of the images that express this—is not recalled, then the whole work threatens to collapse.

So the specificity of images, of images used well, is not enough by itself, even alongside a healthy understanding of resonance. Von Balthasar's use of gestalt presses us to ask how it is that a Christian—more specifically, a theologian—can judge between an effective image and a poor one, between resonance and dissonance. It is a problem of which von Balthasar himself is aware, and so he argues, even in "Revelation and the Beautiful," that the Christian heart that redeems beauty must be an attuned heart, a heart fixed on and formed by God himself: "Only one whose heart is attuned to the art of God can be expected to establish order and due proportion in the confusion and chaos of the present."[71]

A Governed Theo-Poetic

An *attuned heart* necessarily implies something, or rather someone, to which the human heart must be ordered. For von Balthasar, our ultimate "attunement"—whether we speak ontologically, epistemologically, or existentially—is to God. Von Balthasar discusses such an attunement consistently in the trilogy, with the analogy varying from the musical ("attunement"), to the dramatic ("personality" or "role"), to the missiological, ("attestation" or "witness"), among others. Throughout, von Balthasar attempts in diverse ways to order all of creation toward God—particularly the Triune God of Christian revelation. He is interested in introducing a hierarchy by which contingent reality might be understood, and at the height of the (Dionysian) hierarchy is the Trinity revealed in Christ. Von Balthasar's insistence that we reorder our thought and expand it according to Trinitarian revelation is at its most radical in *Theo-Drama V*, where he attempts to find some analogy for all of creation's basic qualities in the Trinity itself.[72]

At no point does von Balthasar consider reality as a single, flat horizon of notions that can be compared equally. To do so would be comparable to what he accuses Heidegger of doing. For von Balthasar, contingent existence has its varied hierarchy, from the one that differentiates plants and animals and so forth (with human beings at the apex) to the immensely complex inner realm of the knowing subject. His interest in hierarchy is not of itself an interest in proclaiming what is *lower* and what is *higher*, as if the mere statement of it were helpful, but rather an interest in seeing things as they are in their unique dignity. It is an attempt to understand, in all seriousness, that rocks are not the same as trees and that this says something good about both. Human beings are not divine and this says something good about humanity and about God. A hierarchy is an attempt to understand *rightly*. What von Balthasar sees through his hierarchy is that the Trinity, from unsurpassable heights, has grounded creation in love—from creation's very depths upward.[73]

Von Balthasar's understanding of hierarchy is influenced by the Christian theological tradition as well as the Christian artistic tradition. Poetry, in its way, receives much of its coherence from a single image or set of images that form a poem's foundational themes. *Conversio Ad Phantasmata*, for example, begins with its image of a beloved figure outlined by fire, which is then impressed on the lover, an "impression" through which the poem describes desire. The poem completes itself by repeating these themes, which govern its course, and inverting them:

> In knowing you I longed for you,
> heart fashioned in a sympathetic scape,
> a likened light. So I bent to
> be near you, reflecting back your shape.
> And I, anxious to give what I had received,
> closed my eyes to kiss you awake.

Now it is the lover who rises to "press" an image into the beloved through a kiss, reversing what has occurred in the poem. The kiss would not make sense were it not for the stanzas that preceded it, and its inversion is their completion. What it is possible to observe in most poetic uses of a governing image is that the basic image helps us to comprehend the other images employed in the poem without demanding strict coherence between all of the images. Without the opening outline of fire, the language of impression and of a kiss as a return of that impression, would not cohere. As is typical with poetry, much of the meaning is left flexible and hidden, to be found in the reading of the whole poem and not only its parts.

Much of the *further* meaning of the poem is announced in the title, *Conversio Ad Phantasmata*, which refers to an epistemological principle that harkens back to the Scholastic era, especially Thomas Aquinas. In the *conversio ad phantasmata*, the sensible impressions of an object that the passive intellect has received from the senses (phantasms, *phantasmata*) are abstracted or converted (*conversio*) into the essence or form of an object. If a reader knows this, then the title—which governs the meaning of the poem, provided it is understood—gives to every stanza a new, or rather another layer, of meaning. Now not only desire and love are at play in the poem, but also knowledge itself. The sensible reception of the beloved (the outline of fire), impressed on the loving knower, elicits not only desire, but also knowledge. In Scholastic language, knowledge of a thing is also conformity to a thing: as Aquinas says at the beginning of *De veritate*, "all knowing is produced by an assimilation of the knower to the thing known, so that assimilation is said to be the cause of knowledge."[74] The knower becomes *like* the object known, which helps us to grasp how in the poem the lover is "impressed" with an image of the beloved and in being so impressed becomes like it: the lover "received the form" of the beloved, and now has a "heart fashioned in a sympathetic scape, / a likened light."[75] Knowing and desiring are each in this way described as con-formity: a shaping-with. The lover, so shaped, is then able to give that shape back through the press of a kiss, which more intensively begins the repetition in the beloved of what has happened in the lover—and here the poem ends. Knowing is also loving, an effect the poem achieves by employing Scholastic language in the midst of its images. Without the poem's title, these further meanings persist, but with less clarity and direction. The poem's title tells us something of what it is about to attempt, and urges our attentiveness.

There are two advantages to this manner of poetic "thinking" or reflection, among disadvantages. One advantage is a constant flexibility, which gives poetry an ability to consider reality under many modes. This is a flexibility anchored by its themes, which restricts a possible infinity of meanings into a range of interpretations. Another advantage is that the all too modern reduction of truth into what is empirically verifiable here receives a counter-response, a deflection away from sheer coherence into a rich interconnectedness. Logical coherence is not, then, the sole or even primary criterion of truth. Therefore, every reductionistic theory of truth is resisted in poetry. Most modern art is radically aware of its critique of an overly narrow conception of (Enlightenment) truth, to the point that it often rejects any notion of truth at all. This introduces art's profound weakness, which is that its own flexibility constantly works against its ability to express what is true—a weakness found in art forms of all sorts in almost countless ways.[76] Art's resonance constantly threatens to dissolve or die. This is why we are, again, reminded that images, art, and poetry are to be beginnings and not ends in themselves, especially when used in theology. This threat to become an end rather than a foundation is another disadvantage.

Von Balthasar adopts this peculiar form of poetic governed-reasoning alongside a more traditional view of the hierarchic structure of being. He buoys the linguistic with the traditional and eschews sheer harmony—or reductionistic coherence—in favor of an *obedient* harmony. This is a harmony that is, in von Balthasar's words, obedient to the form of Christ, as in the case of Church office:

> Church office reminds the community that its unity does not lie in the mere harmonic interplay of personal charisms, or in self-contained, self-satisfied intraworldly order (as in a work of art), but that this harmony itself must be obedient to the crucified and risen Lord. Nowhere does the Church grow on her own.[77]

The obedience of harmony is not automatically established in Christ, as if it rested there for us to observe as one might observe so many blueprints on a table. It requires an ability to perceive, as well as an active (and free) *reception* of harmony—even within the Church. Von Balthasar calls it "skill" and "a Christian art" by which we are capable of seeing what is distorted, even within the Church.[78] The harmony is both objective (in Christ) and subjective (in the Church).

Such "vision" requires our formation in Christ, who governs our understanding of the memories of faith and our perception of the world—both in a subjective sense (since we are formed in it), and in an objective sense (since he bears the form by which things are brought into obedient harmony). In *Glory of the Lord*, von Balthasar calls this a "rightness" (*Richtigkeit*) borne by Christ that illuminates all other forms, and shows their unity with him. So he argues,

> The crucial Illuminating is then up to Christ, and in a double sense: that the figure of Christ has in itself an inner rightness (*Richtigkeit*) and evidence to that which it is, as in—in another, purely worldly area—a work of art or a mathematical theorem, and that this rightness which lies within the proportions of the thing also has the power radiating from itself to radiate in apprehending people, an il-

lumination which is meant not only intellectually, but also illuminates our wandering existence.[79]

The governing "image" of Christian theology is Christ himself, who is one by whom we judge the *rightness* or *attunement* of our statements and their inner relationships to one another. This is not meant in a loose sense, as if Christ were *merely* an image; he is the Incarnate Son, and in this way he governs theology more strictly and comprehensibly—with more concomitant and unsurpassable mystery—than any image or any title in any poem could possibly function. The demands made on theology are harsher and bear greater risk. This of course must mean that the poetic analogy fails, even as it illuminates in partial fashion the way theology is able to reason.[80]

Aquinas, meditating on truth in general and not only truth as it is expressed through images, has a similar "hierarchy" of meaning by which things can be said to be true in the Word and yet also true in themselves. If we ask if things exist more truly in themselves or in the Word, he argues in two ways: "If it refers to the truth of the thing, then undoubtedly the truth of things as they exist in the Word is greater than that which they possess in themselves," since they depend on the Word for their existence and since the Word is truth itself and the true expression of the Father.[81] If "more truly" refers to truth as it is predicated to a thing, then the thing more truly exists in itself and thus has an integrity of its own—but only inasmuch as it is predicated, which is to say known in a relation other than its relation to God. This is because it is possible to consider a thing both in its relation to the Word and in its own nature; not because the Word lacks superiority but because of the Word's superiority over it. So Aquinas is able to link created things with the Word in a profound way, even to the point of saying that "the likeness of a creature in the Word is, in a certain sense, the life of the creature itself."[82] Yet it is a *likeness* at work in the creature and not an identity, and so the Word remains distinct from a creature and the creature also retains an integrity of its own.

Both Aquinas and von Balthasar have a theory of meaning that roots truth in the superiority of the Word over creation, and that in this way presumes a hierarchy of truth. Von Balthasar, however, emphasizes the

Incarnate Word, while for the Aquinas of *De veritate* the emphasis is on the eternal Word. This is a significant difference between the two, and though their agreement is important for the sake of clarifying von Balthasar's position, it is equally as important not to identify them on this point in particular. Von Balthasar's interest in poetic language, his continued use of it in theology, is founded in his emphasis on the Incarnate Word and his desire to keep his theology informed by it. Aquinas, while beholden to the Incarnation and in many ways the foremost defender of its importance in other areas of theology—one thinks in particular of the sacraments—does not arrange his hierarchy of meaning and language according to it in the same fashion von Balthasar does. Both thinkers are Christocentric, but on this point they are so with distinctive emphases. Of this difference, much more could be said and extrapolated, but its acknowledgement must suffice for now.

If we return, by way of closing, to the image of a mother and her child, it is possible to see in this very human image how the love of a mother governs the response of her child. This is not because the child lacks integrity or (in potency) freedom, but rather because a response is always shaped by that to which it responds. A child would not know love if love were not first given. This is an analogy for the Christological governance of theological reflection and theological language. Love does not rule over its object with an iron will, and it does not suffocate though it yet encloses and directs. Love gives identity, which is restrictive inasmuch as it means being *this* and not *that*, and which is also freeing inasmuch as it guides us to understanding what we desire to be.

In this chapter, we have seen how metaphysical questions and questions of language do not oppose one another. D. Stephen Long argues for much of this in his book *Speaking of God* drawing from both von Balthasar and Barth. Asking questions regarding expression and image does not exclude prior or concomitant questions of being. Though often treated divisively, metaphysics and language are not cordoned off from one another in separate realms. Nor, indeed, is language determinative of metaphysics as the exclusive source or determination of reality. Both consistently operate together, and—as Long insists—truth binds them to one another. In a metaphysics such as von Balthasar's, *expression* is both a metaphysical and a linguistic term.

Long also showed us how linguistic and metaphysical concerns each find themselves reliant on the Word for the coherence of either. "The incarnation is true," Long argues. "Truth is the incarnation." Neither language nor metaphysics can render existence intelligible to the profound degree Christ, God Incarnate, does. This is not to say that they are unintelligible of themselves; it is, rather, to insist that the Incarnation brings both fields to a fullness of meaning that they are not intrinsically capable of reaching. Long's constant aversions to Marian theology reveal the integrity of nature and its contribution to grace, and indeed its reliance on grace.

Von Balthasar's corpus contains many of the themes that Long draws upon, though the two men have different interlocutors. Von Balthasar's close arrangement of being and of love, his pairing of the two together, helps us to see his careful union of theological language and metaphysical reflection. His image of a mother's smile is vital here, since it is a natural analogy that serves to describe nature's expressive qualities and also serves as an analogy for God's supernatural, prior love for us.

Von Balthasar's use of such an image, viewed alongside his metaphysical emphasis on expression, helps us to see how he is interested in retaining traditional metaphysics and at the same time accomplishing a different task. This "task," or style, is what I call a *theological poetic*. It is a method of theology that employs poetic devises analogously in its theological reflections. Of the poetic devices it was possible to discuss, I highlighted three: (1) poetic logic, especially *resonance*, (2) poetic imagery, especially its *"flexible" specificity*, and (3) poetic governance, especially a poem's need for *hierarchical patterns of meaning*.

All three characteristics could, in their distinctive ways, serve as what defines a poetic logic. All three have great provenance in the poetic tradition, with degrees varying according to the age. In a *theological* poetic, however, the need for a poem to be patterned according to something that orders it takes a place of primacy. What governs the theological "logic" of poetry is theology itself, or rather, what governs our use of images in theology—to the degrees that we employ them—is Christology. This is not meant in a simple fashion, as if it were easy to determine the way Christ orders our use of images. The case is complex because the Incarnation, language, and metaphysics are all complex. When von Balthasar speaks of gestalt, he means to open the way to just such a complexity.

The "contours" of a theo-poetic have been laid out in a rather disembodied fashion as of yet, extracted into basic principles that can be discussed and compared. Von Balthasar himself never discusses these basic principles, though we have seen how it is possible to draw out their lineaments in his work. It is important for us to understand how von Balthasar works out such a theory of language and being in his corpus, and here the problem is twofold: how it is that he employs a theo-poetic as best we can see it and how it is that he judges the quality of a theo-poetic in others. The first of these can be grasped in principle through the work of this chapter, which gives the theory of von Balthasar's own poetic. This poetic remains rather disembodied when not paired with von Balthasar's careful use of artists, and it is that question to which we now turn in the next chapter. This is the final urgent matter: seeing a theo-poetic at work and asking how it responds to the problem of the modern age as von Balthasar understands it.

FIVE

Art, Metaphysics, and the Sacraments

Dante to Beatrice

I saw you along the pier,
solitary, amid the water and the stars.
Black and silver turning overhead and underneath,
light and dark throwing their shape
against your face.

I saw you at turns bright and dim,
near to me and far. A centerpoint of light,
gathering each ray in to cast it out and back again.
And my eyes followed the light, drawn
to you and pointed toward the stars.

The stars, which themselves seemed
to pull together at angles of light against dark.
Themselves a constellation of your face.
Your heavenly self, sealed in the sky
and calling to me in this, my deepest night.

The stars, aligning along your future self,
your truest self, perfected in God's sight.
Shining in the spheres of time and eternity, gathered in
the dark of death—your heavenly self,
composed of brightest light.

I looked at you here, and there—
heaven and earth present to me, and both
beautiful as they crossed each other in my heart.
You like the waters held something of the stars,
and the sky something of the earth.

I looked and asked, whom do I love?
The one before me, or the one above?
Warm flesh, or flesh fired to light?
I asked myself who, the two or the one or each.
Who, since each self is self, and true.
And I could only answer that I love you.

The last chapter gave the intelligible shape of what might be called von Balthasar's "theo-poetic"—a theological style that takes advantage of basic poetic forms as they are transfigured for the work of theology. A theo-poetic in the sense that von Balthasar plies the style bears three major qualities: poetic logic, poetic imagery, and Christological ordering or governance. The first, logic, emphasizes the flexible resonation of multiple meanings together with one another, so that its exactness is found only in the whole "sound" of theological insight taken as a "symphony." The second, imagery, again emphasizes a certain sensuous flexibility, since an image can of itself bear several meanings at once. Yet an image, since it is sensuous, is also concrete: so an image helps to narrow a valence of implications as much as it calls upon several. The third, which is the Christological ordering of thought, is the most important. It is by this principle that von Balthasar's theology is a *theology*, a *theo*-poetic, and not simply a poetic or work of art alone. The right set of flexible meanings, or sounds, is found only according to their attunement in Christ. Such are, briefly summarized, the major concerns of a theo-poetic.

This chapter must be spent in the effort to understand how von Balthasar's theological poetic works itself out in the length of his corpus, particularly in *Glory of the Lord*. Serving this twin task—of understanding and of implication—can by no means take up every successive section of von Balthasar's efforts and describe how each functions theo-poetically. That would occupy too much time and stray into redundancy. Nor does it indeed always need to be the case that von Balthasar employs a theo-poetic to do the theological "work" he requires. A theological poetic is neither exhaustive for von Balthasar's theological style, nor for theology's efforts in general. This is instructive for the possible relevance of theological poetics outside of *Herrlichkeit*. A theo-poetic style certainly operates in the background of von Balthasar's work to a profound degree—but it is by no means an exclusive one. As we have seen, a theo-poetic itself must presume elements of classical metaphysics to be coherent.

Still, it is necessary to see how such a theo-poetic "style" can and does inform von Balthasar's theological judgment. In this chapter, we will see a theo-poetic in the concrete, especially in an artistic figure that von Balthasar praises: Gerard Manley Hopkins. An aesthetic that lacks specificity, after all, is no aesthetic—it fails to be embodied, and thus fails to be aesthetic in the sense von Balthasar means the word.[1] After a study of von Balthasar's theo-poetic as it operates in specific appropriations of artists, namely the poet G. M. Hopkins as compared with Rilke, it will be possible to understand how the three major qualities discussed in the previous chapter work themselves out in von Balthasar's theology.

RETURNING TO RILKE: ART, DEATH, AND THE HOPE FOR REDEMPTION

Rilke's poetry has served as a consistent interlocutor in the course of this work as much as in von Balthasar's own. The poet haunts von Balthasar in both a positive and a negative fashion. Rilke is, first, a master of the poetic form. Anyone who would desire a comprehension of the German literary tradition must spend time with Rilke, just as it would also be necessary to encounter Goethe. There is genuine beauty in Rilke, and in him is crystalized all the grandeur and misery of human longing. Rilke grapples with our desire for immediacy (what von Balthasar calls *Unmittelbarkeit*), which is to say that he wrestles with our uniqueness and our desire to express that uniqueness—without bars or barriers, in purity.[2] Yet this desire is to our sorrow, since such purity escapes us and disintegrates into solitude. Rilke's famous image of the bowl of roses encapsulates the poet's final reflections on our desire to communicate and the resplendency of its failure:

> But now you see, how such a thing forgets:
> then before you stands the full bowl of roses,
> which is unforgettable and filled
> with the extremity of being and yielding,
> holding out, never-can-be, yet standing there,
> in what might be ours: might also be our extremity.
>
> Soundless life, expansion void of end,
> used-space without space taken
> from this space, which near things decrease,
> almost not, silhouetted hollows
> and pure interiority, so strangely delicate
> and self-illuminating—to the edge:
> are we aware of anything like this?[3]

Rilke inquires after the bowl of roses, which is an image of extreme yielding. Rose petals in their openness live as pure vulnerability, and in that vulnerability they somehow grasp eternity.[4] Yet there is nothing beyond these roses, and their delicate existence folds in upon themselves as "pure interiority." They are an expansive solitude. In other words, the only immediacy to be experienced is the self. Rilke strives to comfort himself with the rose's yielding solitude, but von Balthasar notes its concealed restlessness.[5] We do not, and cannot, really desire such profound solitude. Von Balthasar identifies this tendency in Rilke as both strength and weakness, as a sorrow lent to Rilke's work and as its splendor. Rilke, like other poets, breathes the "sorrow of the gods" (*Göttertrauer*).[6] His is a poetry of *Schreckliche*, terror at the finitude of life and the finitude of beauty.

Rilke provides a strong contrast against which von Balthasar highlights the Christian virtues that Rilke simultaneously rejects and desires.

These again revolve around *Unmittelbarkeit*, but in the case of a Christian appropriation of the concept, immediacy no longer conceals the tragedy of ultimate solitude. The subject instead yields to the genuine otherness of another's existence. The subject also yields to *mediation*, and here there are various sorts—the primary of which in this case is the mediation of self-knowledge through our encounter with objects.[7] Whereas Rilke desires in the end a self-knowledge so absolute that none other than the self-knowing self can mediate it—in an egocentric simulacrum of the Trinity—von Balthasar instead embraces mediation as his prime epistemological principle.[8] Though for both thinkers love might be said to serve as the foundation for knowledge, for Rilke "love" must necessarily involve solitude while for von Balthasar "love" must necessarily have recourse to another. Where the two agree, they immediately part ways.

Von Balthasar is not judging Rilke's art as art, strictly speaking. In other words, it is not a judgment of Rilke's genius, skill, or aesthetic execution. His judgment is theological, and it is also metaphysical. Beneath the epistemological critique of love there exist profound theological-metaphysical presuppositions according to which von Balthasar's concept of love is ordered and moves. Or rather, it would be more accurate to say that love is, for von Balthasar, metaphysical as well as epistemological.[9]

The metaphysical problem with Rilke, identified as early as *Apokalypse*, is a failure to comprehend the analogy of being and thus a failure to understand the asymmetrical relationship between God and the world. For Rilke, the "god" (if there is one, and it is never clear whether the divine is a poetic device or perhaps more substantive) is the torn Orpheus, who persists in the world according to a forever-death that represents the world's own forever-death. Transcendence is, in this fashion, immediately eviscerated, and indeed bound with terror. Transcendence is rendered, if not futile, then at least bound up in inescapable tragedy (death). Von Balthasar responds with an invigorated understanding of the analogy of being, which itself moves according to a Christological directive.

What renders Rilke's poetry ultimately insufficient for a theo-poetic is neither his use of images nor his employment of logic, both of which are masterful. He is missing the third and most important characteristic of a functioning theo-poetic, and that is Christ. Or, to be more specific,

Rilke obfuscates God and the world and so denies both what the Incarnation reveals and what must be presupposed for redemption to be intelligible: a proper understanding of the world and of God. This has been the constant theme of this book.

The corrective that von Balthasar offers is a response not only to Rilke but also to modern philosophy and modern theology. Though he reacts strongly against modern tendencies to absolutize a solitary self and death, especially as found in art, he does not do away with art. Though art is in many ways the nadir of modern tragedy, this by no means renders it anathema to theology. Rather, art—particularly poetic language—must all the more urgently receive resuscitation, so that the full "grammar" of the Incarnation may be rendered more effective.

So von Balthasar looks back on other poets who, while also sympathetic to Rilke's struggles, respond to the problem in a different form than Rilke. Of particular interest in the contrast between Rilke's wounded poetic and a "redeemed" poetic is the figure of Gerard Manley Hopkins, whose poetry bears many of the same interests as Rilke's—this despite a complete lack of historical relationship between the two—and yet Hopkins breaks apart those characteristics in a Christological inversion. As Cyril O'Regan says of von Balthasar's read of Rilke and Hopkins, "If the non-Christian Rilke points in the *Duino Elegies* to the mysterious communion, which can only be glimpsed at an angle, it is G. M. Hopkins who . . . captures 'death as resurrection' and 'resurrection as death.'"[10] After a careful discussion of Hopkins, it will be possible to see in von Balthasar's approval of Hopkins's work the same operant principles that were theoretically discussed in chapter 4.

A REDEEMED THEO-POETIC: HOPKINS AND THE BEAUTY OF THE PARTICULAR

Von Balthasar gives to Hopkins a unique place in the English literary tradition from which he emerges, so that in many ways Hopkins encapsulates the whole of the tradition that he uniquely surpasses.[11] The English tradition is characterized chiefly by two impulses in von Balthasar's eyes: a willing trust in images in religious thought, and a consistent distrust of universal concepts.[12] Hopkins's poetry is thus typified by a free use of imagery to express religious insight and a keen interest in what is unique and irreducible.

So Duns Scotus becomes for Hopkins a muse by which he channels the great English inheritance that is his.[13] The Nominalism of Scotus is, for the poet Hopkins, an insight into the irreducible with which poetry as an art is deeply identified. He even dedicates a poem to Scotus's vision of the world.[14] Von Balthasar notes Hopkins's investment in Scotus without judgment, which is not unusual in his review of an artist's background and scope, but is unusual considering von Balthasar's open distaste for Scotus.[15]

Hopkins's keen interest in the unique does not confuse his desire for, or affirmation of, what is objective. Rather, according to von Balthasar, Hopkins is driven by a desire for truth—indeed the truth that inheres in the unique individual, the most unique (and most true) of whom is Christ. Von Balthasar describes this desire as an *impatience*: "breaking through to the uniquely true glory determines Hopkins's whole ethos; here lies the unity of his personality as poet and religious, that unique of which he was most sharply conscious even when it finally broke him."[16] Hopkins desires the real, and to express the real, but only through an expression of its instantiated uniqueness. Herein for Hopkins rests the glory of creation and the Glory of God in Christ.

Hopkins is fascinated by nature from an early age. He loves the world and in this way shows himself to be a creature of the Romantic tradition that von Balthasar sees him surpass. It is not nature as a broad concept that arrests him but its wild peculiarity: the shape of a cloud or the flight of a skylark, which is "his favourite, untiringly varied picture—the bird in the free, untamable air."[17] So, too, he is more interested in the human person than in *humanity*,[18] though not to the denial of human nature.[19]

The emphasis in his poetry remains unmistakably on what is unrepeatable, and yet that emphasis demands repetition or apprehension in poetic verse and in lived life. Every existent has an *instress*, a favorite word of Hopkins's, which von Balthasar explains as that in beings that is "their deep, unique act, which establishes them, holds them together and holds them in tension." The instress of a thing demands from the observing subject "an answering stress," so that it might be understood by a kind of ontic sympathy through which the subject can speak a word that corresponds to the thing understood.[20] Instress is accompanied by *inscape*, which von Balthasar compares to *form*—a sensual form—that extends out from a thing even while resting in it, and which can be brought to completion.[21] The poet Hopkins speculates at length regarding instress and inscape, his special keywords employed in an attempt to comprehend what it is that poetry does and to which poetry responds. Much of his speculation occurs in his journal notes, with a great deal of his intellectual development occurring in the implicit progression of his use of terms.[22]

While instress emphasizes a kind of activity in an object, a *tendency toward* expression, inscape emphasizes the way in which an object is already expressed while yet incomplete. The first reaches out with the sympathy of all beings for one another at the very heart of their existence; the second shows how their sensual qualities already demand their expression and determine the direction of their completion in expression. Poetry is responsive to the world out of sympathy for the images with which the world speaks; it is shaped by those images, even as it shapes them. Words become, instead of mere designations, the expression of a form. "*Formed*," von Balthasar explains, "can also mean *worded*."[23] For Hopkins, the world is in this way already "worded." The words of a poem do not impose so much as reveal. The world is already, in this sense, poetic. Here is where Hopkins touches the Romantic poetry of his time, enamored as he is with the creativity already inherent in nature, and yet he is forced through great sacrifice to renounce many of its qualities. He praises the wild nature that he adores on long walks, but must also surrender those fields and skies to have them given back to him again. Such a surrender is, in von Balthasar's eyes, necessary to Hopkins the poet and the Christian.[24] Yet this surrender is distinctive from Heidegger's *Hingabe*, because it is not an abandonment to death, but rather an abandonment to Christ. Hopkins's surrender is an abandonment to the world of grace.

Hopkins allies himself more and more strongly with the world of grace and not with the immanent near-pantheism of his artistic contemporaries. He writes with increasing emphasis on offering everything to God, which is itself an image of the "great sacrifice" of the cross. So poems like "Morning Midday and Evening Sacrifice" appear in Hopkins's corpus, with lines that stress how the transient things of the world must be offered to the eternal God:

> The dappled die-away
> Cheek and wimpled lip,
> The gold-wisp, the airy-grey
> Eye, all in fellowship—
> This, all this beauty blooming
> This, all this freshness fuming,
> Give God while worth consuming.[25]

Yet these lines would be incomprehensible if they did not have God at their center, so that all the beauty of the earth that blooms in wildness and passes away has its anchor in God himself. So, too, does the human being, as in this poem:

> Thee, God, I come from, to thee go,
> All day long I like fountain flow
> From thy hand out, swayed about
> Mote-like in thy mighty glow.[26]

For Hopkins, all of creation is an "offering" to God—an offering put in motion and sustained by God and in which creation continually participates. All is a "great sacrifice," much like the wild sacrifice of the shipwreck poems. As von Balthasar explains of Hopkins, "The principle lies in the fact that all truth is grounded in Christ ('Christ is truth') and that all beauty belongs to him, is related to him, is yielded to him in the 'great sacrifice' and must rest with him."[27] Von Balthasar's emphasis on Hopkins's great sacrifice, itself a strong component of scholarship on the poet,[28] resonates strongly with what von Balthasar himself will say of Christ's surrender on the cross in *Theo-Drama*.[29] In Hopkins, von Balthasar sees a poet who comprehends the intimate link between Christology and metaphysics—between Christ and the way the world is—and who expresses it in his poetry with great depth. What holds the wild world together and sustains it, for either man, is God himself.

Hopkins's poetry helps von Balthasar illustrate the coincidence, or rather the entwining, of the unique and the universal. While Dante achieves a similar dimension in his *Divine Comedy*, for von Balthasar the achievement loses its Christological center and thus at most presents us with a Christianized eros.[30] In von Balthasar's assessment, Dante does not quite manage to elevate the particularity of Christ along with love. Here is where Hopkins outdistances the Florentine master and receives von Balthasar's fierce praise. Everywhere Hopkins is concerned for the unique: for the solitary and singular, which he discovers with utmost intensity in the wild fields of nature. Each uniqueness is a "taste" of Christ's uniqueness. Particularity in the world bears an inscape and instress of Christ's particularity. For Hopkins, more than any other poet von Balthasar surveys, such worldly and Christological uniqueness in a particular way corresponds to the realm of poetry. Poetry draws its inspiration from the *taste* of the world and in its singular weave of images helps us also to *taste* the wild and peculiar qualities of the world. We taste something of Christ in poetry, since the curvature of its surfaces trains us to see something of the curvature of Christ.

Hopkins is increasingly convinced that every ounce of the world partakes in the uniqueness of Christ, in the "taste" and instress of Christ. This Christocentric principle is perhaps no better illustrated than in these lines from Hopkins's "Blessed Virgin Compared to the Air We Breathe":

> Of her flesh he took flesh:
> He does take fresh and fresh,
> Though much the mystery how,
> Not flesh but spirit now
> And makes, O marvelous!
> New Nazareths in us,
> Where she shall yet conceive
> Him, morning, noon, and eve;
> New Bethlems, and he born
> There, evening, noon, and morn—
> Bethlem or Nazareth,
> Men here may draw like breath
> More Christ and baffle death;
> Who, born so, comes to be
> New self and nobler me

In each one and each one
More makes, when all is done,
Both God's and Mary's son.[31]

With an intense Marian sensibility, Hopkins describes how the Son takes on flesh "fresh and fresh" in each Christian, becoming Incarnate again through Mary in the believer. This idea, which has a long history, finds in Hopkins a concise poetic expression. Both Mary and Christ receive universal application—since all are "God's and Mary's son"—yet only through profound specificity: in each breath of the believer.[32]

The uniqueness and peculiarity of Christ, of wild nature, and of poetry are not *isolated* coincidences. Otherwise, there would be no way for us to taste Christ in anything, let alone everything; we would perceive a peculiarity unrelated to everything else known, which would pass away without frame or influence. Here is where von Balthasar's description of Hopkins's continued conversion, his intensifying Christocentrism, becomes indispensable. Hopkins's theories of inscape and instress, which were mostly about the natural world, are given a new radiance the more Hopkins locates them in a doctrine of grace. Everything relates back to the "great sacrifice" Christ offers on the cross, and indeed for Hopkins "the cosmos as a whole possesses, either manifestly or secretly, a Christological form."[33]

With Hopkins as his guide, von Balthasar strives to reinforce a lively Christocentrism that is not a threat to created beauty, but rather its fulfillment. While Rilke fears that otherness ultimately swallows the individual, or in any case that desire wrecks all attempts for unity that does not end in solitude, Hopkins throws himself into the unrepeatable and inimitable. The sensible world is for Hopkins a wealth of unique graces, so long as its Christological center is maintained; for Rilke, the sensible world is at best ambiguous. In contradistinction to Rilke and other Gnostic tendencies, von Balthasar exalts Hopkins's profoundly sacramental sensibilities:

Faith is so deeply involved in flesh and blood (the Word indeed has become flesh), that the transfer of interpretation from sacramental signs to the indwelling grace of faith proceeds imperceptibly, ultimately indeed because the christological-mariological has been *understood* as the inner condition of the possibility of the whole natural order.[34]

Flesh, and the sensible signs involved in sensuality, is no threat to grace or redemption. Further, the utterly unique God of redemption is not a threat to created reality. Instead, as von Balthasar stresses, the Christian is permitted a higher "final creative unity" that resides in faith, so much so that the Christian's creative inspiration is drawn from the wellsprings of faith.[35]

Von Balthasar highlights Hopkins's shipwreck poems—"The Loss of the Eurydice," "The Wreck of the Deutschland"—as his greatest poetic achievements, because "here the foundering and shattering of all worldly images and symbols yield a final picture of the sacrament of the world: perishing and ascending to God—death as Resurrection: Resurrection not beyond death, but in death."[36] These poems are, for von Balthasar, the heart of Hopkins's poetic insight. Here is where the insight into what is beautiful and particular in images finds its sacramental anchor. Inscape finds its clearest expression in Hopkins's sacramental shipwrecks.

Of the shipwreck poems, "Wreck of the Deutschland" is the longest and most significant.[37] The poem is dedicated to five Franciscan nuns who drowned in a shipwreck. Hopkins imagines them on the sinking ship in a storm at night and focuses on their faith in the midst of harrowing, considering with them the God of faith and the God of the sea, who is one and the same God. The opening stanza addresses God, who is the "giver of breath and bread;/ world's strand, sway of the sea." Not only is God the master of these, of life and the world, but he is also master of our very flesh: "Thou has bound bones and veins in me, fastened me flesh." With these lines, the stanza sketches out the major themes of the entire long poem—the God who created us gives us life, yet in giving it also plunges us into the dark depths of a transformation through death. Von Balthasar is quick to grasp this thematic trajectory and highlight it.

For von Balthasar, Hopkins has expressed with poetic precision what the Christian tradition is forever attempting to express: the cosmic scope of the Incarnation and cross. Hopkins himself sees how the five shipwrecked nuns speak to a far more universal mystery:

Five! The finding and sake
and cipher of suffering Christ.
Mark, the mark is of man's make
And the word of it Sacrificed.
But he scores it in scarlet himself on his own bespoken,
Before time-taken, dearest prizèd and pricèd—
Stigma, signal, cinquefoil token
For lettering of the lamb's fleece, ruddying of the rose-flake

The five nuns suffer, and Hopkins notes how their suffering indicates something of the mystery of Christ's suffering, a suffering caused by human sin ("of man's make"). In the same breath, however, Hopkins calls the suffering of the five a "mark," a mark and word: "Sacrificed." He immediately folds together human sin, Christ's five wounds, and the sacrifice of the cross. Here in the shipwreck, Christ marks his five nuns (each figure thus related to his five wounds) in scarlet as "his own bespoken," marking them and "wording" them in his five wounds. Using images, Hopkins reaches back to ideas rather similar to Bonaventure's explanation of St. Francis's stigmata, through which Francis experienced the impress of Christ's suffering. By recalling these themes, Hopkins intimately links the tragedy of this shipwreck with the redemption of the cross. The scarlet stigmata of the five nuns drowned is never once viewed as tragic but is rather seen as an image of the profound—cosmically scaled—transfiguration of the Resurrection: these nuns in their deaths see Christ.

This poem, and its sister, "The Loss of the Eurydice," contrasts sharply with Rilke in the poetic account of a crisis with death (the shipwreck). Allied as the two poems are with Christ's cruciform self-offering, they do not see death as an endless end by which life persists. Instead, death is the means by which creation more intimately unites itself to Christ's death and resurrection and—as if carried by that cruciform victory—in this way creation is brought to the fullness of life beyond death. Hopkins, like Dante, is the refutation of Rilke. Or, perhaps more to the point, Hopkins's shipwreck poems take up many of the existential themes of Heidegger's being-toward-death and explode them. Death is no longer *answer* or *finality*; it is no longer that toward which all being tends. Death is an offering.

Though for Hopkins the highest integration of Christ's profound uniqueness with the things of the world in the "great sacrifice" is to be found in our inheritance from Scotus, for von Balthasar this is much more profoundly our inheritance from Chalcedon and Thomas. Von Balthasar's read of Hopkins repeats many of the themes to be found in his short section on Aquinas in *Glory of the Lord IV: Metaphysics and Antiquity*. While acknowledging the importance of Scotus for Hopkins, von Balthasar—shaping the poet's work toward the total argument about worldly beauty and divine glory to give found in *Herrlichkeit's* volumes—emphasizes the way sensible images defend the uniqueness of God and the world and yet how those images must themselves be purified. These are ideas that Hopkins identifies with Scotus, but that von Balthasar identifies with Thomas Aquinas and derides Scotus for forgetting. Hopkins's eye for the form of the world, which for him is also "worded," sounds eerily like von Balthasar's assessment of human beings as "attuned to total reality" through their faculties, and how "no one has shown this more profoundly and more thoroughly than Thomas Aquinas."[38] For von Balthasar, Aquinas's genius is to preserve the beauty of the world and the glory of God through the distinction between *esse* and *essentia*.[39] This distinction is what enables our apprehension of particulars and indeed our apprehension of being itself through sensible particulars (*phantasms*). It is not Scotus who undergirds Hopkins; it is Thomas Aquinas.

SACRAMENTALITY AND ART

Because Hopkins's unique achievement, for von Balthasar, revolves around a highly sacramentalized use of poetic verse, we move now to consider the relationship between the sacraments and poetic language. Here von Balthasar's Thomist use of the Scotist Hopkins plays a fundamental role in the final constitution of a theo-poetic, and that is to show us how metaphysics and language coincide with one another in Hopkins's sacramental construal of language.

The Metaphysical Disagreement: Aquinas and Scotus

While he acknowledges Hopkins's explicit indebtedness to Scotus, especially to Scotus's *haeccitas*, von Balthasar tends to interpret Hopkins with emphases that lean the poet toward Thomas Aquinas and the distinction between *esse* and *essentia*, that is, toward that key idea in Thomas that supports the analogy of being—the analogy that Scotus ultimately rejects in favor of the univocity of being. Von Balthasar reinterprets Hopkins according to the essentially Thomist form of *Herrlichkeit*, and the Thomist undertones become especially clear if we proleptically read the metaphysic von Balthasar gives us in the fourth and fifth volumes into the Hopkins of the third volume. We come now to review how such a reinterpretation operates in the context of von Balthasar's work and why it is important. Von Balthasar's reinterpretation of Hopkins places the poet on an aesthetic trajectory that allows us to better grasp why metaphysics is so fundamental to language and how the opposing Scotist and Thomist schools grasp language distinctively.

Hopkins, von Balthasar stresses, involved himself wholly in the fleshly particularity of the world, and this for the sake of its surrender to the glory of God—a surrender that reveals the glory of God. This poetic involvement in the flesh bears with it the temptation to pantheisms of various sorts—even of a Rilkean sort—yet Hopkins shows resistance to these strains. He is, for example, "convinced by [Coventry] Patmore of [John] Keats's entanglement in a sensuous immanence,"[40] and his suspicion toward these entanglements builds into von Balthasar's assessment that he does not confuse nature and grace.[41] This lack of confusion, embedded in Hopkins's fascination with what is particular, is ultimately founded on a desire for nothing but God, who transcends the world, especially as that desire is expressed in the surrender of the nuns in "Wreck of the Deutschland."[42]

These emphatic articulations of the singularity of God, of a uniqueness that is in turn expressed in an unconfused way in the singularity of nature, is for Hopkins and many of his scholars a Scotist idea. "The 'inscape' Hopkins speaks of," Louis Mackey explains, "is (loosely) the network of forms that you see when you look into a thing through its haecceity."[43] Haecceity (*haeccitas*) is the "thisness" of a thing (alternately its quiddity), which makes it *this* thing and not *that*; in short, haecceity is what individuates beings from one another.[44] So for Hopkins an inscape is always caught up in the "thisness" of any one thing encountered, a *thisness* that for both Hopkins and Scotus must presuppose the univocity of being.

Scotus argues that God and creation are not only related to one another through analogy, thus requiring God's nature to be wholly other than creatures, but also through univocity: a term and perfection shared entirely between the two—and that term and perfection is "being."[45] Without the univocity of being, Scotus argues that we cannot know God. This is because, in order to know a thing, we must share something in common with it—a "middle term"—in order that we may know it. This "middle term" is, then, being.[46] Having united God and the world through a common, univocal concept (being), Scotus must then explain the difference between the two. For him, being is differentiated between God and the world because in the former being is infinite, while in the latter being is finite.[47]

What haecceity helps to explain, in this context, is the individuation of finite being into finite beings; since Scotus has broadened being into a univocal perfection of both God and creature, he cannot explain individuation in the same way Thomas Aquinas does. Since Aquinas argues that it is really only God who has being (who *is* Being), and that creatures have being by participation, then the metaphysical logic of distinction follows as a matter of course: beings, since they have being by participation and not *in se*, may be divided infinitely without a threat to the ultimate unity of Being itself (which only God has).[48] Scotus comes up against the same problem but must explain it in a distinct fashion, since for him both God and creatures "have" being. Haecceity is, then, Scotus's principle of individuation, and for him the term refers both to the distinction of a species (into beings) and the indivisibility of a being. This is what makes *haecceitas* unique: it explains singularity and indivisibility in *one* concept.[49] Thus the "thisness" of a thing takes a special primacy of place in the thought of Scotus, as well as Hopkins, since by it we may know the uniqueness of a thing. The accent on "thisness," on the actuality and concrete expression of things, gives to Scotus's metaphysics a particular emphasis on existence. *Esse* is so wholly bent toward *ens* that they are co-extensive terms. As Etienne Gilson says of Scotus, "Any essence claims an existence of its own, which is for it nothing else than to be."[50]

Richard Cross argues that Scotus's move for the univocity of being is primarily a linguistic argument. It is not, in fact, a metaphysical claim.[51] To presume this seems too much a burden on the text, however, as Scotus himself unites the perfections of being alongside his syllogistic logic, making univocity both metaphysical and linguistic.[52] As with many medieval thinkers, Scotus considers metaphysics and language together. Catherine Pickstock argues in a convincing manner that Scotus is quite serious about the metaphysical import of his univocity theory. For her, univocity and haecceity introduce a metaphysical confusion by which essence necessitates existence—in fact distorting the relationship between the theoretical and the actual—and Scotus's stress on existence conceals a prior logical rupture between what can be thought and what actually exists.[53] The theoretical lurks behind the actual as a sort of virtual realm, secretly governing existence, and thus shifting metaphysical emphases from ontology and actuality to epistemology and rationality—and this in spite of Scotus's concept of haecceity.[54]

Pickstock argues that the rupture Scotus has introduced continues into the Enlightenment, modernity, and postmodernity. Hers is an updated account of a fall that sounds very much like von Balthasar's. For her, even the modern Catholic liturgy falls under its dark shadow.[55] We do not need to follow her down every path, though we can acknowledge the metaphysical problems she describes in Scotus. Rather, more like von Balthasar, it is possible for us to see in this problem an opportunity, one advanced through the retrieval and expansion of Thomas Aquinas—a retrieval that it is possible to apply to Hopkins as well as to Scotus.

In *After Writing*, Pickstock contrasts Aquinas and Scotus, analogy and univocity. Because of the real distinction, which Pickstock calls the "inner kernel of both *analogia entis* and participation," Aquinas is able to account for likeness in ways that Scotus cannot: without destroying the quiddity of a being, Thomas can describe its participation in Being, thus making a being *like* the Source of its being without confusing the two. Scotus is only able to explain likeness in terms of intensity: God has "more" being—is Being infinitely—while the finite being has "less" being, or finitely.[56] Thus Scotus's "middle term," *being*, is revealed to be a unifying linguistic-metaphysical principle only inasmuch as it makes its poles of unity—God and the world—impossible to distinguish save through "less" or "more." Likeness in the Scotist scheme is brought about through degrees of saturation; for Thomas, likeness participates in difference.

What we must recall about Thomas's real distinction of essence and existence is that it allows for him to distinguish between God and the world in the same act of relating them. God, Thomas reminds us in the *Summa Theologica*, is his own essence and his own being.[57] No creature can claim such an identity of being and essence, and yet creatures are able to participate in being. Finitude and infinity cannot be opposed as opposites, because the act of distinguishing the two also relates them. "That which exists in a finite manner," explains Rudi te Velde, "so as to be a particular being of a certain kind, must therefore be intrinsically and positively related to the infinite fullness of being in such a way that it expresses something of this fullness in itself (*similitudo*)."[58] Pickstock and te Velde help us to see how the Scotist *haecceitas*, while striving to emphasize the uniqueness that Hopkins so adored in creation, in fact befuddles uniqueness. Univocity confuses both likeness and difference because they exist on the same plane of understanding: each is a comparative of intensity. Thus compared, uniqueness and similarity become equivocations.

What has happened here, if we expand past Pickstock, is the "flattening" of the world through the univocity of being. Von Balthasar's youthful accounts of the Dionysian and Promethean impulses here find a medieval approximation: Scotus has collapsed finitude and infinity. It would be easy for us at this point to draw identical lines of accusation as in previous chapters, but that would be deceptive. What Scotus assists us in seeing is how individuality—which the early von Balthasar highlights as a disease of the modern age—reaches a crisis through the collapse of the analogy of being.

Scotus cannot account for difference because he has eliminated it through univocity. Now difference may only be explained through degrees of intensity of being, which is to say that difference is described on a horizon equal to itself. Haecceity renders itself an empty term because it has no sense of hierarchy. Univocity forces us to distinguish according to a sliding scale, since the scale is singular and omnipresent (being). An individual is thus only questionably unique because uniqueness is only posited according to a description of varying intensities. A creature is uniquely itself, uniquely creature, if only because we can ascribe finite being to it. We can ascribe no other uniqueness to it, which forces us to question whether it is really possible to call any one thing—in a metaphysic of univocity—really unique, even God. By contrast, analogy allows us to differentiate according to the perfections of the being in question.

We can say that there is a perfection proper to a creature that makes it like God, yet without identifying these perfections according to a shared middle term. Comparisons and distinctions are not made along a sliding scale of intensity because they are made hierarchically. An individual, in the Thomist metaphysic, is legitimate and irreplaceable.

This argument warrants more consideration. If we were to put it colloquially, we might say this: in a metaphysic of univocity, everyone is special, which means that no one is special. Haecceity is everywhere ascribed, "thisness" is posited and emphasized, but only according to an over-arching *sameness* (being) that confuses what makes this thing *this* and not *that*. We can only say that it has more being or less. This makes beings essentially interchangeable. In a metaphysic of analogy, individuality and uniqueness ("specialness") are ascribed through likeness as well as difference. Because creature and Creator relate to one another in a highly disproportionate fashion—God has being (*is* Being), a creature has being by participation—we can orient uniqueness transcendentally. "They are different from one another in what they have in common," writes Rudi te Velde, "the one has *being* in identity with its essence, the other has *being* as distinct from its essence."[59] That is, a creature's being is hierarchically conceived. This makes beings nonfungible.

Here I have attempted to repeat, in metaphysical terms, a specific attribute that Max Horkheimer and Theodor W. Adorno ascribe to the modern era in *Dialectic of Enlightenment* (originally published in 1947).[60] Von Balthasar himself was aware of this work, and has recourse to it in *Theo-Drama IV*.[61] Horkheimer and Adorno claim that modernity is characterized by *fungibility*, where individuality is emphasized only for the sake of rendering every individual the same and thus exchangeable. Scientific language and technology contribute to fungibility by making everything a static object to be controlled and (if needed) replaced. Art falls under the sway of exchange by being transformed into advertisement.[62] Neither Horkheimer nor Adorno look into the theological implications of their thesis, nor indeed its theological roots, and here I have gestured toward such a theological explanation and its resolution.

The resolution, which itself serves as the backdrop for von Balthasar's use of Horkheimer and Adorno in *Theo-Drama IV*,[63] is Thomas Aquinas's analogy of being, which disallows fungibility because it disallows for the flattening of uniqueness into a series of horizontal comparatives of intensity. This is not only a metaphysical claim, but also—to return to Pickstock—a sacramental one. The sacramental "threat" of Scotism, according to Pickstock, is a reduction of sacramentality into quantification: for Scotus, Christ is present in the Eucharist by extension; for Thomas, Christ is present in the Eucharist by substance.[64] Christ is present, for Scotus, by a sort of spatial intensification. Christ is "broadened" out in an almost longitudinal effort. Aquinas, by comparison, is almost bewilderingly simple. Christ's substantial presence in the Eucharist intensifies the uniqueness of our experience of him. There is no question of quantity at all; only of identity and presence.

Individuality, then, is better understood in the Thomist metaphysic than the Scotist. This is because individuality is preserved without descending into an exchangeability of equal interminable uniquenesses; individuality is preserved through the hierarchy of being that the analogy of being presupposes. What is more, the Thomist individual is not—and cannot be—an individual in the negative, atomic, history-less concept that von Balthasar feared from modernity. The Thomist individual is highly personal in the Balthasarian sense: as one who is unique, and whose uniqueness is fundamentally oriented toward the expression of God. For Thomas, every individual is related to the Source of all being.

So the uniqueness that Hopkins praises, that he roots in a deeply sacramental view of the world, is one defended by Thomas Aquinas and not by Duns Scotus. Univocity destroys particularity, while analogy upholds it. This is so because analogy is capable of relating unique things to a supremely unique object—God—who has being in a supreme and incomparable fashion because he is Being. What Scotus desired to defend, uniqueness, is in fact found in Thomas. Yet we may still say that Scotus outdoes Thomas's apprehension through the defense of the Immaculate Conception, that supreme and unique grace given to the Virgin Mary. Here Scotus brilliantly outdistances Aquinas, yet in such a way as to crown Aquinas's own achievements with respect to uniqueness. Hopkins himself is similarly upheld in von Balthasar's aesthetic epic through a placement in a broadly Thomist dialogue with being. The new context that von Balthasar gives to Hopkins highlights what the poet himself was after: a deeply sacramental account of beauty and particularity. The Scotist Hopkins in this way is allowed to bring Thomas to a sort of completion in a manner similar to Scotus and the Immaculate Conception. That is, Hopkins brings the metaphysics of Thomas Aquinas fully into the realm of language; inscape and instress crown Thomas's sacramental theory with sacramental language. Hopkins in this way brings Thomas's theoretical metaphysic to brilliant new life in his poetry.

We have given this "new life" an account in its metaphysical underpinnings, but the reintegration of Hopkins's poetry that von Balthasar accomplishes would not be complete without turning as well to Hopkins's theory of language.

Word and Sacrament

Hopkins's theory of inscape and instress is at once metaphysical and linguistic. Metaphysically speaking, it operates under the presupposition that all things ontically possess sympathy for one another: things are expressive and responsive to expression. This places Hopkins thoroughly within the Romantic tradition of his era, and in that fashion makes him a precursor of linguistic theories like Heidegger's. For Hopkins, the theory is more visceral than for one such as Heidegger: in the mind of Hopkins, even the *sounds* of words reflect something of the inscape they attempt to express. "The act of utterance," Hopkins scholar James Wimsatt tells us, "animates the sounds, and its stress flushes and foredraws, fills and defines the rich iconic significance, manifesting its metaphysical reality."[65] So poetry, with its speech- and sound-repetitions, imitates the patterning of natural utterances and in so doing helps the reader to contemplate the inscape a poem attempts to express.

If we look back to "Wreck of the Deutschland," we can see Hopkins working hard to aurally signify to us the crisis of the foundering ship:

Hope had grown grey hairs,
Hope had mourning on,
Trenched with tears, carved with cares,
Hope was twelve hours gone;
And frightful a nightfall folded rueful a day
Nor rescue, only rocket and lightship, shone,
And lives at last were washing away:
To the shrouds they took, —they shook in the hurling and horrible
    airs.[66]

Reading the stanza out loud makes the repetitions more obvious: the alliterations (*grown grey*, *trenched with tears*, *carved with cares*), the phrase-imitations (hope had . . . hope had . . . hope was . . .), rhyme patterns (fright*ful* . . . night*fall* . . . rue*ful* . . .), and so forth. The effect is a rushing musicality, a soundscape of lyrical desperation. Hopkins's aural patterns are not meant to obscure the panic of the hour, but to make it clearer, more felt.

What scholars perhaps underestimate about Hopkins's poetic technique here is its theological shape. In the sacramentality of inscape resides a confidence that physicality expresses meaning, much as in the sacraments physical symbols can impart grace. This is a quality of Hopkins's poetry that von Balthasar highlights. As von Balthasar also notes, Hopkins's optimistic interest in linguistic sensuality may yet be a pantheism masked in Catholic sacramental language of grace and sign—if this optimism did not increasingly concentrate itself into cruciform self-offering.

> With a mercy that outrides
> The all of water, an ark
> For the listener; for the lingerer with a love glides
> Lower than death and the dark;
> A vein for the visiting of the past-prayer, pent in prison,
> The-last-breath penitent spirits—the uttermost mark
> Our passion-plungèd giant risen,
> The Christ of the Father compassionate, fetched in the storm of his
>   strides.[67]

Christ comes to the sinking ship in mercy—walking across the water, an "ark" that "glides/ Lower than death and the dark," "passion-plungèd"—not in order to halt the descent, but to be with and in it, to be its inner form. This shipwreck represents, for Hopkins, how the wreck of words, of meaning, of event, is redeemed. This is how Christ is "easter in us, be a dayspring to the dimness of us, be a crimson-cresseted east."[68] Mercy is cruciform: which is to say that we do not avoid the cross but cling to it and only so clinging (like the nuns on the failing ship) do we rise to Easter.

In order for Hopkins's sacramental theory of language to hold water, it is necessary to reconsider its ground. We have observed above how his emphasis on uniqueness is better served by a Thomist metaphysic than the Scotist metaphysic he adored. Here his theory of language arrives at a similar crossroad: if meaning and expression, inscape and instress, are too closely identified with one another, then Hopkins's falls into the linguistic trap discussed in chapter 4. Language is not only sacramental—able to physically express the "grace" of meaning—but is in fact hyper-sacrament: so wholly identified with what it expresses as to constitute it totally. There would be no room for analogy, nor indeed mystery, because truth would be exhaustively brought to the surface as raw fact (extending beyond even the Catholic sacraments, which still bear mystery).

What threatens to occur here is an over-application of the Scotist univocity of being in a linguistic mode: just as Scotus can only differentiate between beings by intensity of being, words and meaning are constituted according to their intensity of expression. Speech becomes hyper-critical at this point because it has but one horizon of evaluation, rather than a hierarchical, analogical one. Words threaten to become exchangeable, much as the individual threatens to become fungible, and unique expressions of meaning fade into comparisons infinitely bifurcated and evaluated unto meaninglessness. I may use this word or that, but it cannot in the end matter, because my words may be endlessly substituted with the same mute intensity. Words and images are no longer governed—neither Christologically nor metaphysically—and so their flexible precision is lost. The contours of a theo-poetic fail.

What von Balthasar prefers, when he reenvisions Heidegger through Thomas, is a constitutive theory of language that nevertheless recognizes the difference between expression and expressed—a difference that Thomas supports metaphysically through the analogy of being. This is the theory that upholds Hopkins's sacramental desires, and thus makes the sacramentality of his poetry more obvious in its new context in *Herrlichkeit*. Words are not exchangeable because words contribute to and constitute truth; words are *also* not exchangeable because the truth governs them, because words and truth are not (necessarily) identical. Both statements must be affirmed, or else linguistic sacramentality is rendered either pantheistic or deistic. We might say that, in von Balthasar's

Hopkins, Thomas Aquinas's sacramental metaphysic reaches its most beautiful linguistic dimensions.

We must remember that the world is already worded. God has worded it. This is what happens in Genesis: God speaks, and the world comes into being. And when the Word takes flesh, he takes the worded world upon himself—and speaks it anew, speaks it renewed, speaks it through the dark of the cross and the light of Easter. The life of the Church partakes in the speech of the Word Incarnate: whether in the sacraments or in the words of Scripture. The life of the Church, even more than poetry, is shaped by the Word of God. When we speak in theology, when we speak with our lives, the whole determined drive is to show how we have already been spoken by and spoken for in Christ. The great surrender of Hopkins's shipwreck poems, the careful emphasis on the cross in von Balthasar's theology, these are attempts to allow God to speak through and in us. We and the world have an instress and an inscape that bends us toward Christ, because we have been spoken into existence through him and because he redeems us. Created and redeemed: this makes us "double-worded" in Christ.

What Hopkins loves about the wildness of the world and its beautiful uniqueness becomes a way of admiring the wildness and uniqueness of God himself. This is only possible for him by uniting his love to the cross, which makes him willing to surrender everything into God's hands. Though at first this seems almost like a threat—since surrender means one no longer possesses something—it turns into the redemption of beauty, because God gives us everything back again, and more beautifully. Von Balthasar admires Hopkins for this reason: because he was the rare poet willing to give away everything, even beauty, and this rare willingness allowed him to achieve what few poets ever have. Hopkins writes with a truly Christic passion.

The opening section of this chapter did much to review the way this book began: with *terror*, and the dangers of a beauty wrongly conceived. Von Balthasar sees much to fear in an aesthetics absolutized for the sake of a redemption interior to the world and perceives such an attempt in much of the modern philosophy and art of his time. The poetic figure of

Rilke, perhaps more than any other figure, stands before von Balthasar as the alluring embodiment of a redemption without Christ. Rilke's poetry is at once enticing and repelling, and von Balthasar converses with the poet throughout his long academic career.

Theology *does* need beauty, and von Balthasar's insistence on this point has him constantly wrestling with the caesura between God and the world that he himself will not relent in affirming. From his youthful interaction with Przywara forward, he reaches for *analogy* as the ladder by which he might climb from beauty to glory. Yet analogy is no ladder at all, as if one of its poles might be forsaken for some higher one, and mere analogy is itself insufficient. God himself, Beauty himself, must enter into the world first if worldly beauty is to be embraced in the light of glory. Which is to say that grace illuminates natural beauty—not for the sake of rendering it unnatural, but to bring it to its fullness. For von Balthasar, especially as his theological work progresses, there persists a more and more radical consideration of the primacy of grace and its relationship to beauty. Here von Balthasar will sound the most like Karl Barth and yet in the same breath will sound the most Catholic: for beauty, earthly beauty, really can unveil the glory of God. Not by a simple divine *fiat*, as von Balthasar at times fears from Barth, but because earthly beauty already resembles the Creator who speaks through it.

In this rather complex way, von Balthasar refutes the modern impulse to collapse earthly and divine beauty. He anchors his refutation in an affirmation of God's transcendence and of a broadly Thomist analogy of being, and the coincidence of both is to be found in the Incarnation. The redemption of beauty is to be found in Christ, and moreover in a visceral renunciation and death that leads to Easter. Beauty must, in other words, acknowledge its evanescence and pass through the harrows of death so that it may last. Rilke can only ever acknowledge beauty's lasting death, and while von Balthasar embraces the poet's agonizing insight, he surpasses Rilke by acknowledging beauty's persisting life through the cross.

Von Balthasar responds to Rilke not with mere condemnation, but with artists like Hopkins. This poet, in a unique way, contributes to a vision of beauty beyond Rilke's tragic resplendence. In this chapter, we saw how Hopkins's fascination with the irreducible and unique takes up many notes similar to Rilke's poetry, yet with a radically different outcome. Rilke's "tree," the tree that "grows" in our ears, becomes for Hopkins the wild of nature that speaks everywhere and uniquely of the one Christ. For both poets, God is perceived somehow in every inch of the world. Yet for Rilke, this perception is the torn God scattered across the earth in a kind of partial pantheism; for Hopkins, there can never be such a scattering or else Christ's uniqueness has been compromised. Instead, Christ is wholly present in every uniqueness.

We also saw how Hopkins's almost visceral attachment to sensual images reinforces his interest in the unique. Here we find a marriage between human words and the divine Word, and Hopkins in a peculiar way directs his poetry according to what he finds there in the sympathetic stress in both. Through the inscape of Christ, which is the inscape of the world, Hopkins is able to wrestle with the uniqueness of individual existence, yet without the failure of hope. He instead turns to the surrender of his shipwreck poems and in this way passes through the depths of sorrow without remaining caught in the impasse of its darkness. Rilke can barely hope save in death; Hopkins hopes in the Christ's great sacrifice. It is not a surrender to death merely, as one finds in Rilke, but a surrender to God.

Von Balthasar's interest in what is personal and unique, itself deeply modern, renders his interest in beauty irreducibly modern even as he works to resuscitate the past. Mere beauty alone is unhelpful to the Church, as von Balthasar perceives quite early in his *Apokalypse*. It is no more helpful than philosophy alone. The modern desire for philosophic self-sufficiency is at every turn thwarted in von Balthasar's theology. Yet Christ gathers all things to himself, including beauty, and in this way beauty receives a permanent place in theology and the Church. What is unique, particular, and sensible indeed has a vital role to play in theology, not despite modern insights but due to them. This helps to place modern interests in continuity with the past. For von Balthasar, such continuity is only possible because Beauty himself redeems earthly beauty by taking flesh, dying, and rising—and he does so for the sake of leading us to himself.

Conclusion

This work set out to discover the intersection between Christology, metaphysics, and language in the thought of Hans Urs von Balthasar, an intersection that constitutes the major shape of his oeuvre, that is, a rhetorical and theological disposition that we can summarize with the term "theological poetic." What surfaced was von Balthasar's profound concern for authentic transcendence, which for him is founded in authentic metaphysics. Without being able to imagine or explain a disproportionate, dependent relationship with a God who is infinitely unique and distinct from creation, modern thought descends into terrible despair. In figures like Heidegger and Rilke, finitude is lifted to equal status with infinity and death is rendered a permanent arbiter of life. Both men, the philosopher and the poet, counsel us to surrender (*Hingabe*): this will ease our pain over death and limitation. Von Balthasar asks us at what cost this surrender is accomplished. Does it not contort our desire for life into a consigned despair? So modern art and philosophy threaten to collapse inward, folding into a transcendence that is pure immanence. Beauty itself lives by dying.

In response, von Balthasar offers his theological aesthetic, which resuscitates medieval metaphysics in the face of Christ's form and which redeems modern interests through classical ideas. Here the singular, irreplaceable person is exalted alongside being itself because both individuality and being qua being are rooted in Trinitarian love and participate in it. Dante appears on the stage to show us the way, and his love for Beatrice lays to bare the dark and hidden dimensions of Rilke's despair. In Beatrice, we see that earthly beauty lives not in itself, but in the glory of the Triune God. Dante then makes way for an improved and renewed understanding of the analogy of being, which von Balthasar makes the hinge of his own metaphysical speculations and through which he brings Heidegger into contact with the metaphysics he had rejected. Being, according to von Balthasar, is expressive. This is Heideggerian, but it is a Heidegger transfigured by the force and splendor of Thomas Aquinas.

Christ stands at the center of von Balthasar's transfigurative work. In Christ, the *analogia entis* is lifted into the *analogia personalitatis*, and created being itself is employed as a language to express the inner mysteries of God's infinite life. Through this Christological language, which consists in every aspect of being and of human language, we come to better understand how poetic ways of speaking are able to serve a vital role in theological reflection. If we ignore the interplay of thought and figure, we ignore a fundamental quality of being and of language. Yet all must be ordered by Christ and rooted in metaphysics so that even giants in the Christian literary tradition like Dante and Hopkins receive critique and re-figuration.

We have spent our time exploring the theoretical foundations for von Balthasar's unique use of language and understanding how such a use of language might continue forward in theology. These foundations serve as both a summary of von Balthasar's major critical insights, as well as a place to begin making use of those insights beyond his own work. That is, von Balthasar uses artists and artistic ways of speaking because it fills out theological reflection to greater depth and dimension, and yet we can only make sense of these efforts if we have in mind both Christology and metaphysics. Violating either of these, especially Christological governance, renders a theological poetic at best flawed, at worst in serious error. Von Balthasar's imaginative logic receives explanation through these commitments, while at the same time providing theologians the necessary opportunity to move into concerns of their own. The thesis of this book is not meant to rest always and only with Hans Urs von Balthasar.

The book began by stating that *Hans Urs von Balthasar uses poets and poetic language to make theological arguments, because this poetic way of speaking expresses metaphysical truth without reducing one to the other.* I defended this thesis by showing the way von Balthasar takes the metaphysical presuppositions of his poets seriously, from his early days with Rilke to the Hopkins of the trilogy. Poets ask questions about the way the world is and the way it might be, and von Balthasar takes these questions to heart. I also showed how von Balthasar responds to artists with other artists, highlighting Dante and Hopkins against Rilke's despair. Von Balthasar's responsiveness stretches still deeper, and he appropriates a metaphysic comingled with ideas from Thomas Aquinas, Maximus the Confessor, Karl Barth, and Martin Heidegger among others in order to show how the vitality of art is enriched by a metaphysical vitality. Language itself is enriched, especially as its Christological contours become apparent: in Christ, God uses every quality of created being in order to express divine being, which makes language expressive of divine being as well. It is in the expressiveness of Christ that we find the key to von Balthasar's theo-poetic. He makes the poetic use of language not only possible or appropriate in theology, but also necessary. It is necessary because it allows language, including theological language, to resemble and express a transcendental of being: beauty, along with goodness and truth. Theology as a discipline lacks inasmuch as it does not permit itself this mode of discourse, which is not a mode to be used instead of or against other forms of discourse such as metaphysics. That would be a contradiction. Yet poetic language is *not* necessary in the sense that it is always to be employed. Necessity is not the same as a universal, univocal mandate.

The theological poetic of Hans Urs von Balthasar, as now forwarded, allows us to accomplish two basic and necessary tasks in the future: evaluating von Balthasar's theo-poetic and attempting to expand into new realms of theological-poetic reflection. In each of these two tasks, dozens of avenues open. For now, what must be said of these avenues is as follows: a theo-poetic ought not serve as the sole style of theological speculation because it was never meant to serve as such. Necessary though this language is to theology, its necessity does not permit it to dominate discourse as the sole mode of explanation. So, too, metaphysical rigor ought to be maintained in theological efforts, but this does not make explicit metaphysical discussion necessary in every work of theology. Nor indeed should we collapse art and theology into identical fields, a distinction that von Balthasar was eager to maintain for all his efforts toward mining the theological import of poems and other works of art.

There is a way in which artists should still be allowed to be artists, and theologians to be theologians. Their desires meet at the crossways of authentic transcendence, before the God who redeems all that is and all that we desire. Theologian-poets are possible, indeed welcome, but exceptions should not become the rule for all.

The great optimism we should have is that language indeed expresses reality, and indeed may be employed to express divine reality. It is this confidence that the poems at the opening of each chapter wrestle with, threatening to descend into despair at first and yet rising to greater hope. The poems speak with the texts in which they have been placed, and they speak with one another. That is what poems do: they *resonate* their meaning, and their expression is to be found between the lines and stanzas, and between each other. So if the first poem wonders aloud whether there is anything but demise, and whether love can ever do anything but "touch," "taste," and "caress" the "waking death that lives within," the final poem answers with the shape of Dante's love. Unable to resolve whether he loves the living Beatrice or the heavenly Beatrice, the things of the earth or the things of God, Dante closes with "I love you." It is an ambiguous phrase, since in English the singular and plural of the second person is identical. Yet this ambiguity allows for a precision, inasmuch as the statement is then able to stretch itself across both earth and heaven and claim love for each. So, too, are we able to do so at the end of this book: though at first beauty always seems under threat of death, so we may love it so long as we adore the divine glory that is its inner form.

A l'alta fantasia qui mancò possa;
ma già volgeva il mio disio e 'l velle,
sì come rota ch'igualmente è mossa,

l'amor che move il sole e l'altre stelle.

—Dante Alighieri, *Paradiso*, Canto XXXIII, 142–45

NOTES

Introduction

1. Scholarship on theology and art—whether it be music, poetry, literature, etc.—has flourished. See, for example, Cecilia González-Andrieu, *Bridge to Wonder: Art as a Gospel of Beauty* (Waco, TX: Baylor University Press, 2012); David C. Mahan, *An Unexpected Light: Theology and Witness in the Poetry and Thought of Charles Williams, Micheal O'Siadhail, and Geoffrey Hill* (Eugene, OR: Pickwick Publications, 2009); *Dante's Commedia: Theology as Poetry*, ed. Vittorio Montemaggi and Matthew Treherne (Notre Dame, IN: Notre Dame University Press, 2010); Jeremy Bergbie, *Theology, Music, and Time* (Cambridge: Cambridge University Press, 2000); Malcom Guite, *Faith, Hope and Poetry* (Farnham, Surrey: Ashgate, 2010); Thomas J. Norris, *A Fractured Relationship: Faith and the Crisis of Culture* (New York: New City Press, 2010).

2. For this alternate use of the phrase, see L. B. C. Keef-Perry, "Theopoetics: Process and Perspective," *Christianity and Literature* 58, no. 4 (2009): 579–601; David Miller, "Theopoetry or Theopoetics?" *Cross Currents* 60, no. 1 (2010): 6–23. Another book uses the term theopoetic from a "Balthasarian" perspective, also without apparent lineage in this other movement. See Richard Viladesau, *Theological Aesthetics: God in Imagination, Beauty, and Art* (New York: Oxford University Press, 1999).

ONE. Beauty and Risk

1. Rainer Maria Rilke, *Duino Elegies (Bilingual Edition)*, trans. Edward Snow (New York: North Point, 2000), 4–5. For the sake of consistency, I will always cite from this edition of Rilke's elegies; translations are mine unless otherwise noted.

2. The original dissertation was published under the title *Geschichte des eschatologischen Problems in der modern detuschen Literatur* (Zurich, 1930); it was republished as *Die Apokalypse der detuschen Seele*, 3 vols. (Salzburg, 1937–39); the first volume was republished as *Prometheus: Studien zur Geschichte des deutschen Idealismus* (Heidelberg: F.H. Kerle, 1947). The edition used here is the version published after von Balthasar's death: *Apokalypse der detuschen Seele: Studien zu einer Lehre von lezten Haltungen*, 3 vols. (Einsiedeln, Freiburg: Johannes Verlag, 1998). According to Peter Henrici, there was to be a fourth volume, a theological volume, which was never written. See "The Philosophy of Hans Urs von Balthasar," in *Hans Urs von Balthasar: His Life and Work*, ed. David L. Schindler (San Francisco: Ignatius Press, 1991), 149.

3. See the opening paragraph of the introduction to Balthasar, *GL* I, 17.

4. I am not, in other words, claiming exclusive rights to the singular or most appropriate interpretation of the massive work. It appears in any case designed for multiple interpretations depending on the questions asked of it.

5. The major current work on von Balthasar and Hegel is Cyril O'Regan's *Anatomy of Misremembering*, which he plans to follow with a book on von Balthasar and Heidegger. See Cyril O'Regan, *The Anatomy of Misremembering: Von Balthasar's Response to Philosophical Modernity, Volume 1: Hegel* (New York: Herder & Herder, 2014).

6. With respect to the *affirmation* of transcendence, much of von Balthasar's praise is directed toward the union of the world and of salvation from the perspective of medieval thought. Here, eschatology is viewed according to a "fullness" that includes both creation and redemption. See especially *Apokalypse I*, 21–22. The fullness of the medieval point of view falls apart with the advent of the Reformation: see pp. 27–31.

7. Cf. Friedrich Nietzsche, *Die Geburt der Tragödie: Der Griechische Staat*; or an English translation: *The Birth of Tragedy*, trans. Douglas Smith (Oxford: Oxford University Press, 2000). For a discussion of von Balthasar's tendency to adopt and transform these sorts of loaded terms, see Cyril O'Regan, "Balthasar: Between Tübingen and Postmodernity," in *Modern Theology* 14, no. 3 (1998): 325–53.

Von Balthasar will also call these *principles* "worlds": the *Prometheuswelt* and the *Dionysoswelt* (inconsistently, he will apply a hyphen to the word: *Prometheus-welt*, etc.).

8. Balthasar, *Apokalypse* II, 5. [Prometheus-Prinzip war jene Letzthaltung des Menschen gewesen, die sich als der glorreiche und zugleich tötende Mittelpunkt zwischen Gott und Welt verstand: als Vermittlung zwischen Gott-Alles zu Welt-Nichts und von Welt-Alles zu Gott-Nichts und in diesem doppelten δια als Ruhm und Schmerz der Dialektik.]

9. Balthasar, *Apokalypse* II, 5.

10. Balthasar, *Apokalypse* I, 8.

11. Balthasar, *Apokalypse* II, 12.

12. Cf. Balthasar, *Apokalypse* II, 15.

13. Peter Henrici describes that "method" as follows: "The individual figures (*Gestalt*) are not significant in themselves; what he sees and draws is, rather, a historical movement which is a meaningful form (*Sinngestalt*) above all in its goal, its peripheries, and errors, and above all in the decisions it includes.... Many of the figures he draws are anti-figures (*Gegen-Gestalten*) and von Balthasar's thought defines itself in opposition to them." in "The Philosophy of Hans Urs von Balthasar," 155.

This is an apt summary for von Balthasar's entire "method" throughout his life, and its contours will receive more definition as the dissertation proceeds.

14. Balthasar, *Apokalypse* I, 4.

15. See Nichols' discussion of this in *Scattering the Seed*, 234.

16. All of this he repeats rather complexly in *Apokalypse* I, 21–24. I have done my best to unravel the threads.

17. Nichols, *Scattering the Seed*, 56.

18. Kevin Mongrain situates von Balthasar's other texts along similar lines, and emphasizes the Christological charges that drive von Balthasar's critique of modernity: "Von Balthasar argues that modern intellectuals have been tempted by, and in many cases have succumbed to, rationalist Prometheanism because they have turned away from the aesthetic form of Christ bequeathed to them by ancient and medieval Christianity." See Kevin Mongrain, "Poetics and Doxology," in *Pro Ecclesia* 16, no. 4 (2007), 392.

19. Alois M. Haas councils that there is a Jesuit link here—that the overarching concern with one's "final attitude" must be understood as Jesuit. See "Hans Urs von Balthasar's 'Apocalypse of the German Soul': At the Intersection of German Literature, Philosophy, and Theology," in *Hans Urs von Balthasar: His Life and Work*, 51. Haas also warns, as far as "soul" is concerned, that "one must take note of von Balthasar's emphasis that what is called 'spirit' by the school of intellectual history is to be understood in the direction of a '*concrete* spirit'" (52, cf. 55). In other words, it is not an insight into something unseen, but a concrete attitude displayed in the writing of a particular individual.

20. Karl Barth did write about Anselm, a translation of which is available in *Anselm: Fides Quaerens Intellectum: Anselm's Proof of the Existence of God in the Context of His Theological Scheme*, trans. Ian W. Robertson (Richmond, VA: John Knox Press, 1960). The irony, in Catholic minds, would be Barth's

stubborn rejection of the *analogia entis* and yet exemplifying its perspective in his theology. Von Balthasar argues as much in his *Theology of Karl Barth*.

21. Cited in Balthasar, *Apokalypse* I, 3. Occurs in Rilke, "Erste Elegie," 6. Translation mine.

22. Balthasar, *Apokalypse* I, 26.

23. Balthasar, *Apokalypse* I, 24.

24. Balthasar, *Apokalypse* II, 175. [Die radikale Endlichkeit der Welt ist dann gar nicht wie eine letzte Grenze, an die das Leben zuletzt stößt und an der es sich resignieren muß, sondern sie ist von Anfang an, wenn auch in wachsendem Maße, die innere Begrenztheit des unendlichen Dranges selbst, der inwendige, unaufhebbar Widerspruch zwischen "Grund" und "Form."]

25. Cited in Balthasar, *Apokalypse* II, 175. This one is harder to find in collections of Rilke's work, of which no definitive edition exists. Its title is "Ich lebe mein Leben in wachsenden Ringen." It can also be found in *Selected Poems of Rainer Maria Rilke*, ed. Robert Bly (New York: Harper and Row, 1981), 12. Translation mine.

26. Balthasar, *Apokalypse* II, 117.

27. Hans Urs von Balthasar, *Die Entwicklung der musikalischen Idee: Versuch einer Synthese der Musik* (Braunschweig, 1925). Cf. Aidan Nichols's review of the book in *Scattering the Seed: A Guide Through Balthasar's Early Writings on Philosophy and the Arts* (New York: T & T Clark, 2006), 1–8; and Stefan Klöckner, "Hans Urs von Balthasar und die Musik" in *Letzte Haltungen: Hans Urs von Balthasar's "Apokalypse der detuschen Seele"—neu gelesen*, ed. Barbara Hallensleben, Guido Vergauwen (Fribourg: Academic Press, 2006): 291–304.

28. Balthasar, *Entwicklung die musikalischen Idee*, 7. Here music is the most unfathomable (*unfaßbarste*) because of its immediacy, possessing a nearness (*Nähe*) that also bears within itself an eternal puzzle (*ewigen Rätsel*).

29. Balthasar, *Entwicklung die musikalischen Idee*, 8. The young von Balthasar toys with the meaning of "word" in this passage, playing with its range of meanings. Music is a kind of "word," distinguishable from spoken words, yet sharing similar qualities to a spoken word: "Word and sound stand close to each other, because they are both expression-tools, objective ground material of like meanings." [Wort und Ton stehen sich nahe, denn sie sind beide Ausdrucks-Werkzeuge, Objektivierungsmittel des gleichen Sinnes.]

30. Nichols, *Scattering the Seed*, 1.

31. Balthasar, *Die Entwicklung der musikalischen Idee*, 11. [Welches ist dieses Maximum, diese Vollendung des Sinnes? Es ist die *größt*mögliche Objektivation des Metaphysischen, des Göttlichen, den nichts anderes als das göttliche Urlicht selbst ist jener Sinn, jene Idee, von der oben gesprochen wurde. Es steht im Mittelpunkt des Kreises, von dem die Einzelkünste strahlenhaft ausgehen,

und so wird das Göttliche selbst durch die Strahlen fortgerissen in Zeit und Raum hinein und dort in der immer vollendeter sich entwickelnden Form zu immer hellerem Aufleuchten gebracht.]

32. Balthasar, *Die Entwicklung der musikalischen Idee*, 12.

33. Balthasar, *Die Entwicklung der musikalischen Idee*, 56–57, esp. 57: *"die Kunst ist in sich selbst tragisch."*

34. See "Chapter 4: Central Images 2: Fulfillment and the Circle," in Karen Kilby, *Balthasar: A (Very) Critical Introduction* (Grand Rapids, MI: William B. Eerdmans Publishing, 2012), 71–93.

35. See Balthasar, *Die Entwicklung die musikalischen Idee*, 9–13, 39.

36. Cf. Balthasar, *Die Entwicklung die musikalischen Idee*, 42.

37. Kilby, *Balthasar: A (Very) Critical Introduction*, 91.

38. For the most explicit early discussion of art and metaphysics, see Balthasar, *Die Entwicklung die musikalischen Idee*, 13. He characterizes art as arousing "an inexplicable experience of the metaphysical" (*unerklärlichen Erlebnis des Metaphysischen*). The idea of the metaphysical is rather vaguely formed in von Balthasar's book. It forms the ground of his thought, a contact-point for his discussion of music's relationship to reality, but he does not define it. This very early work is, in Aidan Nichols's words, "the work of a brilliant mind that has not yet reached intellectual integration," *Scattering the Seed*, 8. The trilogy, written by a much older von Balthasar, takes up these same concerns.

39. Balthasar, *Die Entwicklung die musikalischen Idee*, 42–43. Music is a "more beautiful expression of truth" (*ein schöner Ausdruck der Wahrheit*).

40. Hans Urs von Balthasar, "Kunst und Religion," *Volkswohl* 18 (1927): 354–65; "Katholische Religion und Kunst," *Schweizeriche Rundschau* 27 (1927): 44–54.

41. Balthasar, "Kunst und Religion," 361: *"ein verabsolutierter Ästhetizismus das Wesen der Religion nie erfassen kann."*

42. Balthasar, "Kunst und Religion," 364–65.

43. Balthasar, "Katholische Religion und Kunst," 44.

44. See especially Søren Kierkegaard, *The Point of View*, ed. Howard V. Hong and Edna H. Hong (Princeton, NJ: Princeton University Press, 1998). George Pattinson summarizes Kierkegaard's opposition between aesthetics and religion in "Art in an Age of Reflection," in *The Cambridge Companion to Kierkegaard*, ed. Alastair Hannay and Gordon D. Marino (Cambridge: Cambridge University Press, 1998): 76–100.

45. Balthasar, "Katholische Religion und Kunst," 45.

46. Balthasar, "Katholische Religion und Kunst," 52–54.

47. Balthasar, "Katholische Religion und Kunst," 54.

48. On these ideas and their out-working on the cross in the trilogy, see especially David Luy, "Aesthetic Collision: Hans Urs von Balthasar on the Trinity and the Cross," in *International Journal of Systematic Theology* 13, no. 2 (2011): 154–59. See also Graham Ward, "Kenosis: Death, Discourse and Resurrection" in *Balthasar at the End of Modernity*, ed. Lucy Gardner, David Moss, Ben Quash (Edinburgh: T & T Clark, 1999), 15–68.

49. Balthasar, "Katholische Religion und Kunst," 48.

50. Balthasar, "Katholische Religion und Kunst," 51.

51. Hans Urs von Balthasar, "Die Kunst in der Zeit," *Schweizeriche Rundschau* 40 (1940): 239–46; "Antikritik," *Schweizeriche Rundschau* 40 (1940): 453–60.

Paul Silas Peterson argues that these two articles in particular reveal von Balthasar's anti-Semitism. I do not have the space to address these complex claims here, but for Peterson's central argument, see, "Anti-Modernism and Anti-Semitism in Hans Urs von Balthasar," in *Neue Zeitschrift für systematische Theologie und Religionsphilosophie* 52, no. 3 (2010): 314–15; see also his conclusion, 317–18.

52. Balthasar, "Die Kunst in der Zeit," 239.

53. A visual review of these styles can be found in Gabriele Crepaldi, *Modern Art 1900–45: The Age of Avant-Gardes*, trans. Jay Hyams (New York: HarperCollins, 2007).

54. He characterizes this age as the "cynical audacity of pure nihilism" (*zynische Keckheit des reinen Nihilismus*). Balthasar, "Die Kunst in der Zeit," 245.

55. Balthasar, "Die Kunst in der Zeit," 240. This echoes von Balthasar's evaluation of isolated, traditionless individualism in *Apokalypse*, an evaluation that Kevin Mongrain summarizes as, "a critique of modern intellectual life and culture for a twofold forgetfulness: forgetting that the God of the Old Testament is also the God of New Testament; and forgetting Christianity's assimilation and preservation of classical piety. As a consequence of this twofold forgetfulness, modern intellectual life and culture have drifted toward Promethean anthropocentrism in which an 'infinite I' replaces God and, concomitantly, humanity's self-guided spiritual evolution replaces providence." See Kevin Mongrain, "Poetics and Doxology," 387.

56. Balthasar, "Die Kunst in der Zeit," 240.

57. Balthasar, "Die Kunst in der Zeit," 240: "*die immer noch steigende Vergötterung des schaffenden Künstlers selbst.*"

58. Balthasar, "Die Kunst in der Zeit," 241.

59. Balthasar, "Die Kunst in der Zeit," 245.

60. "Balthasar, "Die Kunst in der Zeit," 246. [Heimatschutz genügt nicht. Genügen kann nur die neue lebendige Verbindung mit der ganzen Geschichte.

Diese wäre das Gegenteil von Historismus. Wer heute noch einmal romanisch, gotisch, barock bauen wollte, würde nur den Geist dieser Stile verleugnen, der ein Geist der Lebendigkeit, der Erfindung und des Vorwärtsschauens war.]

61. Balthasar, "Antikritik," 455. [Diese fatale Situation aber, die heute vielleicht auf ihrem Höhepunkt steht und eine weltgeschichtliche, nicht nur den Einzelnen, sondern auch die Länder und Nationen übergreifende ist, diese Situation, für die kein Einzelner etwas "kann", ist, wie ich zu zeigen versuchte, schon seit langem vorbereitet durch die wachsende Auseinanderentwicklung von Einzelnem und Masse.]

62. Balthasar, "Antikritik," 457. Interestingly, Karl Barth is exempt from the charge, which echoes some of the positions taken up in *Apokalypse*.

63. Balthasar, "Antikritik," 457. [Ich glaube nicht, daß diese etwas düsteren Sätze sich mit Defaitismus verwechseln lassen. Es handelt sich nicht darum, die Flinte ins Korn zu werfen. Aber auch ebenso wenig darum, einen leichtfertigen Optimismus, der über die Tragik der Lage hinwegtänzelt, zu verbreiten, vielleicht gar im Namen des Christentums. Sondern zunächst einfach sehen zu lernen, was ist. Dies scheint mir noch immer der erste Schritt zu Überwindung der Krise.]

64. Balthasar, "Antikritik," 460. [Ohnmächtigwerden jenes allmächtigen Geistes selbst, der in dieser Ohnmacht und Vergeblichkeit die Welt erlöste und die Macht vergeistigte: "Wenn ich schwach bin, dann bin ich stark."]

65. Balthasar, "Antikritik," footnote on 458. [einzig aus der höchsten Kraft schöpferischer Persönlichkeiten, ihrem souveränen Berherrschen des ganzen Gewesenen und ihrer feinsten Spürsamkeit für das heute Notwendige wird sich unsere Kunst, auch und gerade unsere kirchliche Kunst, regenieren.]

Von Balthasar does not use the term "whole individual," and I use it here as an attempt to describe several ideas in one phrase. That is, an individual who still has a history (a full history), who is still linked to a community, and who is viewed in terms of God and not merely in terms of the self.

66. Yves Congar, *The Meaning of Tradition*, trans. A. N. Woodrow (New York: Hawthorn Books, 1964); John Henry Newman, *An Essay in Aid of a Grammar of Assent* (Notre Dame, IN: University of Notre Dame Press, 1979). Cf. Aidan Nichols, "Littlemore from Lucerne: Newman's Essay on Development in Balthasarian Perspective," in *Newman and Conversion*, ed. Ian Ker (Edinburgh: T & T Clark, 1997), 100–116.

67. Peter Henrici, "A Sketch of von Balthasar's Life," in *Von Balthasar: His Life and Work*, 14.

68. Henrici, "A Sketch of von Balthasar's Life," 12. Let us also not forget von Balthasar's extensive conversation with philosophers and theologians, most of whom he developed relationships with at this period of time or shortly

afterward. An extensive study on these "Philosophenfreunde" can be found in Manfred Lochbrunner, *Hans Urs von Balthasar und seine Philosophenfreunde: Fünf Doppleportraits* (Würzburg: Echter, 2005).

69. Henrici, "A Sketch of von Balthasar's Life," 31.

70. See Alois M. Haas, "Hans Urs von Balthasar's 'Apocalypse of the German Soul,'" 51. Haas is "convinced that the hour has not yet come to assess its [*Apokalypse's*] true importance in both method and content" (55).

Contemporary reception can be found in *Letzte Haltungen: Hans Urs von Balthasars "Apokalypse der detuschen Seele"—neu gelesen*, ed. Barbara Hallensleben and Guido Vergauwen (Fribourg: Academic Press, 2006). It is often equally as negative as von Balthasar's contemporaries were.

71. There has been some consternation in German literature over the historical context and value of von Balthasar's dissertation: it was published in the 1930s (the height of National Socialism, just before the Second World War), and it references the dreaded concept of a "German soul" (which runs all too close to the popular Nazi phraseology describing the triumphant "German spirit" [*Geist*]). Most scholars, when bringing forward the issue, ascribe it to a willful or dangerous naiveté on von Balthasar's part. Cf. Peter Köster, "Letzte Haltungen? Hans Urs von Balthasars, 'Apokalypse der deutschen Seele'—nach über 60 Jahren wieder erschienen," *ZeitSchrift* 49, no. 3 (2000): 184–90; Sabine Haupt, "Vom Geist zur Seele: Hans Urs von Balthasars theologisierte Geistesgeschichte im Kontext der zeitgenössischen Germanistik und am Beispiel seiner Novalis-Auslegung," in *Letzte Haltungen*, 40–62, esp. 61–62; Stefan Bodo Würffel, "Endzeit-Philologie: Hans Urs von Balthasars germanistische Anfänge," in *Letzte Haltungen*, 63–82, esp. 77.

72. Aidan Nichols, *Scattering the Seed: A Guide through Balthasar's Early Writings on Philosophy and the Arts*; Alois M. Haas, "Zum Geliet," in *Apokalypse der deutschen Seele: Studien zu einer Lehre von letzten Haltungen Band I: Der deutsche Idealismus* (Einsiedeln: Johannes, 1998), 25–48; *Letzte Haltungen: Hans Urs von Balthasars "Apokalypse der detuschen Seele"—neu gelesen*.

73. Others have explored these two figures together, with varying conclusions. See Jenny Y. Hammett, "Thinker and Poet: Heidegger, Rilke, and Death," *Soundings* 60, no. 2 (1977): 166–78; Walter Biemel, "The Finitude of Human Being," in *Being Human in the Ultimate*, trans. Liliane Welch and Cyril Welch (Amsterdam: Rodopi, 1995), 167–87; Ulrich Fülleborn, "Dichten und Denken: Bemerkungen zu Rilke und Heidegger," in *Heidegger und die christliche Tradition* (Hamburg: Meiner, 2007), 245–63.

74. Martin Heidegger, *Being and Time*, trans. John Macquarrie and Edward Robinson (New York: Harper & Row, 1962), 250.

75. Piotr Hoffman, "Death, Time, History," in *The Cambridge Companion to Heidegger*, ed. Charles Guignon (Cambridge: Cambridge University Press, 1993), 199.

76. Heidegger, *Being and Time*, 258–59.

77. Balthasar, *Apokalypse* III, 242–47. As Aidan Nichols notes of von Balthasar's critique, "It is indeed axiomatic for Heidegger that as long as existence persists it never reaches totality," *Scattering the Seed*, 212.

78. Nichols describes a similar trajectory: "Balthasar finds in Rilke a gradually intensifying 'identity' of self-surrender, Hingabe, and creation, receptivity and spontaneity, all of which, however, are carried by a 'tragic' ground which declares itself in 'anxiety' and might be called God—or, alternatively, death and nothingness." *Scattering the Seed*, 215.

79. Balthasar, *Apokalypse* III, 201.

80. Balthasar, *Apokalypse* III, 196.

81. *Sonnets to Orpheus* was written very near the end of Rilke's life while *Duino Elegies* was begun earlier but only finished in proximity to Rilke's death.

82. See Rainer Maria Rilke, *New Poems: A Revised Bilingual Edition*, trans. Edward Snow (New York: North Point, 2001).

83. Cf. "Angel Songs" (1898) in *Book of Hours: Love Poems to God*, ed. Anita Barrows and Joanna Marie Macy (New York: Riverhead Trade, 1996); and these selections from *New Poems*: "Song from the Sea," "David Sings before Saul."

84. Balthasar, *Apokalyse* 3, 255.

85. Balthasar, *Apokalypse* III, 256. "Das ist der Mythus vom tragischen Orpheus: das singende Herz in der Mitte der Wüste der Welt, sie aus der Kraft seines Leidenden Pathos verzaubernd. Insofern nun freilich der Raum dieser Existenz von vornherein für Rilke Diesseits und Jenseits umfaßt, ist seine Problematik des Todes und der Eigentlichkeit eine andere als die Heideggers. Daß aber die Seele überdauert, daß sie als Tote in der Landschaft der Klagen weiterlebt, das ist, so unangefochten es ist, ja noch Gewinn."

86. Rilke, *Sonnets to Orpheus*, Erster Teil 1. Translation mine: "Da steig ein Baum. O reine Übersteigung! / O Orpheus singt! O hoher Baum im Ohr!" German drawn from Rainer Maria Rilke, *Sonnets to Orpheus: A Bilingual Tradition*, trans. M. D. Herder (New York: W. W. Norton, 2006).

87. Rilke, *Sonnets to Orpheus*, Erster Teil, 3.

88. Rilke, *Sonnets to Orpheus*, Zweiter Teil, 1.

89. Rilke, *Sonnets to Orpheus*, Zweiter Teil 12; cf. Zweiter Teil, 29.

90. Balthasar, *Apokalypse* III, 197. [Aber wie "Wahrheit" für Heidegger Dasein ist, so ist auch das dritte transcendentale, "Schönheit", Kunst, für Rilke

Dasein: "Gesang ist Dasein." Denn er ist dessen erhellende Transzendenz ("O reine Ubersteigung! O Orpheus singt!") und damit die Atmosphäre das "göttliche" Nichts, der "Raum der Rühmung," darin Sein zu sich selbst kommt.]

91. They have elevated "becoming" to the status of a transcendental in traditional metaphysics, a move that von Balthasar is diagnosing here as a major problem. This becomes much clearer later in von Balthasar's work, where he responds with a constructive vision of beauty. It is nascent here.

92. For a discussion of this idea, see Hoffman, "Death, Time, History," 211.

93. Martin Heidegger, "What Is Metaphysics?" in *Basic Writings: From Being and Time (1927) to The Task of Thinking (1929)*, ed. David Farrell Krell (New York: Harper & Row, 1977), 110. Von Balthasar notes the use and development of Hegel in several places, one of the most interesting occurring in *Apokalypse* III, 203–4. Both Heidegger and Rilke (and Rilke in a more radically existential mode, "*Rilke bewohnt diesen selben Innenraum des Seins*") grapple with Hegel's negation and distance, but for them negation and distance are *positive*—not necessarily things to be overcome, as in Hegel.

94. Heidegger, "What is Metaphysics?" 112.

95. See Heidegger, *Being and Time*, 263–64; and "What Is Metaphysics?" 98–110. Von Balthasar links these two concepts as a unified argument in *Apokalypse* III, 269.

96. Heidegger, "What Is Metaphysics?" 105.

97. Balthasar, *Apokalypse* III, 242. See also *Apokalypse* III, 196–99, as well as Aidan Nichols's discussion of nothingness in Rilke and Heidegger in these passages from *Apokalypse* in *Scattering the Seed*, 204–5. Others would disagree with this evaluation, and see Heidegger's confrontation with an ontology of nonbeing as an opportunity for religion. See John D. Caputo, "Heidegger and Theology," in *The Cambridge Companion to Heidegger*, ed. Charles Guignon (Cambridge: Cambridge University Press, 1993), 270–88; Hubert L. Dreyfus, "Heidegger on the Connection between Nihilism, Art, Technology, and Politics," in *The Cambridge Companion to Heidegger*, ed. Charles Guignon (Cambridge: Cambridge University Press, 1993), 289–316.

98. Balthasar, *Apokalypse* III, 198. He cites Sonnets to Orpheus, Daseins als Schönheit (O du verlorener Gott! Du unendliche Spur!), no. 26.

99. Rilke, *Sonnets to Orpheus*, Zweiter Teil, 13. Translation mine.

100. Rilke, *Sonnets to Orpheus*, Zweiter Teil, 29.

101. Balthasar, *Apokalypse* III, 204. Von Balthasar describes three "passwords" (*Kennwort*) to Rilke's poetry: positivity of finitude, temporality of existence, and double truth (*doppelte Wahrheit*). These are different from a list he

gives in an article on Rilke before the revision of the dissertation: see "Rilke und die religiöse Dichtung," *Stimmen der Zeit* 63 (1932): 183–92. There the list is "innocence, loneliness, love, suffering" (183).

102. Von Balthasar perhaps suspects Hegel's "solution" ends in death, too.

103. Balthasar, *Apokalypse III*, 274. [Was bei Heidegger das Problem des Seins aus dem Nichts ist, das ist bei Rilke das Schaffen aus dem Nichts, das schaffende Nichts, das der Mensch ist. Und wenn bei Heidegger die Angst vor das Sein brachte, indem sie das Seiende im Ganzen überstieg, so muß nun bei Rilke die Angst der Quellgrund, der Stoff und das Tragende der Schöpfung sein. Das Stundenbuch stellt schon die entscheidende Frage nach dem Medium des Dichters. Ist das Absolute, in dem der atmet, das substantielle sein, Gott? Oder ist es das substantielle Nichts?]

104. Or, as Nichols puts it, "Nothingness is not on the margins of life but at its innards." *Scattering the Seed*, 204.

105. Rilke, "The Poet," *New Poems.*

106. Cf. Balthasar, *Apokalypse* III, 282.

107. Nichols, *Scattering the Seed*, 215.

108. O'Regan, "Von Balthasar's Valorization and Critique of Heidegger's Genealogy of Modernity," 150.

109. Balthasar, *Apokalypse* III, 210. [Die Sonette führen diese innere Plastik bis zur Virtuosität, die Elegien aber geben gleichzeitig die Theorie und die Metaphysik dieses Tuns.]

110. Rilke, "The Seventh Elegy," 45.

111. Rilke, "The First Elegy," 5.

112. Rilke, "The First Elegy," 7; cf. "The Fifth Elegy," 33; "The Seventh Elegy," 43; "The Eighth Elegy," 47.

113. Rilke, "The Fourth Elegy," 27, "The Eighth Elegy," 51.

114. Balthasar, *Apokalypse* III, 247.

115. Balthasar, *Apokalypse* III, 274.

116. Balthasar, *Apokalypse* III, 299. Nichols calls this the "deep incompatibility" Rilke sensed between his absolute position and Christianity's refusal to utter an absolute response to relative terms (relative in relation to God). See *Scattering the Seed*, 212, 218.

117. Rilke, *Duino Elegies.* Translation mine.

118. Balthasar, "Rilke und die religiöse Dichtung," 185.

119. A more detailed discussion of von Balthasar's complex personal and theological relationship can be found in D. Stephen Long's *Saving Karl Barth: Hans Urs von Balthasar's Preoccupation* (Minneapolis: Fortress Press, 2014).

120. Balthasar, "Rilke und die religiöse Dichtung," 188.

TWO. The Redemption of Beauty

1. Cf. von Balthasar's own allusion to Rilke's "Panther" as spiritual fatigue: *GL* I, 29.

2. Rainer Maria Rilke, "Der Panther," excerpt. Translation mine.

3. Hans Urs von Balthasar, "The Fathers, the Scholastics, and Ourselves," *Communio* 24 (1997): 347–96; the original was published as "Patristik, Scholastik, und wir," *Theologie der Zeit* 3 (1939): 65–104. Hans Urs von Balthasar, "On the Tasks of Catholic Philosophy in Our Time," *Communio* 20 (1993): 147–87; the original was published as "Von den Aufgaben der katholischen Theologie in der Zeit," *Annalen der Philosophischen Gesellschaft der Inner Scweiz* 3, no. 2–3 (1946–47): 1–38.

4. Nichols, *Scattering the Seed*, 18.

5. Balthasar, "The Fathers, the Scholastics, and Ourselves," 352.

6. Balthasar, "The Fathers, the Scholastics, and Ourselves," 353–54.

7. Balthasar, "The Fathers, the Scholastics, and Ourselves," 357.

8. The Church stands before the world as the obedient sign of the union of God and humanity achieved in Christ. Cf. Balthasar, "The Fathers, the Scholastics, and Ourselves," 363f.

9. Balthasar, "The Fathers, the Scholastics, and Ourselves," 360.

10. Nichols, *Scattering the Seed*, 22.

11. Balthasar, "The Fathers, the Scholastics, and Ourselves," 371.

12. See especially Balthasar, "The Father, the Scholastics, and Ourselves," 373–74.

13. Balthasar, "The Fathers, the Scholastics, and Ourselves," 373; cf. p. 378: "the correction in scholasticism is anticipated by the fathers."

14. Balthasar, "The Fathers, the Scholastics, and Ourselves," 381. See also Fergus Kerr, *Twentieth Century Catholic Theologians* (Somerset, NJ: Wiley-Blackwell, 2007), 137.

15. Note the balance of ideas in von Balthasar's acceptance of the *potentia oebedentialis* and warning against a *potentia naturalis*: the first is understood as a defense of a robust nature as well as grace, while the second is seen as a threat to revert to pantheism, since nature would have the power to unite itself to God. Cf. "The Fathers, the Scholastics, and Ourselves," 383–84.

16. Cf. Fergus Kerr, *20th Century Catholic Theologians*, 136: "The doctrines of creation and redemption are radically Christological, Balthasar says—a very Barthian thought, which old-fashioned Thomists would no doubt accept also, though after saying a great deal else first." See also Angelo Scola, "Chapter Five: The Chief Bases of the Theological Method II. Christocen-

trism," in *Hans Urs von Balthasar: A Theological Style* (Grand Rapids, MI: William B. Eerdmans, 1995), 45–52

17. Balthasar, "The Fathers, the Scholastics, and Ourselves," 390.

18. Balthasar, "The Fathers, the Scholastics, and Ourselves," 387.

19. Balthasar, "The Fathers, the Scholastics, and Ourselves," 390. Cf. Aidan Nichols, *A Key to Balthasar*, 13: "More widely, in Balthasar's analysis, there must be a reunion of philosophy and theology, and, within theology, a reunion of spirituality and dogmatic thought, if there is to be for Western man—who is now for many purposes global man—a recovery of the sense of the integrity of being, in its co-constitutive transcendent and immanent dimensions."

20. Nichols, *Scattering the Seed*, 245.

21. Balthasar, "The Task of Catholic Philosophy," 147.

22. Balthasar, "The Task of Catholic Philosophy," 149.

23. Balthasar, "The Task of Catholic Philosophy," 150.

24. Cf. Fergus Kerr, *20th Century Catholic Theologians*, 134: "In modern philosophy (idealism, existentialism, personalism, and so on), it is true, the underlying theological motifs are overlooked or denied. Philosophical work is theologically neutral, most philosophers would suppose. That is not how Balthasar sees it." John Dadosky suspects that von Balthasar nevertheless was not able to embrace modern philosophy enough to develop it. See "Philosophy for a Theology of Beauty," *Philosophy and Theology* 19, no. 1–2 (2007), 7: "his suspicion of modern philosophy with its turn to the subject left him unable to articulate the proper philosophical foundations for a modern recovery of beauty. He acclaimed the achievement of Aquinas but did not move beyond him." Dadosky is right that von Balthasar was suspicious of the turn to the subject, but it remains open to question whether it is necessary to move beyond Aquinas in this respect at all, as Dadosky presumes to be the case.

25. Balthasar, "The Task of Catholic Philosophy," 152–54.

26. Balthasar, "The Task of Catholic Philosophy," 170–71, "Now the Christian thinkers must experience the opposite, a *spolatio Christianorum* which they are powerless to resist"; cf. 165, "Modern philosophy is a kind of refuse product of formerly Christian (more precisely, theological) intellectual contents."

27. Balthasar, "The Task of Catholic Philosophy," 167.

28. Balthasar, "The Task of Catholic Philosophy," 174–76.

29. Balthasar, "The Task of Catholic Philosophy," 185–86.

30. Balthasar, "The Task of Catholic Philosophy," 186.

31. Balthasar, "The Task of Catholic Philosophy," 187.

32. Balthasar, *GL* I, 41.

33. See, for example: Peter Stansky and William Miller Abrahams, *London's Burning: Life, Death, and Art in the Second World War* (Stanford: Stanford University Press, 1994); Shearer West, *The Visual Arts in Germany 1890–1937: Utopia and Despair* (Manchester: Manchester University Press, 2000); Barbara McCloskey, *Artists of World War II* (Westport, CT: Greenwood, 2005).

34. For von Balthasar's account of the person in *Theo-Drama*, see especially *TD* II (for the Trinitarian background) and *TD* III (for Christology). See also Hans Urs von Balthasar, "On the Concept of Person," *Communio* 13, no. 1 (1986): 18–26. "Bruch und Bruecke zwischen Wirken und Leiden Jesu," in *Christusglaube und Christusverehrung* (Aschaffenburg: Paul Pattloch, 1982): 14–24; "Das Selbstbewusstsein Jesu," in Internationale katholische Zeitschrift, *Communio* 8 (1979): 30–39. Mark A. McIntosh summarizes von Balthasar's dramatic account in *Christology from Within: Spirituality and the Incarnation in Hans Urs von Balthasar* (Notre Dame, IN: University of Notre Dame Press, 2000).

35. See also Angelo Scola, *Balthasar: A Theological Style*, 1–2; Nichols, *A Key to Balthasar*, 15–19; Holzer, "Christologie de la figure et kenosis," 249.

36. Hans Urs von Balthasar, "Bonaventure," in *GL* II, 260–362. The German original is "Bonaventura," in *Herrlichkeit* II, 267–361. The German original unites in one volume what, in the English version, becomes two volumes: *Volume II: Clerical Styles and Volume III: Lay Styles*.

37. *On Beauty*, ed. Umberto Eco, trans. Alastair McEwen (New York: Rizzoli, 2004), 100. Or, as Eco expands in another book, "Aquinas' functionalist theory of beauty gave systematic expression to a sentiment which was very characteristic of the Middle Ages as a whole. This was its tendency to identify the beautiful and the useful, an identification which itself originated in the equation of the beautiful and the good," *Art and Beauty in the Middle Ages*, trans. Hugh Bredlin (New Haven: Yale University Press, 1986), 79.

Von Balthasar of course resists the identification of beauty and utility, but here Eco means "useful" in a sense closer to the way von Balthasar uses the word "ethic": an action whose end is the good. The medieval understanding of utility, which Eco is out to describe, is to be carefully distinguished from the modern sense of the word.

38. Eco, *Art and Beauty*, 26.

39. Hans Urs von Balthasar, *Herrlichkeit* I, 18. [Gleichzeitig ist da: das Gebild und was von ihm ausstrahlt, es zu einem werten, liebwerten macht.] Cf. Balthasar, *GL* I, 20.

40. Hans Urs von Balthasar, "Theology and Aesthetic," in *Communio* 8, no. 1 (1981): 63.

41. Hans Urs von Balthasar, "Transcendentality and *Gestalt*," in *Communio* 11, no. 1 (1984): 5.

42. More of Hopkins's contributions are discussed in chapter 5 of this book.

43. Veronica Donnelly notes the importance of Christian von Ehrenfels's understanding of form alongside, or rather as a part of, Goethe's understanding of form. See *Saving Beauty: Form as the Key to Balthasar's Christology* (Bern: Peter Lang, 2007), 43–46. See also another work (also noted by Donnelly): Michael Maria Waldstein, *Expression and Form: Principles of a Philosophical Aesthetics According to Hans Urs von Balthasar* (Paris: Editions du Cerf, 1998). There is also Ulrich Simon, "Balthasar on Goethe," in *The Analogy of Beauty: The Theology of Hans Urs von Balthasar*, ed. John Riches (Edinburgh: T & T Clark, 1986), 60–76.

44. Hans Urs von Balthasar, "Personlichkeit und Form," *Gloria Dei* 7 (1952): 1–15. For a lengthy discussion of this article, see D. C. Schindler, *Hans Urs von Balthasar and the Dramatic Structure of Truth: A Philosophical Investigation* (New York: Fordham University Press, 2004), 14–17.

45. Cf. *GL* I, 118: "As form, the beautiful can be materially grasped and even subjected to numerical calculation as a relationship of numbers, harmony, and the laws of Being."

46. Balthasar, "Persönlichkeit und Form," 1.

47. Balthasar, "Persönlichkeit und Form," 2.

48. Balthasar, "Persönlichkeit und Form," 5. [Leben ist Selbstzweck, und Form ist Mittel der Lebenserhaltung und Lebenserhöhung.]

49. Balthasar, "Persönlichkeit und Form," 5.

50. Cf. Balthasar, *GL* V, 363. See also Balthasar, "Persönlichkeit und Form," 7. Here he describes the ultimate disappointment of Goethe's eros, since it is confined only to the world, and its freedom and turmoil is in the end experienced only as "illusory masks" (*illusorische Masken*). Cf. Mongrain, "Poetics and Doxology," 405.

51. Balthasar, *GL* V, 363.

52. Balthasar, *GL* I, 118.

53. It might be helpful to clarify that God does not *have* form, since form (gestalt) in this sense always implies the possession of parts that need to be unified, and implies sensibility. Thomas Aquinas, too, is careful to differentiate: God is not composed of form and matter, but inasmuch as God is an agent (indeed, the first agent), God is in essence form. Still this is not the same as saying God *has* form (*ST* I, q. 3, a. 2). Because gestalt also incorporates the sensible in its range of meanings, von Balthasar centers his reflections on the

Incarnation; Christ *does* have form, and this form is the economic expression of the immanent Trinity. It would be better not to apply gestalt to God in the strict sense, or it would seem von Balthasar makes the mistake of giving God a "body."

54. Balthasar, "Persönlichkeit und Form," 9.

55. Balthasar, "Persönlichkeit und Form," 10. [In diesem Zwei-Eins der Bildnatur des Sohnes lösen sich die Paradoxe des Menschen: das endliche Bild ist überstiegen, aber nicht zerstört, die Fleischwerdung bleibt Funktion des Wortseins, die kreatürliche Bildnatur bleibt Ausdruck und Hinleitung auf die ewige und unendliche Bildnatur.]

56. This sensuality distinguishes von Balthasar's aesthetics from Thomas's. Whereas Thomas refers to the art of the Father, describing the preexistent Son as beautiful, von Balthasar focuses on the Incarnate Son. Cf. Nichols, *A Key to Balthasar*, 26.

57. Balthasar, "Persönlichkeit und Form," 10.

58. Balthasar, "Persönlichkeit und Form," 12.

59. Balthasar, "Persönlichkeit und Form," 13–14.

60. Balthasar, *Herrlichkeit* I, 447–48. Translation mine. Cf. Balthasar, *GL* I, 465–66; Dupré, "Hans Urs von Balthasar's Theology of Aesthetic Form," *Theological Studies* 49 (1988): 309: "The light, then, within which the believer apprehends God's manifestation originates entirely in the manifestation itself."

61. Balthasar, *GL* I, 29.

62. Balthasar, *GL* I, 153.

63. Francesca Murphy, *Christ the Form of Beauty: A Study of Theology and Literature* (Edinburgh: T & T Clark, 1995), 135.

64. Note the way he continues to struggle with how to describe a positive relationship between the aesthetic (earthly) and God's splendor: "The *splendour* of the mystery which offers itself in such a way cannot, for this reason, be equated with the other kinds of aesthetic radiance which we encounter in the world. This does not mean, however, that that mysterious *splendour* and this aesthetic radiance are beyond any and every comparison" (120). At the same time, "The quality of 'being-in-itself' which belongs to the beautiful, the demand the beautiful itself makes to be allowed to be what it is, the demand, therefore, that we renounce our attempts to control and manipulate it, in order truly to be able to be happy enjoying it: all of this is, in the natural realm, the foundation and foreshadowing of what in the realm of revelation and grace will be the attitude of faith" (153).

65. Nichols, *Redeeming Beauty*, 54–55.

66. Hans Urs von Balthasar, "Christliche Kunst und Verkündigung," *Mysterium Salutis*, vol. I, ed. J. Feiner and M. Löhrer (Einseldeine and Cologne, 1965), 708–26; cf. Nichols, *Redeeming Beauty*, 55.

67. Balthasar, "Christliche Kunst," 710–11.

68. See Balthasar, "Being and Beings," in *Epilogue*, 47–50.

Cf. Scola, *Hans Urs von Balthasar: A Theological Style*, 30; Nichols, *A Key to Balthasar*, 7: "the transcendentals somehow point us to the dynamic life going on for ever within God. It seems likely that Balthasar has in mind here the notion that the transcendentals are joined in continuous reciprocal interpenetration"; Nichols, 26.

69. See "Christliche Kunst," 711.

70. Balthasar, "Christliche Kunst," 710. [Die innere Durchgestaltung erfolgt durch die Prägekraft der einmaligen, unverwechselbaren, personalen Wesenheit Jesu Christi: er ist das gültige "Ausdrucks-Bild" des unsichtbaren Gottes (Kol 1,15).]

71. Balthasar, "Christiliche Kunst," 714.

72. Nichols, *Redeeming Beauty*, 55.

73. Balthasar, *Herrlichkeit* I, 229. Translation mine. Cf. Balthasar, *GL* I, 237.

74. For more on the cross and the aesthetic in von Balthasar, see Viladesau, "The Beauty of the Cross," *Theological Aesthetics after von Balthasar*, esp. 143; Stephen M. Fields, "The Beauty of the Ugly: Balthasar, the Crucifixion, Analogy, and God," *International Journal of Systematic Theology* 9, no. 2 (2007): 172–83.

75. Balthasar, *GL* III, 13.

76. Balthasar, *GL* III, 28–29.

77. See Dante, *Paradiso*, Canto XX, 139–43; Canto XIV, 72.

78. Balthasar, *GL* III, 10.

79. Balthasar, *GL* III, 24.

80. Balthasar, *GL* III, 29.

81. Balthasar, *GL* III, 36.

82. Cf. Balthasar, *GL* V, 409.

83. Balthasar, *GL* III, 41: "Rosetti, Tristan, Petrach, Michelangelo, Shakespeare. . . . Indeed, the same wind was blowing in the circle of Dante's friends, where Eros ruled over the heart as an all-powerful *fatum*, a sweet calumny, and this problem was not really overcome. . . . Dante has this air in his lungs . . . only to leave it behind him, once and for all, in Hell."

84. Balthasar, *GL* III, 32. Cf. the opening of *GL* II, which introduces the concept of "studies in theological style": "into the centre of the Platonic and Scholastic world-view there is now brought—for the first time in Christian intellectual history—the mystery of an eternal love between man and woman, *eros* refined by *agape* and drawn up through all the circles of hell and spheres of the world to the throne of God" (18).

85. Balthasar, *GL* I, 193.

86. Balthasar, *GL* III, 34.

87. Balthasar, *GL* I, 29. German notations are from *Herrlichkeit* I, 26–27. This nexus of words—*Wort, Bild, Ausdruck, Exegese*—form a constellation through which von Balthasar builds his account of the expressiveness of being. We will see this developed in chapter 3.

88. Balthasar, *GL* I, 158.

89. Balthasar, *GL* I, 193.

90. Scola, *Hans Urs von Balthasar: A Theological Style*, 24. "In such a horizon, the fact that man both synthesizes and transcends the cosmos means that ontological discourse takes as its starting point the existential analysis of man, that is, of his enigmatic structure (man is limited but is capable of the entirety of being), in order to go beyond it" (25). Cf. Rodney Howsare, *Balthasar: A Guide for the Perplexed* (New York: T & T Clark, 2009), 50–53.

91. Balthasar, *GL* I, 159.

92. Balthasar, *GL* III, 61.

93. Balthasar, *GL* III, 59.

94. Dante, *Purgatorio*, Canto XXX, 28–39. All translations, unless otherwise noted, are mine. The edition of the original Italian I have used is Dante Alighieri, *La Divina Commedia*, 3 vols., ed. Natalino Sapegno (Florence: La Nuova Italia, 1984). A good, readable translation can be found in *The Portable Dante*, trans. Mark Musa (New York: Penguin, 1995).

95. Dante, *Purgatorio*, Canto XXX, 73–75.

96. Balthasar, *GL* III, 60. Von Balthasar paraphrases the moment: "What obstacles have you met with, asks cruel Love, what ditches, what chains, have prevented your love from rising up to me?"

97. Dante, *Purgatorio*, Canto XXXI, 34–36.

98. Dante, *Purgatorio*, Canto XXXI, 133–45. Mount Parnassus was, according to Greek myth, sacred to Apollo—god of poetry—and the home of the Muses.

99. Balthasar, *GL* III, 61.

100. Balthasar, *GL* III, 62–63.

101. Balthasar, *GL* III, 64.

102. Balthasar, *GL* I, 221.

103. Cf. Nichols, *Key to Balthasar*, 2: "Balthasar's approach can be contrasted here with the Kant-inspired methodology of subject-oriented philosophical humanism and, in the Catholic context, the influential movement of philosophical theology known as 'Transcendental Thomism.' These have it in common that they begin their epistemological reflections by examining human

subjectivity from within—on the basis of what has been called the 'I'–'I' relationship. Balthasar, however, puts the human subject—and that by virtue of its created nature—in immediate relation with the truth that lies outside itself. The self-conscious subject exists, knowing that he or she exists as just such a unique subject, yes. But this is always *in relation to other manifestations of being*."

104. Balthasar, *GL* I, 234. "The aesthetic experience is the union of the greatest possible concreteness of the individual form and the greatest possible universality of its meaning or of the epiphany within it of the mystery of Being."

105. Balthasar, *GL* III, 81.

106. Dante, *Paradiso*, Canto XXXIII, 124–45.

107. Balthasar, *GL* III, 50.

108. McIntosh, *Christology from Within*, 26.

109. McIntosh's phenomenal book is an indispensible synthesis of theo-dramatic terms, but in light of the aesthetics, it is necessary to question some underlying presuppositions in his (and like-minded) descriptions of von Balthasar's work. See, for example: "Where Chalcedon speaks of a union of divine and human *essences* in Christ, von Balthasar will speak of a union of divine and human *activity* in Christ" (5), ". . . we can see von Balthasar moving toward a nonessentialist reading of human participation in Christ" (22), ". . . he believes that the largest and truest category for interpreting the divine-human encounter is not metaphysical but covenantal" (26). Is this what von Balthasar favors everywhere, or is it what he favors in the case of dramatic categories of language?

110. Balthasar, *GL* III, 83.

111. Balthasar, *GL* III, 90. "Effigies have no *motus*, no vital interior conative life in the Aristotelian and Thomistic sense, no entelechy, no hope, no *amor*; they are without rapport. That is why the rapport Dante establishes with them is intrinsically impossible" (99).

112. Balthasar, *GL* III, 100.

113. Balthasar, *GL* III, 101.

114. Balthasar, *GL* IV, 395, 404.

115. Balthasar, *GL* V, 12–13.

116. See, for example, Balthasar, *GL* V, 14.

117. Balthasar, *GL* V, 15.

118. Balthasar, *GL* V, 47.

119. Balthasar, *GL* V, 295.

120. Balthasar, *GL* V, 409.

121. Johann Wolfgang von Goethe, "Vermächtnis," excerpt. Translation mine.

122. Goethe's ode, "Prometheus," bears these themes out with almost haunting clarity. Prometheus looks to the gods, turns his back on them, and fixes his gaze on human beings.

123. Balthasar, *GL* V, 295.

124. Balthasar, *GL* V, 421.

125. Balthasar, *GL* V, 412.

126. Balthasar, *GL* V, 409.

127. Rilke, *Sonnets to Orpheus*, Second Part, 29. Translations mine from the German in Rainer Maria Rilke, *Sonnets to Orpheus, Bilingual Edition*, trans. M. D. Herter Norton (New York: W. W. Norton, 2006).

128. Balthasar, *GL* V, 417.

129. Balthasar, *GL* V, 418.

130. See, for example, Rilke's use of Narcissus in "Sonnets to Orpheus," Second Part, 3. Or "Narcissus" from *New Poems*.

131. See Rilke's "A Bowl of Roses" and "The Inner Rose." Both are from *New Poems*. See Rainer Maria Rilke, *New Poems: Bilingual Edition*, trans. Edward Snow (New York: North Point, 2001).

132. Balthasar, *GL* V, 419.

133. Balthasar, *GL* V, 421.

134. Balthasar, *GL* V, 422.

135. Balthasar, *GL* V, 425.

136. Balthasar, *GL* V, 427. See also: "in the clear denial of Christian transcendence, the raiment of glory, which it reserves for the God of love and of the Cross, is removed from these and cast upon the members of the universe, or of that *physis* which Heidegger calls Being"(409).

137. Balthasar, *GL* V, 420.

138. Cited in Balthasar, *GL* V, 423.

THREE. Measuring Metaphysics

1. Balthasar, *GL* I, 118.

2. Balthasar, *GL* I, 29.

3. See von Balthasar's "On the Tasks of Catholic Philosophy in Our Time," *Communio* 20 (1993): 147–87. Cf. Aidan Nichols, *Say It Is Pentecost: A Guide through Balthasar's Logic* (Washington, DC: Catholic University of America, 2001), 4.

4. As Fergus Kerr writes of von Balthasar: "True, the Logos has begun to speak personally, in the Incarnation, but this does not mean, Balthasar insists, that the question that being poses is superseded. On the contrary, the

question is only revealed all the more nakedly." Kerr, "Balthasar and Metaphysics," 229. Cf. David S. Yeago, "The Drama of Nature and Grace: A Study in the Theology of Hans Urs von Balthasar." PhD diss., Yale University, 1992, 35: "This formal creatureliness-as-such is thus in one sense the "presupposition" of all grace, for God's grace is as such grace for a creature which is and yet is not God."

5. Peter Henrici, "The Philosophy of Hans Urs von Balthasar," *Hans Urs von Balthasar: His Life and His Work* (San Francisco: Ignatius Press, 1991), 151.

6. Schindler argues that von Balthasar works against phenomenological positions in two separate articles: "Hans Urs von Balthasar, Metaphysics, and the Problem of Onto-Theology," *Analecta Hermeneutica* 1 (2009): 102–13; "Metaphysics within the Limits of Phenomenology: Balthasar and Husserl on the Nature of the Philosophical Act," *Teología y vida* 50 (2009): 243–48. Contrary to phenomenology's troubled relationship with metaphysics, according to Schindler, von Balthasar thinks that "Because theology does not replace metaphysics, because God is not beyond being in a dialectical sense (perhaps we could say: yes, God is beyond being, but being, too, is beyond being), theology can never simply leave being behind." Schindler, "Balthasar, Metaphysics, and the Problem of Onto-Theology," 112. For an analysis of von Balthasar's positive use of phenomenology, see Larry Chapp, "The Primal Experience of Being in the Thought of Hans Urs von Balthasar: A Response to Theodore Kepes Jr.," *Philosophy and Theology* 20, no. 1/2 (2008): 291–305.

7. Balthasar, *TL* I, 37.

8. Balthasar, *TL* I, 63: "Without the subject's sensory space, it [the object] would not be what it is; it would be incapable of fulfilling its raison d'être, the idea that it is supposed to embody. Cf. *TL* I, 67: "It is not until the other enters into the space of the subject that, like Sleeping Beauty, it awakens from its slumber—at once to the world and to itself."

9. "Classical metaphysics," here, is meant in the way von Balthasar tends to refer to it: that tradition that leads up to and culminates in the thought of Thomas Aquinas. Von Balthasar is much less positive about the "sawdust" neo-Thomism he learned with the Jesuits, and would remain so throughout his life.

10. This statement will receive clarification as the argument of the chapter continues. At this point, it is possible to note, as an example, the way von Balthasar entwines the appearance (or manifestation) of being—a broadly Heideggerian emphasis—with the thought of St. Thomas Aquinas in "A Resume of My Thought" in *Hans Urs von Balthasar: His Life and His Work*: "We add here that the epiphany of being has sense only if in the appearance (*Erscheinung*) we grasp the essence which manifests itself (*Ding an sich*). The infant

comes to knowledge not of a pure appearance, but of his mother in herself. That does not exclude our grasping the essence only through the manifestation and not in itself (St. Thomas)" (3).

11. Balthasar, *TL* I, 37.

12. Kerr, "Balthasar and Metaphysics," 237. Kerr expresses some reservation over whether the version of Thomism to be found in von Balthasar is lasting. Nevertheless, as important as Heidegger is to von Balthasar's understanding, the breadth of his philosophical background and the vital importance of Thomas in that background are not to be underestimated: ". . . he had read Kierkegaard and Nietzsche; he was more interested in Fichte, Novalis, Hölderlin, and especially Goethe, than in Descartes, Hume, and Kant, the standard targets in seminary philosophy. Despite all this, and although he hated the 'sawdust Thomism' then being served up as standard fare by his professors, the metaphysics he was to practise in his maturity was decisively affected by his study of Thomas Aquinas" (225).

13. Heidegger, "On the Origin of the Work of Art," *Basic Writings*, 178.

14. Heidegger, "On the Origin of the Work of Art," esp. 151 and 166. To summarize: art has a "thingly" character, and it is also a *work*, worked out in time.

15. See Junius C. Johnson, "Christ and Analogy: The Metaphysics of Hans Urs von Balthasar," PhD diss., Yale University, 2010; Leonard J. Bowman, "Cosmic Exemplarism of Bonaventure," in *Journal of Religion* 55, no. 2 (1975): 181–98; Michael Schneider, "Die theologische Ausdeutung von Schöpfung und Heiliger Schrift bei Bonaventura," in *Theologie und Philosophie* 69 (1994): 373–83; Therese Scarpelli, "Bonaventure's Christocentric Epistemology: Christ's Human Knowledge as the Epitome of Illumination in 'De scientia Christi,'" in *Franciscan Studies* 65 (2007): 63–86. An inquiry into Bonaventure is beyond the scope of this book.

16. Balthasar, *TL* I, 37–38. Cf. *GL* I, 193.

17. Balthasar, *TL* I, 230.

18. Erich Przywara, *Polarity: A German Catholic's Interpretation of Religion*, trans. A. C. Bouquet (London: Oxford University Press, 1935); *Analogia entis: Metaphysik* (Munich: Josef Kösel & Friedrich Pustet, 1932). See also *Was ist Gott: eine Summula* (Nürnberg: Glock und Lutz, 1953); *Religionsphilosophie katholischer Theologie* (Munich: R. Oldenbourg, 1926). See also Balthasar's article, "Die Metaphysik Erich Przywaras," *Schweizer Rundschau* 33 (1933): 489–99; Edward T. Oakes, "Erich Przywara and the Analogy of Being," in *Pattern of Redemption: The Theology of Hans Urs von Balthasar* (New York: Continuum, 1994), 15–44; John R. Betz, "After Barth: A New Introduction to Erich Przy-

wara's *Analogia* Entis," in *The Analogy of Being: Invention of the Antichrist or the Wisdom of God?* ed. Thomas Joseph White (Grand Rapids, MI: William B. Eerdmans, 2011), 35–87, esp. 40–41.

19. Przywara himself references the Council on p. 31 of *Polarity*. See also Fergus Kerr, "Balthasar and Metaphysics," 226; Manfred Lochbrunner, *Analogia Caritatis: Darstellung und Deutung der Theologie Hans Urs von Balthasar* (Freiburg: Herder, 1981), 108; Rowan Williams, "Balthasar and Difference," in *Wrestling With Angels: Conversations in Modern Theology* (London: SCM, 2007), 79–80; James Zeitz, "Przywara and von Balthasar on Analogy," *The Thomist* 52, no. 3 (1988): 490. What Ulrich Johannes Plaga says of von Balthasar's position also applies to Przywara, "Now the distance between God and creature is so great that the dissimilarity remains greater than the similarity." *"Ich bin die Wahrheit": Die theo-logische Dimension der Christologie Hans Urs von Balthasars* (Hamburg: LIT, 1997), 211.

20. Zeitz, "Przywara and von Balthasar on Analogy," 474. "His question is: what concept of nature is able to relate to *Ubernatur*, while remaining truly a *creaturely* concept of nature? His thesis is that nature cannot be abstract or 'pure' in an eighteenth-century, secularized philosophical sense (e.g., Balus), but—in conformity with the whole tradition of the Church Fathers, where nature means the whole human condition—the concept of nature is always already analogous, since 'man' as creature can never stand aside from his already given, concrete nature within the order of salvation."

21. This plays a major role in von Balthasar's thought as he adopts Nicolas of Cusa's *non aliud* principle. Rowan Williams, "Wrestling with Angels": "God is *non aliud* in respect of creation—not an other, an item enumerable in a list along with the contents of the universe. Analogy is thus emphatically not a correspondence between two or more things exhibiting in varying degrees the same features. . . . There is no system of which God and creatures are both part" (80). The qualitative difference between God and the world effectively eviscerates Heidegger's onto-theological critique, which at first appears to threaten the usefulness of traditional metaphysics. See also Schindler, "Balthasar, Metaphysics, and the Problem of Onto-Theology," 109. The article explores how von Balthasar makes self-transcendence intrinsic to the properties of being because the good is self-diffusive, so that "Opening up beyond itself is therefore not a violence imposed on worldly being, but is the very essence of worldly being."

22. Przywara, *Polarity*, 29.

23. Przywara, *Polarity*, 34.

24. Balthasar, *Theology of Karl Barth*, 255.

25. Cf. Balthasar, "Polarity in Being," in *Epilogue*, 55–58.

26. Here it is almost easy to imagine Pseudo-Dionysius's hierarchies, with the various forms and qualities of being linked together by analogy into the "great chain" that leads to God. But such a conclusion would be all too misleading. Von Balthasar dares not construe the relationship between God and the world as a series of ladder rungs.

27. See especially *TD* V, "The Positivity of the 'Other,'" 81–85; See also *TD* III, 22, discussing *TD* II; this distance is most of all expressed on the Cross: *TD* IV, 320.

The most important work on von Balthasar and the analogy of being is by Georges Schrijver, "Die Analogia Entis in der Theologie Hans Urs von Balthasars: eine genetisch-historische Studie," *Sylloge excerptorum e dissertationibus* 49: 249–81.

28. Balthasar, *GL* V, 613–27.

29. See also Kerr, "Balthasar and Metaphysics," 236. Before reviewing these distinctions, Kerr assesses: "Essentially, Balthasar expands Aquinas's doctrine of the real distinction between existence and essence in created beings in the light of Heidegger's mytho-poetic account of the difference between being (*Sein*, a verbal infinitive referring to the act of 'to-be') and beings (*Seiendes*, an adjectival noun referring to the things that exist) in terms of the Fourfold (*das Geviert*: earth, sky, death, the sacred)." (235). Emilio Brito argues that due to radical uses of Heidegger such as this, von Balthasar emerges as the most Heideggerian of his era, despite his positions against Heidegger. See Emilio Brito, "La reception de la pensee de Heidegger dans la theologie catholique," *Nouvelle revue théologique* 119, no. 3 (1997): 359.

30. Schindler, "Metaphysics within the Limits of Phenomenology," 252.

31. See *Epilogue*, 78, for von Balthasar's own assessment of the place of metaphysics in his work: "we may definitively conclude that the whole unabridged metaphysics of the transcendentals of Being can only be unfolded under the theological light of the creation of the world in the Word of God, who expresses himself in divine freedom as a sensate-spiritual man. But in asserting this, we do so without implying that metaphysics itself needs to become theology."

32. Michael P. Murphy, *A Theology of Criticism: Balthasar, Postmodernism, and the Catholic Imagination* (New York: Oxford University Press, 2008), 52.

33. His move for metaphysics and general omission of causality language is perhaps a deliberate effort to shift the discussion away from causality. Cyril O'Regan notes, for example, that von Balthasar defends Thomas's *esse* but does not link that defense to "a model of efficient causality." See O'Regan, "Von Bal-

thasar's Valorization and Critique of Heidegger's Genealogy of Modernity," 147. It is not necessarily clear, however, that von Balthasar rejects absolutely any traditional models of causality. He will occasionally seek out that language, as he does in *TL* II, 275: "The images were the vehicle that the *causa efficiens* [efficient cause] (the Father) and the *causa exemplaris* [exemplary cause] (the Son) used in order to bring about interior understanding of the faith and of following (*causa finalis* [final cause])." This is not a use of causality with the sort of depth accustomed to those in Thomist circles, but it at least nuances our account of his theology: his reticence toward using causal language is not necessarily a *rejection* of causal language. It rather seems he thinks his theology fits alongside it, as he can use it on occasion to clarify his argument.

34. The overall arc of the narrative in these volumes is a tragic one, though not an irredeemable one. It resembles the basic sketches of his article, "The Fathers, the Scholastics, and Ourselves," though here there is perhaps more pessimism. After the rise and development of metaphysical inquiry in pagan philosophy, that inquiry reaches its zenith in the Middle Ages and quickly disintegrates afterward. John Duns Scotus's nominalist distinctions, the rise of Protestantism, the further bifurcation of knowledge under Kant, all contribute to the demise of metaphysics with both Hegel and Heidegger.

35. Balthasar, *GL* IV, 395; cf., 400. This last point is placed in line with Aquinas's inspired insight: *maxima pulchriudo humanae naturarae consistit in splendore scientiae.*

36. Von Balthasar calls this the first metaphysical question in *GL* V, 613.

37. Balthasar, *GL* IV, 396. See also p. 403: "It is precisely here that a new kind of intimacy of God in the creature becomes clear, an intimacy which is only made possible by the distinction between God and *esse*." See also Michael Hanby, "Creation as Aesthetic Analogy," in *The Analogy of Being: Invention of the Antichrist or the Wisdom of God?* ed. Thomas Joseph White (Cambridge: William B. Eerdmans, 2011), 341–78, esp. 364.

38. Balthasar, *GL* IV, 404. For a review of Thomas Aquinas's use of the transcendentals as a reinforcement of philosophy's disposition of "openness," see O. P. Aberlardo Lobato, "Santo Tomás de Aquina y la via trascendetal en filosofia," in *Die Logik des Transzendentalen: Festschrift für Jan A. Aertsen zum 65. Geburtstag*, ed. Martin Pickavé (New York: W. de Gruyter, 2003), 163–78, esp. his generous construal of this Thomistic openness with von Balthasar's theological aesthetics on page 177: "El clamor se hace mas insisstente a partir de obra del pensador suizo Hans Urs von Balthasar, que ha penetrado a fonde en el tema de la belleza y ha brindado una nueva visión de la teologia y de la teodramatica, desde la penetración de la 'Herrlichkeit.'"

39. This appears as a theme in "The Christian Contribution to Metaphysics," in *GL* V, 646–56, and throughout *GL* VII in its discussion of the New Testament. See also "Confession," in *TL* I, 267–72.

Larry Chapp claims that von Balthasar's concept of mystery is superior to Karl Rahner's because it is more "personalogical," as his metaphysics of the saint emphasizes. Chapp, "The Primal Experience of Being," *Philosophy and Theology* 20 (2008): 291–305. This, however, is a rather unfair assessment of Rahner, leaving out Rahner's most fundamental anthropological presuppositions. If anything, Rahner is more emphatically anthropological than von Balthasar, so much so that von Balthasar worried Rahner was too anthropocentric. See *TD* IV, 273–83.

40. Balthasar, *GL* IV, 405.

41. Balthasar, *GL* V, "The Parting of the Ways," 9–47. There he discusses Scotus and Ekhart. More recent philosophical moves like Kant and Hegel are discussed in "Aesthetics as Science," 597–610.

42. Balthasar, *GL* V, 13ff.

43. Balthasar, *GL* V, 225.

44. As Fergus Kerr argues in "Balthasar and Metaphysics," 224: "For Balthasar, metaphysics and Christian theology are distinct activities, each with its own sources and rules; but neither, he believes, can be properly conducted in ignorance of the other."

45. "The Christians of today, living in a night which is deeper than that of the later Middle Ages, are given the task of performing the act of affirming Being, unperturbed by the darkness and the distortion, in a way that is vicarious and representative for all humanity . . . to pray continually, to find God in all things and to glorify him." *GL* V, 648–49. The whole section ends up being about worship, but here we see it begin to become explicit.

This section fulfills the promise of the opening foreword to *GL* I, which insists "We can be sure that whoever sneers at her name [beauty] as if she were the ornament of a bourgeois past—whether he admits it or not—can no longer pray and soon will no longer be able to love" (18). The collapse of beauty and metaphysics eviscerates Christian worship.

46. Von Balthasar clarifies this elsewhere, as in *Epilogue*, 50: "we must not absolutize anything finite . . . in order to 'construct' God, but rather we have to look out into the direction where the lines of our doubly finite being point. We cannot reckon how these lines are severed in the infinite."

47. Balthasar, *GL* V, 628.

48. Balthasar, *GL* V, 631.

49. Balthasar, *GL* V, 646.

50. See esp. Balthasar, *GL* II, 21; *GL* III, 29 and note 50.

51. For two important reviews of von Balthasar's use of Aquinas from a Thomist perspective, see James J. Buckley, "Balthasar's Use of the Theology of Aquinas," *The Thomist* 59, no. 4 (1995): 517–45; Angelo Campodonico, "Hans Urs von Balthasar's Interpretation of the Philosophy of Thomas Aquinas," *Nova et Vetera* 8, no. 1 (2010): 33–53. Both Buckley and Campodonico acknowledge von Balthasar's indebtedness to Thomas and express puzzlement at his simultaneous distance from Thomas. Of the two, Buckley is perhaps the more negative, concerned as he is that von Balthasar's criticisms of Thomas do not properly apprehend him (525, passim); Campodonico notes that in certain respects von Balthasar de-Aristotelianized Thomas in order to emphasize, over-against the Neo-Scholastics, the Thomas of participation and mysticism— and this also over-against transcendental Thomism (51).

52. See esp. Umberto Eco, *The Aesthetics of Thomas Aquinas*, trans. Hugh Bredin (Cambridge, MA: Harvard University Press, 1988).

53. This perspective sounds a great deal like that of Bernard Lonergan in *Insight*, and there are certainly affinities between Lonergan's move to interiority and von Balthasar's interest in the metaphysics of the saint. We should be careful not to conflate the two, but a kind of kinship persists. See Robert Doran, "Lonergan and Balthasar: Methodological Considerations," *Theological Studies* 58 (1997): 61–84.

54. My summary differs from, but does not disagree with, D. C. Shindler's assessment of von Balthasar's work against the onto-theology critique. Schindler focuses on the self-diffusiveness of the Good as the hinge to von Balthasar's overcoming of Heidegger's position. See D. C. Schindler, "Hans Urs von Balthasar, Metaphysics, and the Problem of Onto-Theology," in *Analecta Hermeneutica* 1 (2009): 102–13. This resembles the position of Matthew A. Daigler, "Heidegger and Von Balthasar: A Lovers' Quarrel over Beauty and Divinity," *American Catholic Philosophical Quarterly* 69 (1995): 375–94, "the question that will finally drive a wedge between Heidegger and Balthasar is the question of who or what gives (*gibt*) Being."

55. Von Balthasar makes a similar inversion of Kant's *cogito ergo sum* when he posits instead *cogitor ergo sum*. See *TL* I, 54; cf. Aidan Nichols, *Say It Is Pentecost*, 17; D. C. Schindler, *The Dramatic Structure of Truth*, 133, esp. n. 117.

56. I am, then, in formal agreement with Aidan Nichols's viewpoint in "Thomism and the Nouvelle Théologie," 18–19. See also Campodonico, "Balthasar's Interpretation of the Philosophy of Thomas Aquinas," 52.

57. See, for example, the way he discusses the midpoint of the Church between Mary, Peter, and John: "But with Mary, John too must come forward in the Church. He takes his place at a strangely veiled midpoint exposed to all minds, between Peter . . . and Mary. . . . With one hand in Peter's and the other

in Mary's, he unites Mary to Peter in terms of their mission. (This does not prevent Mary, as *Ekklēsia*, from being the higher midpoint between both apostles, nor Peter from remaining the visible midpoint.)" Hans Urs von Balthasar, *Razing the Bastions* (San Francisco: Ignatius Press, 1993), 41. Cf. Balthasar, "The Church's Inner Dramatic Tension: Bride and Institution," in *TD* III, 353–60.

58. Hans Urs von Balthasar, *Prayer* (San Francisco: Ignatius Press, 1983), 23: "the highest instance of the *analogia entis* is the *analogia personalitatis*."

59. I use the version published in 1952, translated in 1992: Hans Urs von Balthasar, *The Theology of Karl Barth: Exposition and Interpretation*, trans. Edward T. Oakes (San Francisco: Ignatius Press, 1992). The earlier edition has been heavily edited in the 1952 version, as censors prevented it from publication in the 1940s. Of this first version, two articles emerged: "Analogie und Dialektik," *Divus Thomas* 22 (1944): 171–216; "Analogie und Natur," *Divus Thomas* 23 (1945): 3–56.

60. Balthasar, *Theology of Karl Barth*, 253.

61. Balthasar, *Theology of Karl Barth*, 254. It could even be said that a "closed" metaphysics, for von Balthasar, is not a metaphysic at all, as it would have ceased to be characterized by one of its most important qualities.

62. Balthasar, *Theology of Karl Barth*, 264. Some—though by no means all—Barth scholars, such as Bruce McCormack, vigorously disagree with von Balthasar's thesis with respect to Barth. See, for example, Bruce L. McCormack, "Karl Barth's Version of an 'Analogy of Being': A Dialectical No and Yes to Roman Catholicism," in *The Analogy of Being: Invention of the Antichrist or the Wisdom of God?* ed. Thomas Joseph White (Cambridge: William B. Eerdmans, 2011), 88–144, esp. 116.

63. Steven A. Long, *Natura Pura: On the Recovery of Nature in the Doctrine of Grace* (New York: Fordham University Press, 2010), 55.

64. Balthasar, *Theology of Karl Barth*, 267.

65. Balthasar, *Theology of Karl Barth*, 269.

66. Balthasar, *Theology of Karl Barth*, 287.

67. Balthasar, *Theology of Karl Barth*, 273. He outlines his response in 277–78.

68. In *Theology of Karl Barth*, for example, von Balthasar insists that "the distance between subject and object" has its "deepest foundation" in the distance between Persons in the Trinity but at the same time that the created relationship between subject and object is not *created by* grace (292). Cf. the earlier "Analogie und Natur," esp. 7 and 33–34.

69. Long, *Natura Pura*, 62.

70. See pp. 56–67. Von Balthasar reiterates these sentiments again much later in his career. See Balthasar, "Regagner une philosophie à partir de la théologie," *Pour une philosophie chrétienne: Philosophie et théologie* (Paris: Dessain et Tolra, 1983), 175–87.

71. So von Balthasar would agree with Long's own statement: "But this is a far different thing from supposing that created nature as such, *simpliciter*, is unknowable apart from grace. It is also quite different from holding that created nature *cannot be distinguished in the given multiplex of nature and grace*, for the essential adequation of intellect and nature remains." *Natura Pura*, 67.

72. Long, *Natura Pura*, 80. He continues: "and it is completely consistent with the *abstract intelligibility* of nature and of its being *distinct* from that which affects it (nature is not sin; nature is not grace). The reason? Being and essential nature are really distinct."

73. Balthasar, *Theology of Karl Barth*, 329 [noting Guardini, after Przywara]: "we cannot abstractly define the 'essence' of Christianity, because the historical person of Jesus Christ is himself this essence from whom all general and abstract categories of the being of the world and of nature have their measure." See also Ellero Babini, "Jesus Christ, Form and Norm of Man According to Hans Urs von Balthasar," trans. Thérèse M Bonin, *Communio* 16 (1989): 446–57.

74. Balthasar, *Theology of Karl Barth*, 362.

75. Balthasar, *Theology of Karl Barth*, 363.

76. It would be too much, given all of this, to say with D. Stephen Long (not to be confused with Steven A. Long) that von Balthasar rejected *natura pura* except as a hypothesis to assist in theological reflection. The Janus face of nature is too complex, and von Balthasar's interpretation of nature is able to encounter both Karl Barth and Thomas Aquinas precisely because of its shifting contexts. See D. Stephen Long, *Saving Karl Barth*, 56–58.

77. I use the latter published version as it is nearer to his publication of the trilogy and so reflects its ideas more closely.

78. Balthasar, *Cosmic Liturgy: The Universe According to Maximus the Confessor*, trans. Brian Daley (San Francisco: Ignatius Press, 2004), 37: "The man Jesus's own active doing and willing—not a passive human nature dependent on the activity of a personal divine Logos, as the Monothelites imagined—was more than simply to be defended on the conceptual level; it had to be made plausible within the context of a comprehensive understanding of the world."

79. See, for example, Balthasar, *Cosmic Liturgy*, 66, 161, 207.

80. Balthasar, *Cosmic Liturgy*, 314, and the section that follows: "The Synthesis in the Three Acts of Worship," 314–30.

81. Balthasar, *Cosmic Liturgy*, 248–49. Other mentions of Aquinas include 146, 164, and 175.

82. Balthasar, *Cosmic Liturgy*, 72.

83. Brian Daley, "Translator's Foreword," in *Cosmic Liturgy*, 17. "In 1941 and even in 1961, von Balthasar's concern was to find in the Catholic dogmatic tradition—in patristic thought, but also in the Thomist tradition." A caution ought to be added here with respect to Daley's comments about von Balthasar and the transcendental Thomist Maréchal, with whom Daly associates von Balthasar. Von Balthasar bore great suspicion of transcendental Thomism, and in Fergus Kerr's words, "Fairly or otherwise, he regarded it as unduly anthropocentric, focusing on the knowing and willing human person, rather than on the mystery of being." Kerr, "Balthasar and Metaphysics," 225. See also Angelo Campodonico, "Hans Urs von Balthasar's Interpretation of the Philosophy of Thomas Aquinas," 35.

84. Vincent Holzer calls von Balthasar's Christological-Trinitarian synthesis of metaphysics "an enrichment of the great scholastic tradition, but it extends the latter into unexpected developments." Holzer, "Les Implications," 308. See also p. 309: "If the *analogia entis* constitutes one of the most influential features of Balthasarian theology, then its Trinitarian and Christological sources renew it."

85. For a full review of von Balthasar's use of the analogy of being in his theology, see Nicholas J. Healy, "The Analogy of Being," in *The Eschatology of Hans Urs von Balthasar: Being as Communion* (New York: Oxford University Press, 2005), 19–90.

86. Balthasar, *Epilogue*, 91. The German is from *Epilog* (Einsiedeln: Johannes Verlag, 1987), 71: "Dabei ist aber nicht zu übersehen, daß die in Christus sich gegenwärtigende analogia entis keineswegs zwischen der innerweltlichen Differenz von Sein und Wesen . . . und dem Sein Gottes und seinen freien Weisen des Sich-Offenbarens." The word, gegenwärtigende, is a participle and difficult to translate with the same adjectival sensibility: literally, the *analogia entis* is "presenting" or "actualizing" in Christ. I have sided with the English translation available for the sake of continuity.

87. Balthasar, *Epilogue*, 56.

88. Cf. Balthasar, "Karl Barth," in *Apokalypse III*, 316–45; "The Centrality of Analogy," in *Theology of Karl Barth*, 114–67.

89. See esp. Balthasar, "Analogie und Dialektik," 174–76, esp. 216: "When God creates, then the creature is not per se nothing nor a second God. The creature is thus analogous to the being of God and therefore to God." [Wenn Gott schafft, dann ist das Geschöpf mit schlechthiniger Notwendigkeit weder

ein Nichts noch ein zweiter Gott. Es ist also analoges Sein von Gott her und somit zu Gott hin.]

90. Balthasar, "Analogie und Dialektik," 211: "Analogy, as we saw, has in it the authenticity that is the expression of the ever greater distance . . . of the creature to God." [Die Analogie hat, wie wir sahen, darin ihre Echtheit, daß sie der Ausdruck der je größeren Distanz . . . Geschöpfes zu Gott ist.]

91. See esp. Balthaasar, *TD* III: "Christ's Mission and Person," 149–262; "Chosen and Sent Forth," 263–82.

92. Hans Urs von Balthasar, *A Theology of History* (San Francisco: Ignatius Press, 1994); originally published as *Theologie der Geschicte* as a second edition in 1959. Hans Urs von Balthasar, *A Theological Anthropology* (New York: Sheed & Ward, 1968); originally published as *Das Ganze im Fragment: Aspekte der Geschichtstheologie* in 1963.

93. Balthasar, *A Theology of History*, 7–14.

94. Balthasar, *A Theology of History*, 15.

95. Balthasar, *A Theology of History*, 17.

96. Balthasar, *A Theology of History*, 21.

97. Balthasar, *A Theology of History*, 32.

98 See especially "Christ the Norm of History," in *A Theology of History*, 81–112.

99. Hans Urs von Balthasar, *Das Ganze im Fragment* (Einseideln: Benziger, 1963), 104–5. Translation mine. The English can be found in Balthasar, *A Theological Anthropology*, 84. [Entweder ist der Mensch abermals zum Geist (aus Materie) zu erlösen, unter Verzicht auf seine einmalige Personalität (so bei Hegel und dessen Vor- und Nachfahren), oder der tragische Dualismus bleibt das letzte Wort, das heroisch die Unvollendbarkeit (als ewige Wiederkehr) absolut setzt (bei Nietzsche), oder das Fragment erfährt im "Scheitern" (Jaspers) und in der "Entschlossenheit zum Tod" (Heidegger) ein Aufblitzen der Ganzheit, deren man nur auf sie verzichtend ansichtig und teilhaft wird.]

100. Balthasar, *A Theological Anthropology*, 245: "The eternal Word could not have made himself intelligible to temporal beings by speaking in the form of their existence unless this temporal existence had something like a sense of the eternal: of having come from God and of going to God, a creaturely fullness of meaning and beauty, which reflects the eternal."

101. Balthasar, *Das Ganze im Fragment*, 273. Translation mine. Cf. Balthasar, *A Theological Anthropology*, 249. [Unendlich vielfältig sind die Weisen des Wortes, sich uns verständlich zu machen. Seine Menschheit ist ein Instrument, dem jede Melodie entlockt werden kann; noch das Verstummen, die Pause, kann zur eindrücklichen Art der Mitteilung werden. Ebenso vielfältig

wie deren Weisen sind aber auch die vom Wort geschenkten Weisen, es auf-
zufassen.]

102. Balthasar, *TL* II, 33. Translation mine. The English can be found in
TL II, 35. [Der Mensch Jesus ist die Wahrheit als Ausdruck des Vaters und
wird als solche Wahrheit vom Geist ausgelegt. Aber da dieser Mensch Jesus
darin zugleich der Ausdruck des ganzen Gottes ist (der Vater und der Geist
sind in ihm), kann die menschliche Logik, in der er Gott ausdrückt, selber
nichts anderes sein als ein "Bild und Gleichnis" des dreieinigen Gottes.]

103. This is the theme of *Mysterium Paschale*, especially "Cross and
Church," 129–35. Von Balthasar recapitulates on this theme in *TD* V, "Man in
God's Undergirding," 323–72.

104. Balthasar, *TL* II, 69. See also p. 70, which expands on Christ's humanity by considering his total humility, drawing on language from Phil 2:5–
11: "We see, then, that the total otherness of the man Jesus with respect to all
other human beings (whom he calls his brothers only on the day of Easter [Jn
20:17]) must be interpreted as a total otherness within a perfect equality of
human nature ("*perfectum in humanitate*" [perfect in humanity]: DS 301). . . .
He reveals that he is wholly other precisely in his abasement, his humility, his
service of all (Mk 10:45 par). And this very inimitable quality is what those
who grasp its meaning are to imitate."

105. Balthasar, *TL* II, 73. "This twofold image-character of the incarnate
Son contains, as it were, in a nutshell the whole Chalcedonian dogma."

106. Balthasar, *GL* I, 467–80.

107. This theme begins explicitly in *TL* II, 72, but is already set up in its
foundations as early as *GL* I: "The Mediation of Scripture," 527–55; "The Testimony of the Father," 605–18, which together place Jesus's function as image
in a thoroughly Scriptural and Trinitarian context. All of this is established in
seed form when von Balthasar insists that Jesus is the "archetype," which is
what we might call a broader quality of an image. See *GL* I, "Jesus' Experience
of God," 321–30.

108. Von Balthasar's most concentrated effort to explain this Trinitarian
dynamic occurs in *Explorations in Theology I*, "God Speaks as Man," 69–93.

109. Peter J. Casarella, "The Expression and Form of the Word: Trini-
tarian Hermeneutics and the Sacramentality of Language in Hans Urs von
Balthasar's Theology," in *Glory, Grace, and Culture: The Work of Hans Urs von
Balthasar*, ed. Ed Block (Mahwah, NJ: Paulist Press, 2005), 37–68.

110. See Balthasar, *TL* II, 77–78. Two excerpts in particular are helpful
here: "He speaks to what man, as the 'image and likeness' of God, already possesses in the way of rational and ethical insight . . . as he goes about expositing

divine logic in human logic, the Logos does not find the latter unprepared" (77–78).

111. Balthasar, *Theologik* II, 76. Translation mine. English available in *TL* II, 81–82. Von Balthasar calls this creative relationship an *analogia linguae* based in the *analogia entis*. [geschöpflicher Logik, das Gewicht göttlicher Logik auszuhalten, dank der Kunst der letztern ersichtlich wird: Gott hat ja die Kreatur nach seinem Bild und Gleichnis geschaffen, damit sie durch seine Gnade von innen her fähig würde, ihm gleichsam als Klangkörper zu deinen, durch den er sich ausdrücken und verständlich machen kann. Es geht jetzt somit nicht mehr bloß um die Strukturen der menschlichen Sprache, sondern um die in der Struktur des weltlichen Seins selbst liegende "Sprache."]

112. Balthasar, *TL* II, 82: "This similitude in 'greater dissimilitude' begins already with the nonidentity of being [Sein] and essence [Wesen] within the identity of the creature's existence—a nonidentity that displays the "structural reflection of triune Being." He cites *TD* V, 75, and he later cites *TD* V, 114. See also *TL* II, 248: "Jesus, too, speaks the language of the flesh. It is the language of corporeal-spiritual man, who, as mortal creature exposed to need and danger on every side, is the center of God's creation and speaks to other men."

113. Balthasar, *TL* II, 122

114. Balthasar, *TL* II, 252.

115. Balthasar, *TL* II, 254.

116. Balthasar, *TL* II, 256.

117. Balthasar, *TL* II, 275.

118. Danielle Nussberger, "Saint as Theological Wellspring: Hans Urs von Balthasar's Hermeneutic of the Saint in a Christological and Trinitarian Key," PhD diss., University of Notre Dame, 2007. See esp. 31–32, 78, 81–82. "He [Balthasar] is the artist who looks upon these saints in order to learn how to see the Christ to whom they are transparent. In the end, he recreates their portraits in word so that we might view them as well and train ourselves to take the truth we have perceived and vivify it so that it too can be seen by others" (114).

119. Balthasar, *TL* II, 254.

120. Murphy, *Christ the Form of Beauty*, 150.

121. Balthasar, *TL* II, 254. Von Balthasar cites the *conversio ad phantasma*.

122. Balthasar, *TL* II, 264.

123. Balthasar, *TL* II, 277.

124. Balthasar, *TL* II, 280.

125. Balthasar, *TL* II, 249. This is a section that expands from a discussion of Bonaventure.

FOUR. A Theological Poetic

1. See Scola, *Balthasar: A Theological Style*, esp. 6: "If we consider, for example, the great Trilogy, the expression 'systematic arrangement' explains Balthasar's option of developing the *intellectus fidei* of revelation in the triple scansion of glory, drama, and logic, as well as his peculiar hierarchy of the contents of the faith. They are choices which go beyond stylistic means of expression and correspond to precise reasons, to a specific logic (a systematic arrangement!)."

2. D. Stephen Long, *Speaking of God: Theology, Language, and Truth* (Grand Rapids, MI: William B. Eerdmans, 2009), 2. Long's claim here, as well as his development of it, closely resembles the essays on the Word to be found in Hans Urs von Balthasar, *Explorations I: The Word Made Flesh*, trans. A. V. Littledale with Alexander Dru (San Francisco: Ignatius Press, 1989), especially "The Word, Scripture and Tradition," 11–26; "The Word and History," 27–46; "The Implications of the Word," 47–68; "God Speaks as Man," 69–94.

3. The claims that Matthew Levering makes in *Scripture and Metaphysics*, using Thomas Aquinas to place metaphysical reality in a dynamic relationship to the language of Scripture, Long makes with respect to metaphysics and politics. See Matthew Levering, *Scripture and Metaphysics: Aquinas and the Renewal of Trinitarian Theology* (Malden, MA: Blackwell, 2004). While Long is very positive about von Balthasar's use in these problems, Levering strains toward the negative.

4. There are some, such as Alyssa Lyra Pitstick, who would see the two poles of Long's thought as merely one position, a Protestant one. That is, there are scholars who view von Balthasar and his voluminous insistences on God's utter transcendence as a crypto-Protestantism. See Alyssa Lyra Pitstick, "More on Balthasar, Hell and Heresy," *First Things* 169 (2007): 16–19; Alyssa Lyra Pitstick, "Balthasar, Hell, and Heresy: An Exchange," *First Things* 168 (2006): 25–32; Alyssa Lyra Pitstick, "Development of Doctrine, or Denial? Balthasar's Holy Saturday and Newman's Essay," *International Journal of Systematic Theology* 11, no. 2 (2009): 129–45.

For his part, Long desires to avoid the prominent weaknesses of both Protestant and Catholic thought: "If postliberal (Protestant) theology is tempted to eschew metaphysics for biblical narrative and a kind of historicism, Roman Catholic theology is often tempted to divide metaphysics from theology too thoroughly and make the former the foundation for the latter" (*Speaking of God*, 65). Von Balthasar and Barth, operating together in Long's book, form the ecumenical anchor by which Long is capable of adopting metaphysics without permitting it to "rule" God.

5. Long, *Speaking of God*, 33: "Theology, grounded in faith, claims that the same modes of signifying that reason uses can exceed the language used and give knowledge of God, because it always is a gift from God given in language."

6. Long, *Speaking of God*, 215.

7. See the final chapter, "Truth," in *Speaking of God*, 261–326.

8. Charles Taylor, *Human Agency and Language*, Philosophical Papers, vol. 1 (New York: Cambridge University Press, 1985), 219.

9. Charles Taylor, "Heidegger on Language," in *A Companion to Heidegger*, ed. Hubert L. Dreyfus and Mark A. Wrathall (Malden, MA: Blackwell, 2005), 433.

10. Taylor, "Heidegger on Language," 433–34. Cf. p. 438: "The constitutive theory turns our attention toward the creative dimension of expression, in which, to speak paradoxically, it makes possible its own content."

11. Taylor, "Heidegger on Language," 433.

12. Taylor, "Heidegger on Language," 440.

13. Taylor, *Human Agency and Language*, 229.

14. Taylor, "Heidegger on Language," 441.

15. Taylor, "Heidegger on Language," 445.

16. Taylor, "Heidegger on Language," 451.

17. Taylor, *Human Agency and Language*, 219.

18. Long, *Speaking of God*, 239.

19. This way of describing truth and language is partially drawn from Bernard Lonergan. He discusses a similar position at length in "The Notion of Transcendent Knowledge," in *Insight: A Study of Human Understanding*, Collected Works of Bernard Lonergan, vol. 3 (Toronto: University of Toronto Press, 1992), 662–64. Lonergan calls the relationship between knowledge and language a "genetic inpenetration," which nevertheless does not render the two identical (*Insight*, 578–79). Von Balthasar attempts a comparable differentiation in knowledge with the close of *TL* I, "Truth as Participation," 227–72.

20. Long, *Speaking of God*, 280.

21. Hans Urs von Balthasar, "Who Is the Church?" in *Explorations in Theology II: The Spouse of the Word* (San Francisco: Ignatius Press, 1991), 161.

22. Long, *Speaking of God*, 305.

23. Long, *Speaking of God*, 311.

24. Lonergan, *Insight*, 576–77. "It is one thing to assert and another to judge, for men can lie."

25. Paul J. Griffiths, *Lying: An Augustinian Theology of Duplicity* (Eugene, OR: Wipf & Stock, 2010), 25. "The characteristic mark of the lie is duplicity, a fissure between thought and utterance that is clearly evident to the speaker

as she speaks. Lying words are spoken precisely with the intent to create such a fissure: the liar takes control of her speech, and marks it as her own when she separates it from her thought and grants it autonomy. When this is done, speech becomes the possession and instrument of the speaker. When it is not done, speech comes to birth spontaneously, as an act of gratitude and praise to its giver. Lies require effort; truth none."

26. Charles Taylor, "Heidegger on Language," 452. "Heidegger has no place for the retrieval of evil in his system, and that is part of the reason why Hitler could blindside him."

27. Balthasar, *Herrlichkeit* I, 236. Cf. *GL* I, 245. Translation mine. [Dieses ist seinshaft Resonanz auf Gott und für Gott, ist es in seiner Ganzheit und vor jeder Differenzierung seiner Vermögen in geistige und sensitive, aktive und passive. Weil Gott auf keiner Ebene Kreatur ist und gemeinsames Sein mit ihr hat, ist diese ursprüngliche Einstimmung auf ihn keine Intuition im erkenntnistheoretischen Sinn, sie ist aber auch nicht das Ergebnis eines blossen logischen "Schlusses" vom Endlichen auf das Unendliche; die Unfixierbarkeit dieser Ersterfahrung ist nur der noetische Widerschein der ontischen Unfestlegbarkeit des Seins im ganzen gegenüber Gott. Es ist als solches mit sich selber verweisend auf die unnahbare Quelle.]

28. This highly Thomist assessment of transcendence also sets apart von Balthasar from his friend Karl Barth, who was suspicious of analogy, yet without which von Balthasar cannot rightly understand transcendence. Much as his concern for God's absolute difference from the world was emphasized in sympathy with Barth, von Balthasar construes that difference distinctly: he construes it through the analogy of being.

29. Balthasar, *GL* I, 243–44. "It is not by means of one isolated faculty that man is open, in knowledge and in love, to the Thou, to things and to God: it is *as a whole* (through all his faculties) that man is attuned to total reality, and no one has shown this more profoundly and more thoroughly than Thomas Aquinas."

30. Balthasar, *TL* I, 230. "God is necessarily affirmed concomitantly, whether explicitly or not, in every cognition of truth. At the same time, this implicit affirmation safeguards two things. First, the manifestness of God's being is immediately traced back to his primordial freedom to manifest himself. . . . Second, that God's self-manifestation reveals his lordly freedom and thus his concealment in himself."

31. Thomas Aquinas, *De ver.*, q. 22, a. 1. All quotations taken from Thomas Aquinas, *Truth*, 3 vols., trans. Robert W. Schmidt (Chicago: Henry Regnery, 1952–54).

32. Balthasar, *TL* I, 262.

33. Balthasar, *TL* I, 227.

34. We are able, therefore, to discuss sin and evil, which have no intelligibility or being of their own in classical metaphysics, yet this ability also betrays the possibility of a lie. If we can express what lacks being, then we are capable of attempting to take as truth what has no being.

35. Aquinas, *De ver.*, q. 1, a. 10. There is a "threat" here of understanding Aquinas as if he were a naïve correspondence theorist, a designative language theory of the worst kind. This is by no means the case, as will become apparent later in this chapter. See the section "A Governed Theo-Poetic," 219–27.

36. Aquinas, *De ver.*, q. 1, a. 10. "As was pointed out previously, however, the relation to the divine intellect is essential to a thing; and in this respect a thing is said to be true in itself. Its relation to the human intellect is accidental to it; and in this respect a thing is not true, absolutely speaking but, as it were, in some respect and in potency. Therefore, all things are true absolutely speaking, and nothing is false. But in a certain respect, that is, with reference to our intellect, some things are said to be false. Hence, it is necessary to answer the arguments of both sides."

37. See Henri de Lubac, *The Discovery of God* (Grand Rapids, MI: William B. Eerdmans, 1996), 35. His footnote also cites Joseph Maréchal, and von Balthasar's *Wahrheit*. Other influences on de Lubac's interpretation of Aquinas include the theologian Pierre Rousselot. See Hans Boersma, *Nouvelle Théologie and Sacramental Ontology: A Return to Mystery* (New York: Oxford University Press, 2009), 67.

38. See Aidan Nichols, "Thomism and the nouvelle théologie," *The Thomist* 64 (2000): 1–19; Fergus Kerr, *After Aquinas: Versions of Thomism* (Malden, MA: Wiley-Blackwell, 2002), 134–39. Kerr's discussion includes Barth's critique of the entire Catholic argument, a helpful contrast to the presuppositions that the Catholics share even as they argue bitterly with one another.

39. Balthasar, *Theologik*, 64. Translation mine. Cf. Balthasar, *TL* I, 67. [Ohne ein im Raum seiner Rezeptivität sich anzeigendes Objekt bleibt das Subjekt unfähig, seine Erkenntnismöglichkeiten in wirkliche Erkenntnis überzuführen. Die aufgeschlagene Bühne bleibt leer; das Drama der Erkenntnis wird nicht gespielt. Erst wenn das Fremde in den Raum des Subjekts eintritt, erwacht es aus dem Dornröschenschlaf: zugleich zur Welt und zu sich selbst.]

40. Balthasar, *TL* I, 77–78.

41. Balthasar, *TL* I, 78.

42. Hans Urs von Balthasar, *Love Alone Is Credible*, trans. D. C. Schindler (San Francisco: Ignatius Press, 2004), 76. Cf. Balthasar, *My Work*, 115, and *TL* I, 78: "even the gaze with which God looks upon his creatures is not only the judging gaze of justice but also the loving gaze of mercy."

43. Balthasar, *TL* II, 256. "[T]he I and the Thou bear the trace of the Logos, of the expression of God, in themselves—and not only they, but everything that can be considered as being and that, therefore, itself possesses the power of *expressio*, the capacity to express itself." See also chapter 3, "Christological Language."

44. Balthasar, *GL* III, 63.

45. Aidan Nichols also alludes to the "vertical" and "horizontal" axes of von Balthasar's thought. Cf. *A Key to Balthasar*, 17–18.

46. Balthasar, *TL* II, 254–56.

47. Charles Taylor, *A Secular Age* (Cambridge, MA: Belknap, 2007), 757.

48. Taylor, *A Secular Age*, 759.

49. Taylor, *A Secular Age*, 758.

50. Poetry also resonates or echoes themes within a single poem and echoes previous poetic tradition. Artistic tropes, one of the most prominent being the rose, draw on a complex series of meanings that are part of poetic tradition and wider cultural imagination. Poetry will even echo sound patterns, as in a tightly ordered rhyme scheme.

51. The Latin word for reading, *legere*, bears a similar implication at the etymological level: it literally means, "to pick out," since for Latin readers there were neither spaces nor punctuation to differentiate words and sentences. A reader had to draw out even the words to understand them.

52. Hans Urs von Balthasar, *GL* VII, 131.

53. Taylor, *A Secular Age*, 759.

54. Taylor, *A Secular Age*, 756.

55. Balthasar, *TL* I, 81–82. See my discussion of this passage in chapter 3.

56. Balthasar, *GL* I, 443. "[I]n God the distances between work and creator are infinite; no natural bridge mediates between them, no ready-made system of expressions of an organic-spiritual kind provides a grammar, as it were, in terms of which an individual work could be spelled out and understood. Nor can the general 'concept' of Being (*analogia entis*) be regarded as such a grammar. It is the art of the artist, rather, that in the worldly form which he has invented as his image and likeness, he has on his own initiative also placed and conferred that expressive and revelatory power which allows us to look from this particular surface and understand this particular and unique depth."

57. Balthasar, *Epilogue*, 51–57.

58. Balthasar, *TL* I, 229–31.

59. The self-diffusive goodness of being is a concept drawn from both Scholastic thought, as in Thomas Aquinas, as well as from Pseudo-Dionysius. Cf. Thomas Aquinas, *ST* I, qq. 5–6; Pseudo-Dionysius, *Celestial and Ecclesiastical Hierarchies*.

60. Balthasar, *Herrlichkeit*, 425. Translation mine. Cf. Balthasar, *GL* I, 442. [Mit der gesehen Oberfläche der Erscheinung wird die nicht erscheinende Tiefe wahrgenommen, erst das gibt dem Phänomen des Schönen seinen hinreissenden und überwältigenden Charakter, wie es dem Seienden auch erst seine Wahrheit und Güte sichert. Das gilt ebensosehr für das Naturschöne wie für das Kunstschöne.]

61. Aquinas, *De ver.*, q. 1, a. 4.

62. Aquinas, *De ver.*, q. 1, a. 12.

63. See Aquinas, *De ver.*, q. 10, a. 6: "it is true that our mind receives knowledge from sensible things; nevertheless, the soul itself forms in itself likenesses of things, inasmuch as through the light of the agent intellect the forms abstracted from sensible things are made actually intelligible so that they may be received in the possible intellect."

64. See Thomas Aquinas, *The Division and Methods of the Sciences: Questions IV and V of His Commentary on the De Trinitate of Boethius*, trans. Armand Maurer (Toronto: Pontifical Institute of Medieval Studies, 1986), q. 4, a. 2.

65. The repetition of words and actions in the liturgy bears this sort of specificity, especially when the priest lifts the host and repeats, "Do this in memory of me."

66. For an extended reflection, see Balthasar, *TL* I, "Subject and Object," 61–78.

67. There are entire books about this phenomenon. A prominent one by Daniel Tiffany, *Infidel Poetics: Riddles, Nightlife, Substance* (Chicago: University of Chicago Press, 2009) gives a broad sense of the varying forms of obscurity in poetry and its critique. The book imitates the form of the art at hand as much as it speculates about it.

68. Hans Urs von Balthasar, *Explorations* IV, 47. Cf. "The Christian Form," in *Explorations in Theology IV: Spirit and Institution*, trans. Edward T. Oakes (San Francisco: Ignatius Press, 1995), 50–51. [Vergessen wir nicht, daß "Gestalt" doch vornehmlich der Kunst zugeordnet ist, die im hegelschen System ihren klassischen Ort bei den Griechen hat und für die Gegenwart eigentlich passée ist. . . . Hier liegt die entscheidende Herausforderung an das Christentum.]

69. Hans Urs von Balthasar, "Revelation and the Beautiful," in *Explorations in Theology I: The Word Made Flesh*, trans. A. V. Littledale and Alexander Dru (San Francisco: Ignatius Press, 1989), 109.

70. Aquinas, *Division and Methods*, q. 4, a. 2.

71. Balthasar, "Revelation and the Beautiful," 126.

72. See Balthasar, "The World Is from God," in *TD* V, 61–190.

73. This interpretation of von Balthasar's hierarchy as I work it out here runs counter to many feminist interpretations thereof. These latter are suspicious of hierarchy as a presupposition for an oppressive system of thinking. My interpretation sees hierarchy as a supposition for the sake of freedom, and as not an exclusively evaluative system (i.e., a system that posits the greater or lesser worth of something or someone in the eyes of God). Whereas authors such as Linn Marie Tonstad view von Balthasar's Christological hierarchy as an investment, and entrapment, in tragedy, I understand that Christological hierarchy to secure the overcoming of tragedy and indeed of investments in over-evaluative statements. Cf. Linn Marie Tonstad, "Sexual Difference and Trinitarian Death: Cross, Kenosis, and Hierarchy in the Theo-Drama," *Modern Theology* 26, no. 4 (2010): 603–31, esp. 623–25. Of this disagreement, more would have to be written.

74. Aquinas, *De ver.*, q. 1, a. 1.

75. The poem also adopts G. M. Hopkins's language of inscape and instress, and would also require familiarity with his theory to grasp it—as well as to grasp the way the poem adjusts the meaning of Hopkins's words for the sake of allying it with Thomas Aquinas. While Hopkins's theory will receive attention in the next chapter, a long exegesis of "Conversio Ad Phantasmata" is beyond the scope of the book.

76. See, for example, Gabriel Torretta's critique of modern art in "Art's Irrational Infanta," in *First Things, On the Square,* June 20, 2011, http://www.firstthings.com/onthesquare/2011/06/artrsquos-irrational-infanta.

77. Balthasar, "Christology and Ecclesial Obedience," in *Explorations IV*, 158.

78. Balthasar, "Christology and Ecclesial Obedience," 161.

79. Balthasar, *Herrlichkeit*, 447–48. Translation mine. Cf. Balthasar, *GL* I, 465–66. [Das entscheidend Einleuchtende liegt dann bei ihm, und zwar in der doppelten Hinsicht: dass die Figur, die Christus bildet, an sich eine innere Richtigkeit und Evidenz hat, wie sie—auf anderem, reinweltlichem Gebiet—ein Kunstwerk oder ein mathematischer Satz hat, und dass diese in den Verhältnissen der Sache liegende Richtigkeit zudem die Macht hat, von sich ausstrahlend in den auffassenden Menschen einzustrahlen, was keineswegs nur intellektuell, sondern existenzwandelnd gemeint ist.]

80. Nor is poetry by any means the exclusive analogue for theology's "logic"!

81. Aquinas, *De ver.*, q. 4, a. 6. Cf. q. 4, a. 4: "because the Son is a word that perfectly expresses the Father, the Son expresses all creatures."

82. Aquinas, *De ver.*, q. 4, a. 8. Cf. the rest of a. 6.

FIVE. Art, Metaphysics, and the Sacraments

1. Aidan Nichols reminds us that the sensual (sense-oriented) qualities of von Balthasar's aesthetics, which scholarship often overlooks, form one of the basic pillars of von Balthasar's definition of the term "aesthetic." His definition is a combination of the Scholastic (*pulchrum*) and the Romantic (sublime). Cf. Nichols, *A Key to Balthasar*, 15–18.

2. See Balthasar, "Rilke und die religiöse Dichtung," 184.

3. Excerpt, Rilke, "Bowl of Roses," translation mine.

4. See also Rilke's poem "Das Rosen-Innere," which concentrates on many of the same themes: "Wo ist zu diesem Innen / ein Außen?"

5. From *Apokalypse* forward, von Balthasar notes the way Rilke draws from but a few basic themes and explores them with increasing urgency. This is the poetic form of his circling restlessness. Cf. Balthasar, *Apokalypse III*, 201; "Rilke und die religiöse Dichtung," 189–92; a poetic restlessness that even bleeds into his life, TD V, 417: "Innumerable women will follow Lou and his wife Clara, but they are no more than occasions for awakening anew that 'intransitive' love which has no 'Thou', for which Rilke strives, which he demands from others and which in all his works is the object of his teaching."

6. See *GL* I, 60 and *GL* V, 321 for references to this concept in von Balthasar, both drawn from the author Walter Rhem, a literary and philosophical critic of training similar to von Balthasar's original advanced degree. Von Balthasar's unique response to the concept is best summarized in *GL* I, 237.

7. See especially *TL* I, "The World of the Images," 132–78.

8. This is quite similar to Bernard Lonergan's concept of a "world mediated by meaning." See especially Bernard Lonergan, "The World Mediated by Meaning," *Philosophical and Theological Papers 1965–1980*, Collected Works of Bernard Lonergan, 107–18.

9. See Balthasar, *Love Alone Is Credible*, esp. "The Third Way of Love," 51–60.

10. O'Regan, *Anatomy of Misremembering I*, 454.

11. Balthasar, *GL* III, 353–54. Other work on Balthasar and Hopkins includes Bernadette Waterman Ward, "Hopkins, Scotus and von Balthasar: Philosophical Theology in Poetry," 68–77, and Fergus Kerr, "Balthasar, Hopkins, and the 'English Tradition,'" 81–95, both of which can be found in *Theological Aesthetics after von Balthasar*, ed. Oleg V. Bychkov and James Fodor (Burlington, VT: Ashgate, 2008).

12. Balthasar, *GL* III, 354–55. In the case of Hopkins, the resistance to universal concepts is displayed with a unique radicality. Von Balthasar notes the poet's reticence toward mythology, for example (355), which is itself a further sign of his willingness to move freely past his own tradition—whose poetry took great advantage of ancient mythology—to reach into its very "origins," which makes Hopkins a creature of "astonishing independence" (353).

13. Cf. Balthasar, *GL* III, 355 and 357.

14. See "Dun Scotus's Oxford." All of Hopkins's poems are taken from *Gerard Manley Hopkins: Poems and Prose*, ed. W. H. Gardner (New York: Penguin, 1984).

15. Scotus serves as one knot in a great tangle of broken metaphysical history. Note, for example, the succession here: "how small the steps are, and how internally consistent, from an ontological formalism (Scotus) to empiricism (Ockham), and from pure theological voluntarism and 'positionism' to a positivism which possesses no values, and from there, quite consistently, to materialistic atomism." Balthasar, *GL* V, 21.

16. Balthasar, *GL* III, 357. Elsewhere, von Balthasar will describe Hopkins's breaking-through as "A tense, utterly objective contemplation of the primal power of nature, the language of nature expressing itself free from any hindrance" (360).

17. Balthasar, *GL* III, 361.

18. Balthasar, *GL* III, 377.

19. Balthasar, *GL* III, 390.

20. Balthasar, *GL* III, 365. Cf. Wimsatt, *Hopkins' Poetics of Speech Sound: Sprung Rhythm, Lettering, Inscape* (Toronto: University of Toronto Press, 2006), 104.

21. Balthasar, *GL* III, 366. Cf. Wimsatt, *Hopkins's Poetics of Speech Sound*, 106.

22. See Gerard Manley Hopkins, *The Note-Books and Papers of Gerard Manley Hopkins*, ed. Humphrey House (New York: Oxford University Press, 1937).

23. Balthasar, *GL* III, 366.

24. See esp. Balthasar, *GL* III, 370, 387.

25. G. M. Hopkins, "Morning Midday and Evening Sacrifice," excerpt.

26. G. M. Hopkins, "Thee, God, I come from, to thee go," excerpt.

27. Balthasar, *GL* III, 285–86.

28. See, for example, a book written before most of von Balthasar's trilogy was translated: David Anthony Downes, *The Great Sacrifice: Studies in Hopkins* (Lanham, MD: University Press of America, 1983). Or there is a work heavily influenced by von Balthasar's read of Hopkins: Phillip A. Ballinger, *The Poem*

as Sacrament: The Theological Aesthetic of Gerard Manley Hopkins (Lueven, Belgium: Peeters, 2000).

29. Von Balthasar's description of Hopkins's "great sacrifice" sounds especially like his description of the Son's Eucharistic surrender on the cross as in *TD* V, "Christ the Trinitarian Meaning of the World," 118–30, and "Existence in the Life/Death of Christ," 323–45, both of which serve as a reworking of large themes in *Mysterium Paschale*. Christ surrenders himself to the Father on the cross, and this surrender is the economic expression of his eternal disposition as Son: always to be giving himself over in thanksgiving (*eucharistein*) to the Father. Note the similarity of these themes as compared with his analysis of Hopkins, as in *GL* III, 384: "Christ girds chaos in his descent into Hell—and his coming is always a descent—but he determines too the decisive selving of all created persons who achieve their 'pitch' only in their victory over self for him."

30. See *GL* III, 86–107.

31. G. M. Hopkins, "The Blessed Virgin compared to the air we breathe," excerpt.

32. Von Balthasar exegetes the theme, though not the poem, in *GL* III, 378: "Now if we are indeed from all eternity predetermined and called by God to be brothers and members of Christ, the core of our personal 'pitch' lies in the supernatural, and thus our self-choice can only be perfected concretely within the grace of God." See also Francesca Ann Murphy, *Christ the Form of Beauty: A Study in Theology and Literature* (Edinburgh: T & T Clark, 1995), 172: "Hopkins exercises what Maritain takes to be the poetic prerogative of seizing upon the irreducibility of objects. He finds the finite image he seeks in the Form of Christ." Cf. p. 173.

33. See Balthasar, *GL* III, 383–87, esp. 387: "This doctrine of grace changed the natural doctrine of instress and inscape, for the true inscape of all things is Christ. For now it is really God who has the true taste of the human self in his mouth." Cf. Ward, "Hopkins, Scotus and von Balthasar: Philosophical Theology in Poetry," 77.

34. Balthasar, *GL* III, 396–97.

35. Balthasar, *GL* III, 392. This is opposed to the perspectives of Idealism.

36. Balthasar, *GL* III, 398–99.

37. All quotations taken from "The Wreck of the Deutschland," in *Gerard Manley Hopkins: Poems and Prose*, ed. W. H. Gardner (New York: Penguin, 1984), 12–24.

38. Balthasar, *GL* I, 243–44.

39. Cf. Balthasar, *GL* IV, 393–50, esp. 395.

40. Balthasar, *GL* III, 355.

41. Balthasar, *GL* III, 390.

42. Balthasar, *GL* III, 398.

43. Louis Mackey, *Peregrinations of the Word: Essays in Medieval Philosophy* (Ann Arbor: University of Michigan Press, 1997), 179. Cf. the whole section, "Singular and Universal: A Franciscan Perspective," 147–80.

44. See Scotus, "Concerning Metaphysics," in *Philosophical Writings*, 1–12. *Ordinatio* for his full discussion of the concept. Cf. Etienne Gilson, *Being and Some Philosophers* (Toronto: Pontifical Institute of Mediaeval Studies, 1952), 94.

45. John Duns Scotus, *Philosophical Writings*, ed. and trans. Allan Wolter (Edinburgh: Nelson and Sons, 1962), 19: "God is conceived not only in a concept analogous to the concept of a creature, that is, one which is wholly other than that which is predicated of creatures, but even in some concept univocal to Himself and to a creature."

46. Scotus, *Philosophical Writings*, 5, 20. Cf. Richard Cross, *Duns Scotus on God* (Burlington, VT: Ashgate, 2005), 110: "Scotus believes that, in order for God and creatures to fall under the extension of the same concepts, the various divine and human features in virtue of which the same concepts are applicable must be, at root, the same."

47. Scotus, *Philosophical Writings*, 2.

48. Cf. Thomas Aquinas, *The Summa Theologica of Thomas Aquinas*, trans. Fathers of the English Dominican Province, vol. 1. (Chicago: University of Chicago Press, 1952), q. 47, "The distinction of things in general."

49. See Richard Cross, "Haecceity in Duns Scotus," in *The Stanford Encyclopedia of Philosophy* (Stanford: Stanford University Press, 2010), http://plato.stanford.edu/entries/medieval-haecceity/#3.

50. Gilson, "Being and Some Philosophers," 89.

51. Cross, *Duns Scotus on God*, 254.

52. See Scotus, *Philosophical Writings*, 24; cf. 6.

53. Catherine Pickstock, *After Writing: On the Consummation of Philosophy* (Malden, MA: Blackwell, 1998), 123–26.

54. Pickstock, *After Writing*, 127.

55. See "Chapter 4: I Will Go Unto the Altar of God: The Impossible Liturgy," in *After Writing*, 169–219.

56. Pickstock, *After Writing*, 128–29.

57. Aquinas, *ST* I, q. 3, aa. 3–4.

58. Rudi te Velde, *Aquinas on God: The 'Divine Science' of the Summa Theologiae* (Burlington, VT: Ashgate, 2006), 139–40.

59. Rudi A. te Velde, *Participation and Substantiality in Thomas Aquinas* (New York: Brill, 1995), 116.

60. Max Horkheimer and Theodor W. Adorno, *Dialectic of Enlightenment: Philosophical Fragments*, ed. Gunzelin Schmid Noerr, trans. Edmund Jephcott (Stanford: Stanford University Press, 2002), 2–29.

61. Balthasar, *TD IV*, 92.

62. Horkheimer and Adorno, "Culture Industry," in *Dialectic of Enlightenment*, 94–136.

63. The framing device in *Theo-Drama IV* is the Book of Revelation, in which von Balthasar works through both human time and God's actions, imitating many of his familiar uses of the analogy of being. My interpretation here makes these metaphysical assumptions explicit. See Balthasar, "Under the Sign of the Apocalypse," in *TD IV*, 15–70.

64. Pickstock, *After Writing*, 133–34.

65. Wimsatt, "Hopkins's Poetic Speech of Sound," 107.

66. Hopkins, "Wreck of the Deutschland," §15.

67. Hopkins, "Wreck of the Deutschland," §33.

68. Hopkins, "Wreck of the Deutschland," §35.

BIBLIOGRAPHY

The Analogy of Beauty: The Theology of Hans Urs von Balthasar. Edited by John Riches. Edinburgh: T & T Clark, 1986.

The Analogy of Being: Invention of the Antichrist or the Wisdom of God? Edited by Thomas Joseph White. Grand Rapids, MI.: William B. Eerdmans, 2011.

Babini, Ellero. "Jesus Christ, Form and Norm of Man According to Hans Urs von Balthasar." Translated by Thérèse M Bonin. *Communio* 16 (1989): 446–57.

Ballinger, Phillip A. *The Poem as Sacrament: The Theological Aesthetic of Gerard Manley Hopkins.* Lueven, Belgium: Peeters, 2000.

Balthasar, Hans Urs von. "Analogie und Dialektik." *Divus Thomas* 22 (1944): 171–216.

———. "Analogie und Natur." *Divus Thomas* 23 (1945): 3–56.

———. "Antikritik." *Schweizeriche Rundschau* 40 (1940): 453–60.

———. *Apokalypse der deutschen Seele: Studien zu einer Lehre von letzten Haltungen.* 3 vols. Freiburg: Johannes Verlag, 1998.

———. "Bruch und Bruecke zwischen Wirken und Leiden Jesu." *Christusglaube und Christusverehrung.* Aschaffenburg: Paul Pattloch, 1982, 14–24.

———. "Christliche Kunst und Verkündigung." *Mysterium Salutis,* vol. 1. Edited by J. Feiner and M. Löhrer. Einseldeine and Cologne, 1965, 708–26.

———. *Cosmic Liturgy: The Universe According to Maximus the Confessor.* Translated by Brian Daley. San Francisco: Ignatius Press, 2003.

———. *Das Ganze im Fragment.* Einsiedeln: Benziger, 1963.

———. "Das Selbstbewusstsein Jesu." *Internationale katholische Zeitschrift Communio* 8 (1979): 30–39.

———. *Die Entwicklung der musikalischen Idee: Versuch einer Synthese der Musik.* Braunschweig, 1925.

———. "Die Kunst in der Zeit." *Schweizeriche Rundschau* 40 (1940): 239–46.

———. "Die Metaphysik Erich Przywaras." *Schweizer Rundschau* 33 (1933): 489–99.

———. *Die Wahrheit ist Symphonisch: Aspekte des Christlichen Pluralismus.* Einsiedeln: Johannes Verlag, 1972.

———. "Earthly Beauty and Divine Glory." *Communio* 10, no. 3 (1983): 202–6.

———. *Epilog.* Einseideln: Johannes Verlag, 1987.

———. *Epilogue.* Translated by Graham Harrison. San Francisco: Ignatius Press, 1991.

———. *Explorations I: The Word Made Flesh.* Translated by A. V. Littledale and Alexander Dru. San Francisco: Ignatius Press, 1989.

———. *Explorations II: Spouse of the Word.* Translated by A. V. Littledale and Alexander Dru. San Francisco: Ignatius Press, 1999.

———. "The Fathers, the Scholastics, and Ourselves." *Communio* 24 (1997): 347–96.

———. *Glory of the Lord: A Theological Aesthetics I: Seeing the Form.* Translated by Erasmo Leiva-Merikakis. San Francisco: Ignatius Press, 1982.

———. *Glory of the Lord: A Theological Aesthetics II: Studies in Theological Style: Clerical Styles.* Translated by Erasmo Leiva-Merikakis. San Francisco: Ignatius Press, 1984.

———. *Glory of the Lord: A Theological Aesthetics III: Studies in Theological Style: Lay Styles.* Translated by Erasmo Leiva-Merikakis. San Francisco: Ignatius Press, 1986.

———. *Glory of the Lord: A Theological Aesthetics IV: The Realm of Metaphysics in Antiquity.* Translated by Erasmo Leiva-Merikakis. San Francisco: Ignatius Press, 1989.

———. *Glory of the Lord: A Theological Aesthetics V: The Realm of Metaphysics in the Modern Age.* Translated by Erasmo Leiva-Merikakis. San Francisco: Ignatius Press, 1990.

———. *Glory of the Lord: A Theological Aesthetics VI: Theology: The Old Covenant.* Translated by Erasmo Leiva-Merikakis. San Francisco: Ignatius Press, 1991.

———. *Glory of the Lord: A Theological Aesthetics VII: Theology: The New Covenant.* Translated by Erasmo Leiva-Merikakis. San Francisco: Ignatius Press, 1990.

———. *Herrlichkeit: Eine Theologische Äesthetik I: Schau Der Gestalt.* Einsiedeln: Johannes Verlag, 1961.

———. *Herrlichkeit: Eine Theologische Äesthetik II: Fächer Der Stile.* Einsiedeln: Johannes Verlag, 1962.

————. *Herrlichkeit: Eine Theologische Äesthetik III/1: Im Raum Der Metaphysik.* Einsiedeln: Johannes Verlag, 1965.

————. *Herrlichkeit: Eine Theologische Äesthetik III/2: Theologie Teil 1: Alter Bund.* Einsiedeln: Johannes Verlag, 1967.

————. *Herrlichkeit: Eine Theologische Äesthetik III/2: Theologie Teil 2: Neuer Bund.* Einsiedeln: Johannes Verlag, 1969.

————. "Katholische Religion und Kunst." *Schweizeriche Rundschau* 27 (1927): 44–54.

————. "Kunst und Religion." *Volkswohl* 18 (1927): 354–65.

————. *Love Alone Is Credible.* Translated by D. C. Schindler. San Francisco: Ignatius Press, 2005.

————. *Mysterium Paschale.* Translated by Aidan Nichols. San Francisco: Ignatius Press, 2005.

————. "On the Concept of Person." *Communio* 13, no. 1 (1986): 18–26.

————. "On the Tasks of Catholic Philosophy in Our Time." *Communio* 20 (1993): 147–87.

————. "Patristik, Scholastik, und wir." *Theologie der Zeit* 3 (1939): 65–104.

————. "Personlichkeit und Form." *Gloria Dei* 7 (1952): 1–15.

————. *Prayer.* San Francisco: Ignatius Press, 1983.

————. "Regagner une philosophie à partir de la théologie." In *Pour une philosophie chrétienne: Philosophie et théologie,* 175–87. Paris: Dessain et Tolra, 1983.

————. *Theo-Drama Theological Dramatic Theory Volume I: Prolegomena.* Translated by Graham Harrison. San Francisco: Ignatius Press, 1988.

————. *Theo-Drama Theological Dramatic Theory Volume II: The Dramatis Personae: Man in God.* Translated by Graham Harrison. San Francisco: Ignatius Press, 1976.

————. *Theo-Drama Volume III: The Dramatis Personae: The Person in Christ.* Translated by Graham Harrison. San Francisco: Ignatius Press, 1992.

————. *Theo-Drama Volume IV: The Action.* Translated by Graham Harrison. San Francisco: Ignatius Press, 1994.

————. *Theo-Drama Volume V: The Last Act.* Translated by Graham Harrison. San Francisco: Ignatius Press, 1998.

————. *Theodramatik I: Prolegomena.* Einsiedeln: Johannes Verlag, 1973.

————. *Theodramatik II: Das Endspiel.* Einsiedeln: Johannes Verlag, 1983.

————. *Theodramatik II: Die Personen Des Spiels Teil I: Der Mensch in Gott.* Einsiedeln: Johannes Verlag, 1976.

————. *Theodramatik II: Die Personen Des Spiels Teil II: Die Personen in Christus.* Einsiedeln: Johannes Verlag, 1978.

————. *Theodramatik III: Die Handlung.* Einsiedeln: Johannes Verlag, 1980.

———. *Theo-Logic Volume I: The Truth of the World*. Translated by Adrian J. Walker. San Francisco: Ignatius Press, 2000.

———. *Theo-Logic Volume II: The Truth of God*. Translated by Adrian J. Walker. San Francisco: Ignatius Press, 2004.

———. *Theo-Logic Volume III: The Spirit of Truth*. Translated by Graham Harrison. San Francisco: Ignatius Press, 2005.

———. *A Theological Anthropology*. New York: Sheed & Ward, 1968.

———. *Theologik: Dritter Band: Der Geist der Warheit*. Einsiedeln: Johannes Verlag, 1987.

———. *Theologik: Erster Band: Wahrheit der Welt*. Einsiedeln: Johannes Verlag, 1985.

———. *Theologik: Zweiter Band: Warheit Gottes*. Einsiedeln: Johannes Verlag, 1985.

———. "Theology and Aesthetic." *Communio* 8, no. 1 (1981): 62–71.

———. *A Theology of History*. San Francisco: Ignatius Press, 1994.

———. *The Threefold Garland: The World's Salvation in Mary's Prayer*. Translated by Erasmo Leiva-Merikakis. San Francisco: Ignatius Press, 1982.

———. "Transcendentality and *Gestalt*." *Communio* 11, no. 1 (1984): 4–12.

———. "Von den Aufgaben der katholischen Theologie in der Zeit." *Annalen der Philosophischen Gesellschaft der Inner Scweiz* 3, no. 2–3 (1946–47): 1–38.

Balthasar at the End of Modernity. Edited by Lucy Gardner, David Moss, Ben Quash. Edinburgh: T & T Clark, 1999.

Barth, Karl. *Anselm: Fides Quaerens Intellectum: Anselm's Proof of the Existence of God in the Context of His Theological Scheme*. Translated by Ian W. Robertson. Richmond, VA: John Knox Press, 1960.

Block, Ed. "Hans Urs von Balthasar and Some Contemporary Catholic Writers." *Logos: A Journal of Catholic Thought and Culture* 10, no. 3 (2007): 151–78.

———. "Poetry, Attentiveness and Prayer: One Poet's Lesson." *New Blackfriars* 89 (2008): 162–76.

Boersma, Hans. *Nouvelle Théologie and Sacramental Ontology: A Return to Mystery*. New York: Oxford University Press, 2009.

Bourgeois, Jason Paul. *The Aesthetic Hermeneutic of Hans-Georg Gadamer and Hans Urs von Balthasar*. New York: Peter Lang, 2007.

Brito, Emilio. "La reception de la pensee de Heidegger dans la theologie catholique." *Nouvelle revue théologique* 119, no. 3 (1997): 352–74.

Bowman, Leonard J. "Cosmic Exemplarism of Bonaventure." *Journal of Religion* 55, no. 2 (1975): 181–98.

Buckley, James J. "Balthasar's Use of the Theology of Aquinas." *The Thomist* 59, no. 4 (1995): 517–45.

Bychkov, Oleg V. *Aesthetic Revelation: Reading Ancient and Medieval Texts after Hans Urs von Balthasar*. Washington, DC: Catholic University of America Press, 2010.

The Cambridge Companion to Heidegger. Edited by Charles Guignon. Cambridge: Cambridge University Press, 1993.

Campodonico, Angelo. "Hans Urs von Balthasar's Interpretation of the Philosophy of Thomas Aquinas." *Nova et Vetera* 8, no. 1 (2010): 33–53.

Chapp, Larry. "The Primal Experience of Being in the Thought of Hans Urs von Balthasar: A Response to Theodore Kepes Jr." *Philosophy and Theology* 20, no. 1/2 (2008): 291–305.

A Companion to Heidegger. Edited by Hubert L. Dreyfus and Mark A. Wrathall. Malden, MA: Blackwell, 2005.

Congar, Yves. *The Meaning of Tradition*. Translated by A. N. Woodrow. New York: Hawthorn Books, 1964.

Crepaldi, Gabriele. *Modern Art 1900–45: The Age of Avant-Gardes*. Translated by Jay Hyams. New York: HarperCollins, 2007.

Dadosky, John. "Philosophy for a Theology of Beauty." *Philosophy and Theology* 19, no. 1–2 (2007): 7–34.

Daigler, Matthew A. "Heidegger and Von Balthasar: A Lovers' Quarrel Over Beauty and Divinity." *American Catholic Philosophical Quarterly* 69 (1995): 375–94.

Dante Alighieri. *La Divina Commedia*. 3 vols. Edited by Natalino Sapegno. Florence: La Nuova Italia, 1984.

———. *The Portable Dante*. Translated by Mark Musa. New York: Penguin, 1995.

Dante's Commedia: Theology as Poetry. Edited by Vittorio Montemaggi and Matthew Treherne. Notre Dame, IN: University of Notre Dame Press, 2010.

de Lubac, Henri. *The Discovery of God*. Grand Rapids, MI: William B. Eerdmans, 1996.

Donnelly, Veronica. *Saving Beauty: Form as the Key to Balthasar's Christology*. Bern: Peter Lang, 2007.

Doran, Robert. "Lonergan and Balthasar: Methodological Considerations." *Theological Studies* 58 (1997): 61–84.

Downes, David Anthony. *The Great Sacrifice: Studies in Hopkins*. Lanham, MD: University Press of America, 1983.

Dupré, Louis. "Hans Urs von Balthasar's Theology of Aesthetic Form." *Theological Studies* 49 (1988): 299–318.

Eco, Umberto. *The Aesthetics of Thomas Aquinas*. Translated by Hugh Bredin. Cambridge, MA: Harvard University Press, 1988.

————. *Art and Beauty in the Middle Ages.* Translated by Hugh Bredlin. New Haven: Yale University Press, 1986.

Edwards, Michael. *Towards a Christian Poetics.* Grand Rapids, MI: William B. Eerdmans, 1984.

Fields, Stephen M. "The Beauty of the Ugly: Balthasar, the Crucifixion, Analogy, and God." *International Journal of Systematic Theology* 9, no. 2 (2007): 172–83.

Fülleborn, Ulrich. "Dichten und Denken: Bemerkungen zu Rilke und Heidegger." In *Heidegger und die christliche Tradition,* 245–63. Hamburg: Meiner, 2007.

Glory, Grace, and Culture: The Work of Hans Urs von Balthasar. Edited by Ed Block. Mahwah, NJ: Paulist Press, 2005.

González-Andrieu, Cecilia. *Bridge to Wonder: Art as a Gospel of Beauty.* Waco, TX: Baylor University Press, 2012.

Griffiths, Paul J. "Is There a Doctrine of the Descent into Hell?" *Pro Ecclesia* 17, no. 3 (June 1, 2008): 257–68.

————. *Lying: An Augustinian Theology of Duplicity.* Eugene, OR: Wipf & Stock, 2010.

Gross, David. "The Religious Critique of Culture: Hans Urs von Balthasar and Paul Tillich." *Philosophy Today* 54, no. 4 (2010): 392–400.

Guite, Malcolm. *Faith, Hope and Poetry.* Farnham, Surrey: Ashgate, 2010.

Haas, Alois M. "Hans Urs von Balthasars 'Apokalypse der deutschen Seele.'" *Internationale katholische Zeitschrift Communio* 18, no. 4 (1989): 382–95.

Hammett, Jenny Y. "Thinker and Poet: Heidegger, Rilke, and Death." *Soundings* 60, no. 2 (1977): 166–78.

Hans Urs von Balthasar: His Life and Work. Edited by David L. Schindler. San Francisco: Ignatius Press, 1991.

Heidegger, Martin. *Basic Writings: From Being and Time (1927) to The Task of Thinking (1929).* Edited by David Farrell Krell. New York: Harper & Row, 1977.

————. *Being and Time.* Translated by John Macquarrie and Edward Robinson. New York: Harper & Row, 1962.

Holzer, Vincent. "Christologie de la figure (Gestalt) et christologie de la kénose chez Hans Urs von Balthasar." *Revue des sciences religieuses* 79, no. 2 (2005).

————. "L'esthétique théologique comme esthétique fondamentale chez Hans Urs von Balthasar." *Recherches de science religieuse* 85, no. 4 (1997).

————. "Les implications métaphysico-religieuses d'une dramatique trinitaire chez Hans Urs von Balthasar." *Gregorianum* 86, no. 2 (2005): 308–29.

————. "Phenomenology and Theology: A Contemporary Exit Strategy from Metaphysics." In *Naming and Thinking God in Europe Today: Theology in*

Global Dialogue, edited by Norbert Hintersteiner, 265–74. New York: Rodopi, 2007.

Hopkins, Gerard Manley. *Gerard Manley Hopkins: Poems and Prose*. Edited by W. H. Gardner. New York: Penguin, 1984.

———. *The Note-Books and Papers of Gerard Manley Hopkins*. Edited by Humphrey House. New York: Oxford University Press, 1937.

Howsare, Rodney. *Balthasar: A Guide for the Perplexed*. New York: T & T Clark, 2009.

Imperatori, Mario. "Heidegger dans la Dramatique divine de Hans Urs von Balthasar." *Nouvelle revue théologique* 122, no. 2 (2000): 191–210.

Johnson, Junius C. "Christ and Analogy: The Metaphysics of Hans Urs von Balthasar." PhD diss., Yale University, 2010.

Keef-Perry, L. B. C. "Theopoetics: Process and Perspective." *Christianity and Literature* 58, no. 4 (2009): 579–601.

Kerr, Fergus. *After Aquinas: Versions of Thomism*. Malden, MA: Wiley-Blackwell, 2002.

———. "Balthasar and Metaphysics." In *The Cambridge Companion to Hans Urs von Balthasar*, ed. Edward T. Oakes and David Moss, 224–40. New York: Cambridge University Press, 2004.

———. *Twentieth Century Catholic Theologians*. Somerset, NJ: Wiley-Blackwell, 2007.

Kierkegaard, Søren. *The Point of View*. Edited by Howard V. Hong and Edna H. Hong. Princeton, NJ: Princeton University Press, 1998.

Kilby, Karen. *Balthasar: A (Very) Critical Introduction*. Grand Rapids, MI: William B. Eerdmans, 2012 .

Köster, Peter. "Letzte Haltungen? Hans Urs von Balthasars 'Apokalypse der deutschen Seele'—nach über 60 Jahren wieder erschienen." *Reformatio* 49, no. 3 (2000): 184–90.

Lafontaine, Rene. "Quand K. Barth et H. Urs von Balthasar relisent le 'de Trinitate' de Thomas d'Aquin." *Nouvelle revue théologique* 124, no. 4 (2002): 529–48.

Lauber, David. "Response to Alyssa Lyra Pitstick, Light in Darkness." *Scottish Journal of Theology* 62, no. 2 (2009): 195–201.

Letzte Haltungen: Hans Urs von Balthasars 'Apokalypse der detuschen Seele'—neu gelesen. Edited by Barbara Hallensleben and Guido Vergauwen. Fribourg: Academic Press, 2006.

Levering, Matthew. *Scripture and Metaphysics: Aquinas and the Renewal of Trinitarian Theology*. Grand Rapids, MI: Wiley-Blackwell, 2004.

Lobato, Aberlardo. "Santo Tomás de Aquina y la via trascendetal en filosofia." In *Logik des Transzendentalen: Festschrift für Jan A. Aertsen zum 65. Geburtstag*, edited by Martin Pickavé, 162–78. New York: W. de Gruyter.

Lochbrunner, Manfred. *Analogia caritatis: Darstellung und Deutung der Theologie Hans Urs von Balthasars.* Vienna: Herder, 1981.

———. *Hans Urs von Balthasar und seine Philosophenfreunde: Fünf Doppleportraits.* Würzburg: Echter, 2005.

Lonergan, Bernard. *Insight: A Study of Human Understanding.* Collected Works of Bernard Lonergan. Vol. 3. Toronto: University of Toronto Press, 1992.

———. "The World Mediated by Meaning." *Philosophical and Theological Papers 1965–1980,* Collected Works of Bernard Lonergan, 107–18.

Long, D. Stephen. *Saving Karl Barth: Hans Urs von Balthasar's Preoccupation.* Minneapolis: Fortress Press, 2014.

———. *Speaking of God: Theology, Language, and Truth.* Grand Rapids, MI: William B. Eerdmans, 2009.

Long, Steven A. *Natura Pura: On the Recovery of Nature in the Doctrine of Grace.* New York: Fordham University Press, 2010.

Lösel, Steffen. "Love Divine, All Loves Excelling: Balthasar's Negative Theology of Revelation." *Journal of Religion* 82 (2002): 586–616.

Love Alone Is Credible: Hans Urs von Balthasar as Interpreter of the Catholic Tradition. Edited by David L. Schindler. Grand Rapids, MI: William B. Eerdmans, 2008.

Luy, David. "Aesthetic Collision: Hans Urs von Balthasar on the Trinity and the Cross." *International Journal of Systematic Theology* 13, no. 2 (2011): 154–59.

Mackey, Louis. *Peregrinations of the Word: Essays in Medieval Philosophy.* Ann Arbor: University of Michigan Press, 1997.

Maeseneer, Yves De. "Horror Angelorum: Terroristic Structures in the eyes of Walter Benjamin, Hans Urs von Balthasar's Rilke and Slavoj Zizek." *Modern Theology* 19, no. 4 (October 2003): 511–27.

Mahan, David C. *An Unexpected Light: Theology and Witness in the Poetry and Thought of Charles Williams, Micheal O'siadhail, and Geoffrey Hill.* Eugene, OR: Pickwick Publications, 2009.

McCloskey, Barbara. *Artists of World War II.* Westport, CT: Greenwood Press, 2005.

McCormack, Bruce L. "Karl Barth's Version of an 'Analogy of Being': A Dialectical No and Yes to Roman Catholicism." In *The Analogy of Being: Invention of the Antichrist or the Wisdom of God?,* edited by Thomas Joseph White, 88–144. Cambridge: William B. Eerdmans, 2011.

McDermott, Ryan. "Poetry against Evil: A Bulgakovian Theology of Poetry." *Modern Theology* 25, no. 1 (January 2009): 45–70.

McIntosh, Mark A. *Christology from Within: Spirituality and the Incarnation in Hans Urs von Balthasar.* Notre Dame, IN: University of Notre Dame Press, 2000.

Miller, David Leroy. "Theopoetry or Theopoetics?" *Cross Currents* 60, no. 1 (2010): 6–23.

Mongrain, Kevin. "Poetics and Doxology: Von Balthasar on Poetic Resistance to Modernity's Turn to the Subject." *Pro Ecclesia* 16, no. 4 (2007): 381–415.

Murphy, Francesca Aran. *Christ the Form of Beauty: A Study in Theology and Literature*. Edinburgh: T & T Clark, 1995.

Murphy, Michael Patrick. *A Theology of Criticism: Balthasar, Postmodernism, and the Catholic Imagination*. New York: Oxford University Press, 2008.

Newman, John Henry. *An Essay in Aid of A Grammar of Assent*. Notre Dame, IN: University of Notre Dame Press, 1979.

Nichols, Aidan. *Divine Fruitfulness: A Guide through Balthasar's Theology Beyond the Trilogy*. London: T & T Clark, 2007.

———. *A Key to Balthasar: Hans Urs von Balthasar on Beauty, Goodness, and Truth*. Grand Rapids, MI: Baker Academic, 2011.

———. "Littlemore from Lucerne: Newman's Essay on Development in Balthasarian Perspective." *Newman and Conversion*. Edited by Ian Ker. Edinburgh: T & T Clark, 1997, 100–116.

———. *No Bloodless Myth: A Guide Through Balthasar's Dramatics*. Washington, DC: Catholic University of America Press, 2000.

———. *Redeeming Beauty: Soundings in Sacral Aesthetics*. Burlington, VT: Ashgate, 2007.

———. *Say It Is Pentecost: A Guide Through Balthasar's Logic*. Washington, DC: Catholic University of America Press, 2001.

———. *Scattering the Seed: A Guide Through Balthasar's Early Writings on Philosophy and the Arts*. New York: T & T Clark, 2006.

———. "Thomism and the nouvelle théologie." *The Thomist* 64 (2000): 1–19.

———. *The Word Has Been Abroad: A Guide Through Balthasar's Aesthetics*. Washington, DC: Catholic University of America Press, 1998.

Norris, Thomas J. *A Fractured Relationship: Faith and the Crisis of Culture*. New York: New City Press, 2010.

Nussberger, Danielle. "Saint as Theological Wellspring: Hans Urs Von Balthasar's Hermeneutic of the Saint in a Christological and Trinitarian Key." PhD diss., University of Notre Dame, 2007.

Oakes, Edward T. "Balthasar, Early and Late." *Modern Theology* 23, no. 4 (2007): 617–23.

———. *Pattern of Redemption: The Theology of Hans Urs von Balthasar*. New York: Continuum, 1994.

———. "The Surnaturel Controversy: A Survey and a Response." *Nova et Vetera* 9, no. 3 (2011): 625–56.

O'Meara, Thomas F. "Of Art and Theology." *Theological Studies* 42, no. 2 (1981): 272–76.

On Beauty. Edited by Umberto Eco. Translated by Alastair McEwe. New York: Rizzoli, 2004.

O'Regan, Cyril. *The Anatomy of Misremembering: Von Balthasar's Response to Philosophical Modernity Volume 1: Hegel.* New York: Herder & Herder, 2014.

———. "Balthasar: Between Tübingen and Postmodernity." *Modern Theology* 14, no. 3 (1998): 325–53.

———. "Von Balthasar and Thick Retrieval: Post-Chalcedonian Symphonic Theology." *Gregorianum* 77, no. 2 (1996): 226–60.

———. "Von Balthasar's Valorization and Critique of Heidegger's Genealogy of Modernity." In *Christian Spirituality and the Culture of Modernity,* edited by Peter J. Casarella and George P. Schner, 123–58. Grand Rapids, MI: William B. Eerdmans, 1998.

Ouellet, Marc. "Hans Urs von Balthasar et la métaphysique: Esquisse de sa contribution." *PATH* 5 (2006): 473–83.

Pattinson, George. "Art in an Age of Reflection." In *The Cambridge Companion to Kierkegaard,* edited by Alastair Hannay and Gordon D. Marino, 76–100. Cambridge: Cambridge University Press, 1998.

Peterson, Paul Silas. "Anti-Modernism and Anti-Semitism in Hans Urs von Balthasar's 'Apokalypse der deutschen Seele.'" *Neue Zeitschrift für systematische Theologie und Religionsphilosophie* 52, no. 3 (2010): 302–18.

Pitstick, Alyssa Lyra. "Development of Doctrine, or Denial? Balthasar's Holy Saturday and Newman's Essay." *International Journal of Systematic Theology* 11 (2009): 129–45.

———. *Light in Darkness: Hans Urs von Balthasar and the Catholic Doctrine of Christ's Descent into Hell.* Grand Rapids, MI: William B. Eerdmans, 2007.

———. "Response to Webster and Lauber." *Scottish Journal of Theology* 62, no. 2 (January 1, 2009): 211–16.

Plaga, Ulrich Johannes. *"Ich bin die Wahrheit": Die theo-logische Dimension der Christologie Hans Urs von Balthasars.* Hamburg: LIT, 1997.

Przywara, Erich. *Analogia entis: Metaphysik.* Munich: Josef Kösel & Friedrich Pustet, 1932.

———. *Polarity: A German Catholic's Interpretation of Religion.* Translated by A. C. Bouquet. London: Oxford University Press, H. Milford, 1935.

———. *Religionsphilosophie katholischer Theologie.* Munich: R. Oldenbourg, 1926.

———. *Was ist Gott: Eine Summula.* Nürnberg: Glock und Lutz, 1953.

Rilke, Rainer Maria. *Book of Hours: Love Poems to God.* Edited by Anita Barrows and Joanna Marie Macy. New York: Riverhead Trade, 1996.

———. *Duino Elegies (Bilingual Edition).* Translated by Edward Snow. New York: North Point, 2000.

————. *New Poems: A Revised Bilingual Edition.* Translated by Edward Snow. New York: North Point, 2001.

————. *Sonnets to Orpheus: A Bilingual Edition.* Translated by M. D. Herter Norton. New York: W. W. Norton, 2006.

Rosenberg, Randall. *Theory and Drama in Balthasar's and Lonergan's Theology of Christ's Consciousness and Knowledge: An Essay in Dialectics.* PhD diss., Boston College, 2008.

Scarpelli, Therese. "Bonaventure's Christocentric Epistemology: Christ's Human Knowledge as the Epitome of Illumination in 'De scientia Christi.'" *Franciscan Studies* 65 (2007): 63–86.

Schindler, David C. *Hans Urs von Balthasar and the Dramatic Structure of Truth: A Philosophical Investigation.* New York: Fordham University Press, 2004.

————. "Hans Urs von Balthasar, Metaphysics, and the Problem of Onto-Theology." *Analecta Hermeneutica* 1 (2009): 102–13.

————. "Metaphysics within the Limits of Phenomenology: Balthasar and Husserl on the Nature of the Philosophical Act." *Teología y vida* 50, no. 1–2 (2009): 243–58.

————. "Towards a Non-Possessive Concept of Knowledge: On the Relation between Reason and Love in Aquinas and Balthasar." *Modern Theology* 22, no. 4 (2006): 577–607.

Schneider, Michael. "Die theologische Ausdeutung von Schöpfung und Heiliger Schrift bei Bonaventura." *Theologie und Philosophie* 69 (1994): 373–83.

Schrijver, Georges. "Die Analogia Entis in der Theologie Hans Urs von Balthasars: eine genetisch-historische Studie." *Sylloge excerptorum e dissertationibus,* vol. 49: 249–81.

Scola, Angelo. *Hans Urs von Balthasar: A Theological Style.* Grand Rapids, MI: William B. Eerdmans, 1995.

Stansky, Peter, and William Miller Abrahams. *London's Burning: Life, Death, and Art in the Second World War.* Stanford: Stanford University Press, 1994.

Taylor, Charles. *Human Agency and Language.* Philosophical Papers, vol. 1. New York: Cambridge University Press, 1985.

————. *A Secular Age.* Cambridge, MA: Belknap, 2007.

Theological Aesthetics after von Balthasar. Edited by Oleg V. Bychkov and Jim Fodor. Aldershot, Surrey: Ashgate, 2008.

Thomas Aquinas. *The Division and Methods of the Sciences: Questions IV and V of His Commentary on the De Trinitate of Boethius.* Translated by Armand Maurer. Toronto: Pontifical Institute of Medieval Studies, 1986.

————. *Summa Theologica of Thomas Aquinas.* Translated by the Fathers of the English Dominican Province. Chicago: University of Chicago Press, 1952.

———. *Truth*. 3 vols. Translated by Robert W. Schmidt. Chicago: Henry Regnery, 1952–54.

Tiffany, Daniel. *Infidel Poetics: Riddles, Nightlife, Substance.* Chicago: University of Chicago Press, 2009.

Tonstad, Linn Marie. "Sexual Difference and Trinitarian Death: Cross, Kenosis, and Hierarchy in the Theo-Drama." *Modern Theology* 26, no. 4 (2010): 603–31.

Torretta, Gabriel. "Art's Irrational Infanta." *First Things, On the Square*, June 20, 2011.

Viladesau, Richard. "*Theosis* and Beauty." *Theology Today* 65 (2008): 180–90.

Waldstein, Michael Maria. *Expression and Form: Principles of a Philosophical Aesthetics According to Hans Urs von Balthasar.* Paris: Editions du Cerf, 1998.

Webster, J. B. "Webster's Response to Alyssa Lyra Pitstick, Light in Darkness." *Scottish Journal of Theology* 62, no. 2 (January 1, 2009): 202–10.

Weinandy, Thomas G. *Does God Suffer?* Notre Dame, IN: University of Notre Dame Press, 2000.

West, Shearer. *The Visual Arts in Germany 1890–1937: Utopia and Despair.* Manchester: Manchester University Press, 2000.

White, Thomas Joseph. "On the Universal Possibility of Salvation." *Pro Ecclesia* 17, no. 3 (June 1, 2008): 269–80.

Williams, Rowan. *Wrestling with Angels.* London: SCM Press, 2007.

Wimsatt, James I. *Hopkins' Poetics of Speech Sound: Sprung Rhythm, Lettering, Inscape.* Toronto: University of Toronto Press, 2006.

Yeago, David S. *The Drama of Nature and Grace: A Study in the Theology of Hans Urs von Balthasar.* Ann Arbor: University Microfilms International, 1996.

Zeitz, James. "Przywara and von Balthasar on Analogy." *The Thomist* 52, no. 3 (1988): 473–98.

INDEX

ANNE M. CARPENTER

is assistant professor of Catholic systematic theology at
Saint Mary's College of California